THE FUNDAMENTALS OF FAMILY MEDIATION

SUNY Series in Transpersonal and Humanistic Psychology
Richard D. Mann, editor

The Fundamentals of Family Mediation

by

John M. Haynes

State University of New York Press

Published by
State University of New York Press, Albany

For information, address State University of New York Press,
90 State Street, Suite 700, Albany, N.Y. 12207

Production by Marilyn P. Semerad
Marketing by Nancy Farrell
Composition by John Haynes

Library of Congress Cataloging-in-Publication Data

Haynes, John M.
        The fundamentals of family mediation / by John M.
Haynes.
        p.   cm. — (SUNY series in transpersonal and
humanistic psychology)
        Includes bibliographical references.
        ISBN 0-7914-2035-3 (alk. paper). — ISBN
0-7914-2036-1 (pbk.:
alk. paper)
        1. Family mediation.   I. Title. II. Series.
HQ10.H39   1994
93-38027
306.85 — dc20
CIP

10 9

For Charlotte and Oliver

Contents

Preface

This is a cook book for family mediators. It is based on the author's world famous training program, Fundamentals of Divorce By Mediation. He has delivered this training program to over 15,000 professionals in 14 countries.

The book provides a clear model of mediation, an understanding of the theory of negotiations, and a knowledge of the context of divorce.

The book has two purposes:

- To provide people who have taken the training with a hands-on source of advice as they enter the practice.
- To provide future training programs with a text dealing with the how-to and context of family mediation so that the trainees can concentrate on the skills necessary to practice successfully.

The Organization of the Book

Chapter 1 details the process of mediation and applies general mediation theory to the practice of family mediation. It develops a model which meets the special needs of families and divorce.

Chapters 2-5 examine the context of divorce, explaining the step-by-step activities of the mediator and all of the forms and materials needed to conduct the practice. The areas covered are:

> the intake
> budgeting and support
> dividing the assets and
> parenting.

Chapter 5 explores the negotiating behavior of clients and presents clear strategies for the mediator in managing the negotiations. This section is designed to provide the reader with an understanding of the theory of negotiations as it is applied to families.

Chapter 6 examines different ways to write the memorandum of understanding, the product of every successful mediation. It provides examples for various situations which can be incorporated into the reader's practice.

Chapter 7 provides the reader with clear and simple steps to create and build a successful mediation practice. This chapter includes sample letters, brochures and a client handbook which can be used by the reader.

An annotated bibliography identifies books which mediators should read as the foundation of their understanding about mediation and the role of the mediator as manager of other people's negotiations.

The author, John M. Haynes, Ph.D., has mediated over 5,000 cases and trained over 15,000 professional in divorce mediation. He is the author of two earlier books, Divorce Mediation. A Practical Guide For Therapists and Counselors, Springer, N.Y. 1981 and (with his wife Gretchen) Mediating Divorce: A Casebook of Successful Family Negotiations, Jossey Bass, San Francisco, 1989. He has contributed more than 20 articles to the professional journals.

Dr. Haynes was the Founding President of the Academy of Family Mediators (1981 - 1985) and the first recipient of its Distinguished Contribution Award in 1989. He was awarded Peacemaker of the Year Award in 1991, by the Community Mediation Services, Inc., "For International Contribution to the Development of Divorce Mediation."

Dr. Larry Fong, Calgary, Alberta provided all of the material to make the book applicable to Canada. In addition, he made numerous suggestions and ideas that helped to clarify the text based on his extensive experience as a mediator and trainer.

This book is being published in four language editions simultaneously. This one; a British edition by The Old Bailey Press, London; a German edition published by Kösel Verlag, Munich, Germany; and a Norwegian edition published by Tano, Oslo, Norway.

Chapter One
The Mediation Process

Mediation is a process in which a third person helps the participants in a dispute to resolve it. The agreement resolves the problem with a mutually acceptable solution and is structured in a way that helps maintain the continuing relationships of the people involved.

In order to resolve the dispute, the participants must negotiate a solution. Problem solving is part of negotiations. Because the problem solving involves more than one person, the chosen solution must satisfy *all the participants in the dispute.* The participants must negotiate which solution or combination of solutions is acceptable to all of them. That is why mediation is ideally suited to family disputes.

The process of mediation is the management of other people's negotiations, and the mediator is the manager of the negotiations who organizes the discussion of the issues to be resolved. The more coherent and organized the process, the easier it is for the participants to arrive at solutions that are mutual and appropriate for them. There are generic aspects of mediation, and specialized parts of the process that apply to different contexts. This book concentrates on family mediation. Therefore, it first examines the generic mediation process and then applies the unique aspects to family and divorce mediation.

The Generic Process

The generic process of mediation includes nine stages:

1. Recognizing the problem
2. Choosing the arena
3. Selecting the mediator
4. Gathering the data (fact finding)
5. Defining the problem
6 Developing options
7. Redefining positions
8. Bargaining
9. Drafting the Agreement

The Fundamentals of Family Mediation

Recognizing the Problem

Negotiations can take place when the parties to a dispute recognize that they have a dispute, agree on the need to resolve it, and actively engage in a process designed to settle the dispute.[1]

Sometimes not everyone agrees that there is a dispute. Informal attempts to negotiate an agreement are frustrated if one person does not agree that he is in a dispute. When this happens the other person has only one obvious choice: to make the disagreement a legal dispute. By engaging counsel and filing a suit, one person forces the other to engage in the resolution of the dispute, since the other person is defined by the judicial system as a respondent who must then engage in a process determined by the legal system.

Choosing the Arena

Once the disputants agree they must solve the problem, they need to decide on the appropriate method. They choose an arena in which to settle the problem; in this case, mediation. People are increasingly selecting mediation as the arena in which to settle disputes. In family matters, courts are using mediation as an alternative arena to the court room to help families resolve problems. The choice of mediation as the arena in which to settle the dispute is usually made on one of four grounds:

- **Mediation is nonadversarial.** The nature of the legal system requires the participants to be adversaries. Many people in dispute are not adversaries, and even if they are, they are not always inclined to be adversarial. Rather, they want to problem solve because they understand the importance of maintaining their ongoing relationship. People with this approach to life choose mediation.
- **Mediation is private.** Interpersonal disputes are best solved privately and most people prefer to settle their family matters within the confines of the family. Choosing a mediator limits outside intervention to one professional.[2]

---

[1] P. H. Gulliver, *Disputes and Negotiations: A Cross Cultural Perspective* (New York: Academic Press, 1979).

[2] Some mediators prefer to work in teams.

- **Mediation is cheaper.** Since only one professional is involved, the cost of resolving the dispute is much less in mediation than in the legal system.[3]
- **Mediation is faster.** Since all discussions are held face-to-face, resolving the dispute takes less time in mediation than in the adversarial legal system.

Selecting the Mediator

Selection of the specific mediator is based on the clients' knowledge of the process, the reputation of the mediator, and the extent to which other professionals refer cases to the mediator. This book will help the reader develop the skills and reputation to become a chosen mediator. You will also find simple steps in chapter 7 that you can take to develop your mediation practice.

Gathering the Data (Fact Finding)

The mediator begins by gathering the data about the nature of the dispute, the participants' views of the dispute and any other relevant information. He ensures that all information is revealed to all of the participants. The data are shared, verified, and exchanged.

The fact finding stage helps the participants to clarify the bargaining issues and to learn about each other's positions on the issues. Prior to these discussions, each has thought little about what the other wants, concentrating on making their own argument, rather than understanding the needs of the other. Hearing the other's version of the situation and the data the other brings to the mediation helps participants measure their own position more realistically.

In most cases, prior to entering mediation, the people in dispute have exchanged threats and counter threats about what they will and will not do in the negotiations. These threats reinforce the fears the family members carry for their individual futures and limit the number of options each feels is available. Threats work only in the absence of concrete data, thus fact finding minimizes their impact.

The mediator insists on full disclosure of all issues and facts to all participants. Sharing information is part of power balancing since

---

[3] Joan Kelly, "Is Mediation Less Expensive? Comparison of Mediated and Adversarial Divorce Costs" *Mediation Quarterly* 8. no. 1 (Fall 1990): 15-26.

knowledge is power, and when the mediator uses the process to ensure disclosure of all the information he

- empowers the less knowledgeable participants,
- assures that all participants use the same data to define the problem, and
- improves the ability of each participant to choose the options most beneficial to them.

Disclosure has a special meaning in divorce negotiations. In order to determine the appropriate level of support and the fair distribution of the family assets, all participants must have full and complete knowledge of all the income and assets. Attempts by either spouse to withhold information are prevented by the mediator's process control in insisting on complete disclosure. This is discussed more fully in the budget and asset division chapters.

Defining the Problem

Using the shared data, the mediator helps the people in dispute define the problem. The problem must be defined in a way that does not benefit any one person over the others and, therefore, is a mutual problem definition.

In any dispute, control of the problem definition is crucial. In the legal arena, defining the legal issue is often more important than trying the case. In arbitration, defining the precise issue to be arbitrated is as important as arguing the case once the issue is defined. All participants attempt to define the problem in a way that (a) minimizes their responsibility for the problem and (b) moves the onus for change to the other participants. However, the mediator cannot allow the discussion to focus on solving a unilaterally defined problem since that benefits the participant who determines the problem definition. Rather, the mediator helps the participants negotiate a mutual definition of the problem that does not benefit one client at the expense of the others.

Developing Options

When all the people involved agree on the definition of the problem, the mediator helps them generate options for solving the problem. These options tend to be mutual, since the problem is now mutual, and unilateral solutions are more easily seen as one-sided. Old

4

options, based on a one-sided definition are discarded, and new, mutual options are considered.

Many times participants are in dispute simply because they do not perceive options for solution. They tend to view all situations in the same way, and their limited options prevent them from solving the problem without the assistance of a third party. In these cases, the mediator helps the participants expand the range of options by brainstorming. In brainstorming, a few simple rules help the parties to generate new ideas:

- Any idea they think of should be shared
- Every idea, no matter how unusual, is added to the list
- No idea can be dismissed by the other party
- Nobody may criticize any idea or explain why it won't work

In the first stage of the brainstorming process, the goal is to list every conceivable idea, without assessing each idea as it listed. Once the clients list every idea they can think of, they go back and examine each one individually. The mediator helps them categorize the ideas into *highly possible, possible, unlikely, and impossible.*

After eliminating the latter two groups the participants focus on the remaining ideas, exploring the consequences of each idea, the costs associated with it, and the benefits its implementation will bring.

When brainstorming does not provide a wide range of options, the mediator suggests options from similar cases; if acceptable to the clients, these options are added to the list.

When the list of options appears complete, the mediator moves to the next stage: redefining positions.

Redefining Positions

All participants enter the mediation process with a position. It is part of their problem definition. Positions are usually taken in an emotional climate and do not always match the disputant's self-interest. Most people bargain from positions rather than interest, and bargaining about positions often results in a stalemate. The mediator helps the people bargain from their self-interest.[4] He initially ignores

---

[4] Roger Fisher and William Ury, *Getting to Yes: Negotiating Agreement Without Giving In* (Boston: Houghton Mifflin, 1981), state a cogent case for bargaining from interests, not positions.

the positions introduced at the beginning of the session and helps the participants use the rational process of problem solving to identify their true self-interests, which then form the basis of their subsequent bargaining. They do this by selecting the options most useful to them.

When the positions have been translated into interests, the participants are ready to select the options that seem to provide the most benefits at the least cost to each of them. One option may be more useful to one person, and a different option proves more useful to another. When they select options, they take informed positions based on self-interest leading into the bargaining phase of the negotiations.

Bargaining

The mediator helps them negotiate over the choice of solutions so that the agreement is acceptable to all involved. In this stage positions are modified, options are traded, and the give-and-take of bargaining occurs. Participants can bargain only when they have

- all of the facts,
- an appropriately mutual definition of the problem,
- a range of options to solve the problem, and
- one or more options as their primary goal.

The ways people actually bargain is discussed in chapter 6.

Drafting the Agreement

The mediator drafts a memorandum of understanding (MOU) detailing the agreements and gives a copy to each participant. Drafting the MOU is a simple matter when the mediator keeps track of the issues, the data, and each agreement the participants reach.

At the conclusion of the bargaining he drafts the understandings in plain language that is clearly understood by each participant. Sometimes the agreement needs to be used in the legal arena. In that case the participants' attorneys have responsibility for translating the MOU into legal language. The MOU includes

- the background data,
- the definition of the problem,
- the options chosen, and the reason for the choice, and
- the goal of the agreement.

Cycles of the Mediation Process

Every mediation consists of the generic process plus unique parts, depending on the context. Those parts unique to the context are also made up of the same cycle of the mediation process. The cycle consists of the middle five stages of the generic process described on page 1. These five stages are:

- Gathering the data (fact finding), during which the mediator verifies, displays, and shares the data
- Defining the problem (from the data)
- Developing options to solve the problem
- Redefining positions from self- to mutual interests
- Bargaining over the options to reach a mutual agreement

The cycle is repeated over and over again within the larger mediation process to deal with each issue. For example, in the divorce process it is used in the budgeting/support, asset division, and parenting sections. This is shown in fig. 1.1.

Figure 1.1 Cycles in the Mediation Process

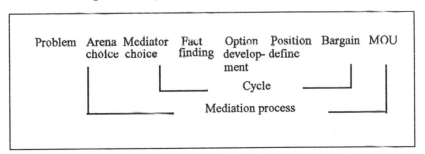

Being a Mediator and Not a Judge

The mediator manages and is responsible for maintaining the process. Frequently, clients act to draw the mediator away from managing the negotiations into other roles.

When the mediator enters the dispute, he is confronted by clients who have thought a great deal about how to convince him they are right and the others are wrong. The disputants have an image of the mediator as a judge who must be convinced. The mediator, on the other hand, must convince them he is not a judge and cannot be "won over" to one side or the other. The mediator helps the clients to accept him as one who

- is committed to the agreement, not to any one person,
- is balanced between the disputants,
- controls the process while yielding control of the content to the clients,
- does not accept any one person's unilateral definition of the problem,
- helps them develop options to solve their problem, and
- holds no secrets from them and allows no participants to withhold information from the others.

Helping Clients Define a Solvable Problem

When people have an intractable dispute that appears unresolvable, the mediator enters to assist them to settle the dispute by negotiating a mutually acceptable agreement. However, a significant part of the problem is the inability of parties to agree on the *content* of the dispute. Indeed, the participants often have quite different versions of the nature and history of the dispute.

When the mediator first meets with the disputants each person has a story to tell. The stories consist of three parts.

The first is their specific version of the events and the past. The basic data of the versions may be similar, or even the same, but the interpretation each places on the facts colors that view of the situation. Each version is designed to show the mediator how good they are; how each is the innocent victim of the situation.

The second part is their complaint about the other, which is designed to show the mediator how bad the other is. The third part is their definition of the problem. The hallmark is that each person defines the problem in such a way that the problem can be solved only by a change in the behavior or position of the *other*. For example, A's problem can be solved only by a change in B, and B's problem can be solved only by a change in A.

These three elements represent each party's definition of the problem. Their inability to agree on the content of the dispute means that the mediator's role in the early stages is to obtain agreement on the problem to be resolved. Thus, the mediator helps the clients to define a mutual and neutral problem definition that, when solved, benefits all participants.

Neither A nor B will change unilaterally, and neither will change to conform with the other's definition of the problem, since both have their own definition. Therefore the mediator's task is to help the participants discard their individual problem definitions and adopt a mutual and common definition of the problem. Only then can problem solving begin.

The mediator begins to take control of the problem definition by first creating doubt in both parties minds about the validity and fairness of their original stories. This is done *without* challenging either side's image of self. In order to achieve this elemental goal, the mediator engages in a set of generic strategies. By "generic" I mean those strategies that are common to all mediation contexts: *normalizing* and *mutualizing*, which create doubt in the original version, and maintaining a *future focus* and *summarizing*, which solidify the new problem definition.

Normalizing

In order to arrive at the point where the dispute needs a third person to assist in its resolution, the participants must believe that their problem is unique enough to justify bringing in an outsider. Normal problems, after all, are solved normally. But clients often frame their problem as abnormal or as having unusual aspects. The mediator must convince them that theirs is a normal, resolvable problem.[5]

Most people engaged in a dispute requiring a mediator have convinced themselves that their situation is unique, and its very uniqueness justifies their position. Given the unique characteristic of the situation, the person also holds an equally unique (or unilateral) solution. The mediator undermines the uniqueness of each problem definition by normalizing the situation. Because, if the situation is normal, it is also resolvable within normal bounds. Let's look at a divorce case to illustrate these points.

---

[5] Obviously, in cases where the participants do have an abnormal problem, the mediator does not try to convince them otherwise. To do so is disrespectful to the clients and undermines the mediator's credibility.

A Case Example

The wife, Debra's, opening statement concluded with "I have let him see the children on several occasions, but the children aren't happy seeing their father. They said they don't want to see him. They are unhappy about the separation. When they've come back home, they're very upset. They're crying and it takes me hours to settle them down and I just don't know how they're going to cope with this."

If the mediator accepts this problem definition as *the* definition, the solution is to maintain either the status quo with the father seeing the children under conditions set by the mother or for Michael to move back home with Debra. Neither of these solutions would be acceptable to the husband.

Michael has his own definition of the problem. "I've seen these kids now five times over the past month. They are happy to come with me, we have a good time. We have done a lot of things together, they enjoy being with me. Now when they come and see me they're apprehensive about their visits. I know that, but I don't think Debra is helping them. I'm having great difficulty coming back and watching her dissemble. When I bring the kids back home she starts crying."

If Michael's definition of the problem is accepted, the children would spend most of the time with him, and Debra would accept the separation and not cry when Michael returns the children. These solutions to the problem as Michael defines it are equally unacceptable to Debra.

Each parent claimed that the children cried when transferring to the other and each blamed the other for this. In commenting to Michael and Debra, the mediator said, "It's not unusual for them, by the way, to have this tension and lots of crying when they go back and when they come forward and some apprehension. Obviously they're still trying to sort out how to behave in relationship to each of you, when you're living apart as distinct from when you were living together. So it is perfectly possible for them to have a good time when with you, Michael, but also express real concerns and reservations when they're with you, Debra. That's not an unusual situation."

In this commentary the mediator accepts the description of the children's behavior according to each parent and presents it as normal and to be expected, thus robbing each parent of the uniqueness of their version of the facts. This carefully balanced commentary addresses both parents' concerns without siding with either one. The more the mediator can normalize the clients' problem the more resolvable it becomes in their eyes and the more chance the mediator has of moving them towards a common definition of the problem that, of course, is not only normal but also mutual.

Mutualizing

Participants in a dispute usually frame the problem in a way that blames the other and denies personal responsibility for the problem. It is a rare person who admits to being a part of the problem. The initial articulation of the problem includes an attack on the other, blaming them for the problem. The mediator's task, as part of creating doubt in order to move towards a mutual problem definition, is to help the participants let go of their individual definitions. When each person makes a strong case that is unilateral, the mediator attempts to reframe the issue as a mutual one.

The daughter may say about her father, "He never listens to me. I might as well not exist." The father responds, "She never listens to me. I'm her father, yet she ignores everything I say." The mediator says, "I assume you both want to be heard." That statement turns the negatives "he doesn't"/ "she doesn't" into a positive "you both want to be heard." The statement also makes not listening a *mutual* problem, and points the way to a *mutual* answer: each being heard.

In a child custody case, the father may complain, "But the children need their father." The mother quickly responds, "But they need their mother more so." The mediator interjects, "I assume they need both of you." This statement does not contradict what either of them said. It merely states their problem as being mutual. The options to solve mutual problem definitions tend to be mutual solutions.

When each person takes a position, they rarely think about the other's view, and thus strategies such as normalizing and mutualizing, which help them look at the situation from different viewpoints, also help to create doubt as to the certainty of the original positions. This opens the way for developing alternative, mutual positions that meet their self-interests.

Once the doubt has been created and the disputants are willing to look at alternatives, the mediator helps solidify the changes by maintaining a future focus in the discussions.

Future Focus

When people first appear in the mediator's office all they want to do is to talk about the past. Their complaints are about past actions and behaviors. The dispute is about the past. The origin of the problem lies in the past, and the fact that they have come to mediation indicates that the past was unsuccessful and without hope. However, determining who was right and wrong about the past is the function of a judge, not the mediator. Any discussion about the past inevitably casts the mediator into a judge role.

The wrongs of the past are unchangeable. Talking about the past does not resolve it; the dialogue simply reinforces the disputants' individual views of their joint past. Searching for solutions requires a future focus because the solution lies in the future. Thus the mediation process is future focused. The mediator is not interested in discussing or evaluating complaints about the past but redirects the disputants to talking about their aspirations for the future.

Mediation is concerned not with who was right and wrong in the past but how the disputants want to reorganize for the future. Returning to our divorce case example, when the husband says to the mediator, "Can't you tell her that what I'm doing is normal, it happens all the time. Can't you explain to her where I am coming from?" The mediator responds to the husband, "I was not so much interested in where you are coming from as in where you want to go in the future with this issue."[6]

Most of the time, clients complain about what they don't want: a continuation of the other's past behavior. It is somehow easier for us to articulate what we don't like or want than it is to articulate what we do want. Thus, the mediator asks questions about what people want in the future rather than what they did not like about the past.

The mediator moves the clients from complaining about the past to stating what they want in the future. The solution lies in the future and hope is also there. As long as the clients talk and complain

---

[6] J. M. Haynes and G. L. Haynes, *Mediating Divorce: A Casebook of Successful Family Negotiations* (San Francisco: Jossey Bass 1989), 68.

about what happened last week, they cannot talk about what they would like to happen differently next week. The mediator asks very few past-focused questions. He prefers to stay in the present and the future tense. Change, hope, and solutions lie in the future.

There is a serendipitous benefit to talking about the future: *clients rarely complain about the future.* As soon as they talk in the past tense, their communication is full of recriminations, complaints, and hopelessness. When talking about the future there are no complaints or recriminations. We can complain about yesterday's weather, but we can't complain about tomorrow's. When the mediator keeps the focus on what people want in the future the clients are not in a complaining mode. The clients benefit, since while talking about their hopes for the future they are also talking about possible solutions to their problems.

A good example of this type of a past-to-future focus occurred in a session where the couple argued about whether the husband could care for their diabetic daughter. [7]

> Tom (husband): I can do those things. I can do those things.
> Pat (wife): No you can't. You've never done them. You don't
> know how to do them.
> Tom: Well, I can learn. I'm not stupid.
> Mediator: Pat, would you like for Tom to be able to do them
> in the future?

Pat's answer must be yes, she would like Tom to be able to care for the daughter. The question moves her from the past and Tom's *inability* to provide care to the future and the benefits of his *ability* to provide the care.

In normalizing, mutualizing, and moving people into a future focus, the mediator does not deny what the clients have said. Rather, he summarizes the key mediation points the clients make, directing them towards problem solving.

Summarizing

The mediator moves the mediation session forward through the summarizing. The summary drives the session. Clients are not sure of

---

[7] Ibid., 197-98

what to expect from the mediator and how to behave as mediation clients. The process of summarizing clarifies their expectations and helps them adopt an appropriate mediation client role.

The mediator does not summarize everything the clients say. He chooses to summarize what he believes is important. If the client says, "It was raining yesterday," the mediator does not summarize, "It was wet yesterday." However, if she says, "It was raining yesterday, and Jimmy went off again without his raincoat even though I asked him to wear it," the mediator summarizes. "So you are concerned when Jimmy goes out in the rain without his raincoat."

The mediator is constantly faced with choices as to what to summarize and what to ignore. Whatever the mediator focuses on becomes important in the eyes of the participants. The mediator uses the summary to

- ignore information that is *not* useful to the conduct of the session,
- focus on those items of information that are useful,
- ignore all attempts to cast him in a legal or therapy role.

In general, we can say that non-useful information includes

- social talk,
- emotional and emotive statements,
- legal and therapy questions.

What is useful in a mediation session is

- information and data about the dispute,
- the clients' goal statements,
- indications of their bargaining behaviors and strategies.

By focusing on the useful and ignoring the nonuseful information, the mediator stays in role and keeps the couple in role as mediation clients. An attorney asks legal questions and summarizes back to the client the *legal* aspects of their response. He ignores the non-legal matter. Similarly, a therapist asks therapy questions and summarizes back the therapeutically relevant aspects of the clients responses. Obviously, the mediator cannot screen out every nonmediation communication of the clients. Frequently, they insist on a response to these other matters. When that happens, the professional responds to the needs of the client.

While the mediator cannot avoid all legal questions or emotive behavior, he can limit the nonuseful dialogue. The primary method is by focusing on what he believes is relevant to the clients. He tests and clarifies the difference between relevant and unuseful information. He clarifies for the clients what is important, directing them away from emotive behavior towards their self-interests that are contained in the information about the problem and solutions to it.

He can limit the nonuseful dialogue by redirecting the clients, cutting off long monologues, and explaining to the clients his function as manager of the negotiations. By limiting the emotive behavior he can concentrate on ways to be most helpful to the clients in solving the problems that brought them to mediation. Most clients monitor the mediator's response, noting what is important and unimportant to the mediator and adjusting their behavior to match the mediator's behavior. Being aware of this helps the client model appropriate and useful mediation behaviors.

Figure 1.2 Sorting Information in Mediation

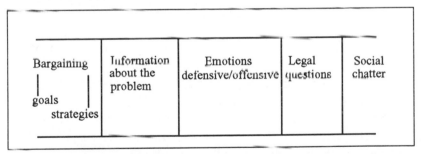

Bargaining ↓ ↓ goals strategies	Information about the problem	Emotions defensive/offensive	Legal questions	Social chatter

The client dialogue is divided into two sectors. The left-hand sector is useful client information, and the right-hand sector is unuseful client information. When the mediator collects the data, he looks for useful data: information about the problem, the clients' bargaining goals, and strategies. He summarizes this information for the client. The data are collected and noted and form the basis of the next line of questioning. Client information that falls into the right sector is ignored unless the client is persistent. Faced with client persistence, the mediator attempts to deal with the behavior by acknowledging it and engaging in other strategies to limit it.

15

The Fundamentals of Family Mediation

Although we have drawn a clear line between the useful and nonuseful dialogues, the distinction is less clear when in the session with the clients. It is helpful to think about client emotional behavior in two ways: offensive and defensive behaviors.

Offensive behaviors are unuseful and are best ignored by the mediator unless they prevent progress in the mediation process. Offensive behavior includes attacks by the clients on each other, fights about the marriage, and arguments. Defensive emotional statements are often useful because they alert the mediator to underlying issues or they indicate emotional issues that, if dealt with, enable the mediator to continue the mediation process.

For example, in one case the couple were fighting about an issue they had as spouses, and the mediator could not bring them back to the mediation issues. Finally, in the middle of an offensive statement about his wife, the husband said, "I'm hurting and she just doesn't know how much I hurt." The mediator, who had been ignoring all of the offensive fighting, acknowledged the hurt by summarizing: "I believe you are both hurting and I sense that neither of you understands just how much the other hurts. That's O.K. in a sense, because it's part of the process of divorce." Upon hearing these comments, the couple relaxed and let go of the offensive fighting and followed the mediator as he led them towards a discussion of the mediation issues.

When the mediator verifies, displays, and shares the data, he works with the data in the useful sector. In a divorce, for example, he concentrates on budget information in the support session. He displays the concrete needs and does not verify, display, or share with the clients their emotional behavior or legal requirements. The same is true as he helps the clients develop a mutual problem definition. The definition is about practical matters falling into the useful sector. When the mutual problem has been defined, the options to solve that problem are useful, as is the outcome to the clients.

When clients ventilate their emotions or ask legal questions, the mediator ignores that part of the communication and summarizes the useful parts. The clients respond to the summary and, if they find it acceptable, do not challenge the omissions. If they do challenge the omissions, the mediator responds by accepting their insistence that the omitted item be dealt with by adding it back into the summary.

Using the case example introduced on page 10, the wife told the mediator that the children lived with her and that they visited their father and added a complaint that the children were not happy seeing their father. The mediator summarized her opening statement with, "So they are currently living in the family home, and they are spending time with their dad."

In addition to focusing the clients' attention on relevant information and suggesting its relative importance to their goals, summarizing also

- tests the clients statements and positions
- helps to determine what is useful and non-useful in mediation
- clarifies data and adds to the common knowledge of all the participants.

We test a hypothesis as to whether the goals are strategic or not. We can determine the priority of various goals by varying our responses to the clients' stated goals.

The client may say that she needs 1, 2, and 3. The mediator can test the relative importance of 1, 2, 3 by reordering them in the summary such as "So you feel 2, 1, 3 are important to you." If the client does not challenge the reordered list, the mediator proceeds using the new list.

If the mediator believes the client is engaging in a strategy of enlarging the number of goals, thinking that this would give him extra room to compromise, the mediator responds to a 1, 2, 3, statement with the summary, "So you think that 1 and 2 are important to you." The client's acceptance of that statement tends to confirm the mediator's belief that number three was added as a strategy. If the client rejects the mediator's summary and reminds him of item three, the mediator apologizes and restores number three to a revised summary.

Professional Bias

Our views and understanding of events are shaped by our experience. We learn from our accumulated experiences in life and also in a formal way through education and reading. Our life events shape our attitudes and values. They provide a prism through which we separate the parts of each new event we encounter so that we can categorize and understand the event in a way that makes sense to us.

This way of looking at experiences is called "biases" or "prejudices." Everyone has them, and everyone is controlled by them, since the biases filter all new information we receive and all new events we experience. We operate continually under a preset catalogue of biases/prejudices.

In addition to looking at events through life-learned ways, we also learn through formal education, which provides a different way of looking at and receiving events. This usually begins during our undergraduate years and increases in importance in graduate and particularly in graduate professional schools.

Thus, if a client takes the same problem to an attorney, a therapist and a mediator, the professional in each situation will define the problem differently.

As attorneys we are taught to look at all new professional events and experiences through a legal prism. As mental health professionals, we are taught to look at all new professional events through a mental health prism.[8] As mediators, we look at each new professional experience through a mediation prism. The mediation prism separates out the legal and mental health issues and focuses on the mediation issues.

When a professional is at work, his personal and professional prisms are in frequent conflict. That is, his personal biases and prejudices may be in conflict with his professional training. Hopefully, the professional training provides an awareness of the conflict, enabling the professional to concentrate on his professional reaction rather than the personal one. For example, a couple negotiating over the level of support may indicate a figure for housing that seems totally unreasonable to the mediator as a private person. However, the figure to the professional mediator is perfectly reasonable in the context of the client's lifestyle.

---

[8] Mental health professionals have an additional problem: their different professional training tends to provide radically different prisms. Thus, given the same client, a psychoanalytical practitioner might see a narcissistic personality disorder and a family systems therapists might see a disorganized family. The different diagnosis leads to radically different treatment.

The Hypothesis

How does the professional ensure that his professional prism is at work? He is aware of the hypothesis he develops about the clients' situation. The hypothesis is about those aspects of the information provided to him that are relevant to him *as a professional.*

Every professional constructs a hypothesis about what is happening in each session as a way of guiding him through the session. Without a hypothesis the professional would not know which question to ask once the basic information has been gathered. When the intake information has been presented to the professional and the clients define the problem that brought them to the office, the professional develops a hypothesis about the situation in order to determine the next line of questions.

At any given moment in an interview, the professional could ask dozens of different questions, and each would make sense to the client. However, in order to make sense to the professional, the chosen question must come from his professional hypothesis. Without a hypothesis, social chatter is as relevant as issue data.

The professional, therefore, selects one from a dozen or so relevant questions, and the hypothesis helps him decide which of a group of relevant questions is the *most useful* at that moment. It is not *whether* we work under a hypothesis, it is *which* hypothesis we are working under at a given moment. We can see that the hypothesis helps the professional to

- maintain a focus on his professional relationship with the client,
- choose the appropriate line of questioning,
- select the specific, most useful question within that line.

Different professions develop different hypotheses about the same situation. A lawyer develops a hypothesis about the legal theory; the family therapist, about the dynamic interaction of the participants; an accountant, about the accounting method, and so on. A mediator develops a hypothesis about

- the problem to be resolved through negotiations,
- the client's goals,
- their negotiating behavior.

19

So, we now have an additional value of the hypothesis, it *helps the mediator to be a mediator.* This is particularly important in mediation because most mediators come to the profession from another profession. The lawyer/mediator has his personal bias/prejudice, his legal hypothesis, and his mediation hypothesis. The same trilogy is found with mediators from other professions.

Ideally the mediator disattends to any hypotheses about the clients' dynamic behavior or their legal posturing, since these do not help him to move the clients towards a mutual definition of the problem and the subsequent problem solving that follows from the acceptable definition.

The only relevance of a therapeutic hypothesis is whether the disorder impacts the client's ability to negotiate an agreement: if it does it requires a referral to a therapist. The only relevance of a legal hypothesis is whether the client has a legal problem requiring a referral to counsel. If the behavioral hypothesis is about a condition that might affect but not prevent an agreement, the mediator lays the nonmediation hypothesis aside.

To be useful, a hypothesis must be generally correct and must also be relevant. The mediator can develop a hypothesis about the client's psychological problem and hypothesize, for example, that one client has a narcissistic personality disorder. The hypothesis may be more or less correct but it would not be useful. Even a person with this disorder must negotiate an agreement in order to solve the problem.

Similarly, the mediator might hypothesize that a client is greedy. This might make the negotiations more difficult, but it does not prevent the other person from holding firm and insisting on a fair settlement, and it does not prevent the mediator from managing the negotiations leading to a fair settlement.

Let's see how different hypotheses affect the mediator's behavior and ability to help the couple solve their practical problems.

The Case of Mary and Peter

Mary and Peter lived in a home purchased by Peter before the marriage. Mary, who is in her mid-thirties, initiated the divorce two years ago. They fought about the children and money. She took the two children, Tony age nine and Greta, age five. She remarried and has a baby with her new husband, Arnie.

The Mediation Process

Arnie and Mary live in a small house. They have a difficult time economically because Arnie has a low-paying job and Mary is home full-time caring for the children. Arnie has three children from his former marriage, and the children spend alternate weekends with him and Mary. At the time of the mediation, the son by her former marriage and the new baby live with Arnie and Mary. Times when Arnie's three children are also with them are difficult because the house is so small.

Peter, who is also in his mid-thirties, has not remarried but has recently found a younger girlfriend. Peter was depressed when Mary left and was unemployed for almost two years. His family of origin is well off and they have helped him to start his own business, which demands a lot of his time. He is happy with his new work and, in order to make it a success, must work many evenings and weekends in addition to the normal hours.

When Mary and Arnie's child was born, Peter, who was not working at that time, took full-time care of Greta, a very demanding and noisy child. She has minor cerebral palsy. Peter agreed to care for her to help Mary, who had a difficult time with the birth of her new child. Now Peter wants to return Greta to Mary's full-time care because his new job is demanding - and will be for the next couple of years. In addition, his new girlfriend does not want Greta around.

Arnie does not want Greta around either because of her difficulties. In addition, he says that the smallness of the house increases the effect of her difficult behavior. Greta's extra expenses are also a problem for him and Mary.

At one session of the mediation, Peter agreed that if Mary would take the daughter he would give her $25,000 to enable Arnie and Mary to build an extra room to accommodate Greta, who has difficulty climbing stairs. Peter thought he could get the money from his family and $25,000 did not seem to be difficult for him. Peter proposed that, in return, he would have alternate weekends with both of the children. He stated he wanted this arrangement because Tony, the nine-year-old son, could care for the five-year-old daughter. Mary agreed to this arrangement.

Greta has repeatedly said she wants to live with her mother and is angry with Mary for leaving her with her father when the new child was born.

At the following session one week later, Peter arrived very angry, rejecting the proposal to pay Mary $25,000. He refused to give a reason although it seemed clear he had talked to his family about the money and to the girlfriend about the weekends. His new proposal was for no money and that he would have Tony on alternate weekends and Greta once a month for one of those weekends.

This case was presented for consultation in Oslo, Norway. A group of twenty mediators analyzed the case, developed hypotheses, about the problem, and then developed strategies for implementing each hypothesis: they offered ten hypotheses. The presenting mediator chose the most useful hypotheses and strategies for her.

We will examine each of the hypotheses to see which are useful, that is, whether they deal with the goals of the parties or the strategies to reach those goals. We will also identify the less useful ones and, based on each hypothesis, determine how the mediator would act in the next part of the session.

It is also useful to ask which of the hypotheses came from the data and which came from a supposition of the mediator. The latter come from the mediator's bias or prejudice. When the mediator is clear that the hypothesis does not come from the data presented by the family, he can discard it and focus on hypotheses about the goals that come from the data they have presented to him.

> 1. The husband feels he is a loser. *(a)* He is a loser as a parent: he cannot manage the daughter. *(b)* He is a loser as a spouse: he could not manage his marriage and Mary left him. *(c)* He is a loser as a businessman: the proposal would make him lose $25,000.

This hypothesis is mostly about emotions/feelings. Whether or not he is a loser is a perception he may or may not share. Developing a line of questions based on this hypothesis leads the mediator towards individual therapy with Peter. The mediator would have to discover the basis of Peter's sense of loss in each of these situations, determine what they have in common and how to deal with the underlying sense of loss in all the three situations, and then decide how to move the discussion back to the practical issues of Greta. During this work, Mary would be ignored, since the hypothesis does not deal with her problems. It might be possible to translate this to a mediation goal by stating it as, How can Peter and Mary reach an agreement without either of them feeling they are losers?

2. Both parents are acting as lovers in their new relationships rather than as parents. The new relationships seem more important than the children.

This is a therapeutic hypothesis about both of them, but as individuals and as spouses, not in relationship with each other as parents. The line of questioning that follows this hypothesis requires the mediator to spend time discussing each of their relationships with their new spouses, focusing on the nonparents, Arnie and Peter's girl friend, rather than Greta and Tony. Clearly, discussing the other partners will not lead the couple to the possible solutions of their practical parenting problems.

3. The new partners are pushing the issue. The wife is afraid that if she takes Greta, she will lose her new husband. Peter is afraid if he keeps Greta, he will lose his new girlfriend. (See also the first hypothesis.)

This is a feeling hypothesis about their spousal needs, which could be dealt with by inviting the other people to a mediation session to explore with them whether this is true and then what they could do to relieve Peter and Mary's concerns. If the mediator invited the other people to a session, he would focus on the children, and his work with the new adults would not be in their adult spousal relationships but as assistant parents of Peter and Mary's children.

4. The husband's fear of losing his new girlfriend is greater than his fear of losing his children.

This is an emotional/behavior hypothesis. One could ask whether this hypothesis is based on the facts of the case as reported by the mediator or upon some other basis. The facts indicate that Peter had cared for the daughter voluntarily. The facts indicate that he might want to shift that responsibility back to Mary but do not indicate that he would make the shift at the cost of losing his children. If Peter's concern for his new relationship is indeed greater than his concern for the children, the mediator would explore the extent of this change and help Peter examine the consequences of losing his children and the relative permanence of his girlfriend.

5. The wife finds the two children from her marriage with Peter, the one child with Arnie, and Arnie's three children from his previous marriage too much to handle.

Put into goal terms this might read, Mary would like to lighten the load of caring for all of the children. This hypothesis would lead the mediator to explore with Peter whether he understands her plight and what he could do to alleviate her situation in the best interests of his children.

6. The husband is seeking the fountain of youth.

An interesting observation not borne out by the data. Not a useful mediation hypothesis.

7. Both parents are afraid the daughter has significant problems that will get worse in the future.

The mediator would follow a line of questioning to clarify this hypothesis. Once it was confirmed, he would explore what the couple could do cooperatively to find out whether the daughter is likely to develop more problems and what they could do, as a team, to help avoid this. A referral could be made to a specialist who works with children with disabilities.

8. If the parents could see their children's needs they would respond to them.

This hypothesis comes close to being an imperative; that is, a belief that they should deal with the children's needs as better parents. A goal hypothesis might read, They would like to be better parents but don't know how. A mediator would pursue a line of questioning to establish each parent's commitment to parenting the children. With this clear he would help them find ways to meet the children's needs according to their definition of good parenting.

9. The daughter is a classic Identified Patient.

This therapeutic hypothesis does not tell us about the parents' goals. This hypothesis would lead the mediator to develop a line of questioning designed to redefine the family and the problem using systemic family therapy. He would also focus on the other children of the marriages as a way of making this redefinition. To be a useful mediation hypothesis, the idea would need to be framed in goal terms, such as, What do the parents need in order to feel good about Greta?

10. The couple is fighting over the money for the extra room: Mary sees it as a way to keep her marriage; Peter sees it as a loss of face with his family.

The hypothesis concerning the money is a useful one. If the mediator uses this hypothesis, he will pursue with the wife whether having extra space at her house will solve some of the problems raised about Greta. He would question the husband as to whether he wanted to solve those same problems for Greta. Then the mediator would explore an understanding of the self-interest of the two people. He would use their self-interest as a basis for further questioning in line with this hypothesis. The mediator would explore with the parents how the extra space at the mother's home would solve the problem between them regarding Greta and how could they get that extra space. The discussion might focus on what is the least such a room would cost; how much could be done by Mary and Arnie, and how much by contractors. The couple would be encouraged to explore other ways of solving the problem such as moving to a larger house and possibly sharing the additional cost. This discussion would lead the couple to explore many ways of solving the problem, hopefully with each of them contributing to the possible solution.

The Hypothesis Drives the Summaries

We can now see that the summaries are not accidental. They are based on the mediator's hypothesis:

- What he chooses to ignore are those matters that, based on his mediator training, are defined as non-mediation issues
- What he chooses to include in the summary is based on his hypothesis of which goals are most important to the participants

The mediator continually checks his hypothesis in order to determine whether it is useful. Once it is formed, the first line of questions is designed to test it. The clients' response to the questions helps the mediator decide whether his hypothesis is generally correct. If it proves to be correct, he acts on it. If the clients' responses indicate that it is more or less correct, the mediator modifies the hypothesis based on this new information.

If the clients indicate that the hypothesis is incorrect, the mediator discards his hypothesis and begins to gather information that enables him to develop an alternative hypothesis. Selvini-Palazzoli et. al.[9] warn of the danger of marrying a hypothesis. Since we develop a hypothesis from our professional training, we are often reluctant to give it up when the client indicates that it is incorrect. We hold on to the hypothesis. I know when that happens to me. I usually find myself sitting on the edge of my seat, leaning forward and saying to the clients, "No, you don't understand. What I really meant was . . ." I am trying to convince them of the correctness of my hypothesis rather than listening and taking my cues from them as to its value and relevance.

This happens because, while we can intellectually understand the difference between our personal biases and our professional hypotheses, it is not always easy to keep them clearly separate in our work. Therefore, consciously testing, modifying, adapting and discarding hypotheses is also the best safeguard to the participants that the mediator is keeping his personal bias out of the session and using only (or primarily) his professional hypothesis.

Maintaining the Mediator Role

In divorce mediation, a couple either has exhausted all known possibilities of reaching agreement known to them or is bereft of options to solve the problems that caused the deterioration of the relationship. Despite this, society requires that in order to end the relationship they must resolve the issues of support, asset division and future parenting. They must agree on some important areas governing the rest of their lives and the rest of their children's minor years.

---

[9] M. Selvini-Palazzoli, L. Boscolo, G. Cecchin, and G. Prata, "Hypothesizing, Circularity, Neutrality: Three Guidelines for the Conductor of the Session," *Family Process* 19 (1980): 3-12.

The Mediation Process

In addition to being asked to make important decisions about their futures from the nondecision context of their past, they must deal with the various levels of guilt, frustration, disappointment, betrayal, anger, and regret. They must deal with each other as exspouses and continuing parents.

Divorce mediation requires the settlement of complex emotional issues as well as mundane practical matters. Each person must be able to let go of the past emotions and relationships long enough to settle the amount of support, how to divide the assets fairly, and how to be separate yet cooperative parents.

Family and business mediation requires a similar focus. There may be complex emotional/dynamic issues causing the teen to rebel or the partners to fight about business decisions. However, the parents and teen want and need to work out an appropriate curfew, and the business must be kept running. These are very practical matters resolved only in practical ways.

When a family also works together in a business, complex family dynamics often cloud and, at times, confuse the very practical differences the family members have about the daily operation of the business. While the mediator must be aware of these dynamics and incorporate the awareness into his management of the business negotiations, he must also remember that the issues presented for resolution are practical issues.

Thus, while the founding father may have dominated the business when he ran it, and some of the inheriting children want to change his practices and others do not, the mediator recognizes that the various family alignments are highly emotional. On the other hand, questions of whether and how to change the business practices require a practical level of problem solving.

The mediator helps the clients understand what he can and cannot do as a mediator and helps them behave as mediation clients. Most people come to mediation expecting to be judged. Some also want the mediator to be a lawyer or a therapist. They do this by asking legal or therapeutic questions. A client wanting a therapist/mediator raises many emotional issues and tries to have the mediator behave as a therapist rather than a mediator. A client wanting a lawyer/mediator asks many legal questions in the hope of obtaining legal advice. The mediator, on the other hand, presents himself solely as a mediator and provides only problem-solving advice.

It is important for the mediator to be able to distinguish among those tasks that can be accomplished in mediation, those that can be accomplished in therapy, and those that can be accomplished in the legal arena. The couple's emotional problems are best dealt with by a therapist. The final legal document is drafted by the attorneys who also provide legal advice.

The mediator provides mediation, which is, after all, ideally what the clients come to him for: to negotiate an agreement on practical issues. That the clients have feelings of frustration and betrayal is a fact of life. They must live with them or resolve them. Even if they decide to take steps to resolve them with the help of a therapist, they must still live with them while they are attempting to resolve them. There is no magic wand that makes emotions disappear.

People in emotional turmoil continue to function in the rest of their lives. They still work and make important decisions. The divorcing airline pilot must take-off and land the jumbo jet and make all of the decisions necessary for a safe flight. The majority of divorcing people manage to conduct their lives relatively normally even though they are going through the pain of the divorce. The divorcing salesperson does not unburden his emotions to every customer. He must act as an employee. Every family suffers one or more traumas over the years. While we all sympathize with them at the time, they must still function in their other capacities during a trauma.

A myth has developed that a mediator must deal with the emotions involved in a conflict in order to resolve the conflict.[10] The myth becomes self-fulfilling if the mediator permits the emotional problems to dominate the mediation session. When the emotions are allowed to dominate, they are reinforced and given precedence over the

---

[10]I accept a large measure of responsibility for this confusion. My first book, *Divorce Mediation: A Practical Guide for Therapists and Counselors* (New York: Springer, 1981), made the case that mediation was essentially a social work role that demanded a combination of social work problem solving and therapy skills. I have come to realize that combining these roles confuses the clients and the mediator, preventing them from concentrating on negotiating an agreement about practical matters to end the dispute.

practical negotiations issues. The clients are held in a position of therapy clients, unable to negotiate an end to their practical disputes normally. The mediator's first response to the emotions is to acknowledge the pain and move on with his task. If that does not work he determines whether the emotions will prevent the individual from negotiating from their legitimate self-interest and, if he decides they cannot, refers the client to a therapist. If the question is whether the marriage is over, the clients should be referred to a family therapist. Once the decision to divorce has been made *by either spouse*, the dispute to be mediated is *how* to implement that decision not *whether* to implement it.

Creating doubt by the generic strategies of normalizing, mutualizing, and maintaining a future focus through summarizing form the basis of all mediation. In the following chapters we will look at how these generic strategies are embellished with other mediation strategies that are specific to the context of family mediation. Chapters two through five deal with the phases specific to divorce mediation: the intake, budgeting and support, asset division, and future parenting.

Chapter Two

The Intake

THE TELEPHONE INTERVIEW

Mediation begins when a client calls the mediation service. When a prospective client calls, the mediator is presented with a classic dilemma: how to provide sufficient information so she can make an intelligent decision about the suitability of mediation while at the same time not developing a relationship with the client. The mediator must provide the information without collecting the facts of the specific case. Although the caller may be the wife (the majority of initial contacts are by women), the mediator's work is with both spouses. If the husband believes the mediator has established a relationship with his wife, he will view the process and the mediator with suspicion.

What the Clients Need to Know

The client making the initial call needs to know about the process of mediation:

- how it works
- what it covers
- who conducts it
- what the outcome is

Clients do not need to know how the mediation applies to any of the specific issues of their situation. The information the wife gleans from the initial telephone call will be relayed to her husband, who will be able to accept the general description of the process but be wary if he learns from his wife what the mediator thought about his specific situation. Any discussion of the details leads him to believe that his wife has gained an advantage over him by influencing the mediator in the discussion. Thus, the mediator provides the caller with information on a general level while avoiding the specifics of the client's situation.

Designating the Intake Person

If the mediator has a support staff, one member can be trained to provide the basic information and set the initial consultation date. An agency can designate one person to conduct all telephone intakes. When a third party conducts the intake, the caller has no special advantage over the spouse and no special information that the other spouse may believe is unavailable to him. Thus, the desirable structure is for the secretary or one staff member to handle telephone intake calls on all cases.

A Useful Monologue

The intake person gathers the basic data: names, telephone numbers, and ages of the children. This is noted on the intake form and provided to the mediator. The secretary delivers a monologue such as:

The mediator will work with you to identify all the issues that need to go into your separation agreement.[1] She[2] will begin by helping you to do budgets showing what it costs to live apart and, using that information together with the income data, help you negotiate the issues of support. She will ask you to complete a net worth statement and help you to negotiate how to divide your assets fairly. Lastly, she will help you think through all of the future parenting issues for each of you and the children. She will make sure you cover all of the details in each of these areas. And she will do that in a way that there are no losers.

The outcome of your work with the mediator is a memorandum of understanding. The mediator drafts this to cover all the agreements you reach in mediation. You take this to your respective attorneys for review and incorporation into the formal legal documents. The mediation takes from eight to twelve hours, depending on the complexity of your dynamics and economics. You meet weekly. During an initial free one-half-hour consultation, you and your spouse can meet the

---

[1] The final legal document has a different nomenclature in different states. Most no-fault states provide for a period of separation under a Separation Agreement before a divorce is granted.

[2] In this chapter the female gender is used to identify the mediator.

mediator and ask any questions you may have. There is an additional three-hour charge for the time taken outside sessions and spent drafting the memorandum of understanding which you take to your attorneys. Have you talked to your husband (or wife) about mediation?

This monologue by the secretary provides the caller with the essential overview of mediation, while arranging that the mediator will cover everything. The secretary ends the monologue with a question. This leaves her in control of the dialogue. If the caller responds that she has talked to her husband, she is asked whether the couple would like an appointment. If the spouses have not talked, the secretary offers to mail a package of information to both spouses.[3]

Avoiding Content

The secretary is trained to avoid discussing any specific issues. When a client asks, "Can I stay in the house?" or "What am I entitled to in support?" or "Can I keep my pension?" the secretary responds, "The mediator will talk to *both* of you about those issues when you meet with her." If pressured by the client, the secretary can avoid discussing details by saying, "The mediator prefers to talk to both of you about those issues at the same time. That way you both get the same information, and one of you does not have an advantage over the other." The secretary notes on the intake form any specific questions or issues the caller raised. The mediator reviews the form prior to meeting with the couple so she is aware of the issues in her first meeting with the couple.

In this initial interaction the secretary has:

- Given the basic information about the three content areas of mediation: support, asset division, and parenting
- Explained the basic process indicating that the mediator will take care of "all the details"
- Avoided discussing any issue specific to the couple
- Defined the mediator's balanced role
- Explained the win-win idea in a way that makes sense by referring to reaching agreement with no losers. (Most people find it difficult to believe that they can be a winner in

---

[3] The contents of this package are found in chapter 7.

33

divorce but most accept the idea that they should not be losers.)

When the Mediator Conducts the Intake Interview

If the mediator answers her own telephone, she must be able to assert her balanced role even more clearly. She provides the same descriptive information about the process and avoids content discussion. Since she is talking directly to the client, she must take responsibility for everything she says. The secretary can indicate she can't talk about these issues because that is not her job. However, the mediator cannot use this reason. Instead, she states explicitly that it is unfair to discuss issues without the presence of the other spouse.

This statement is usually received warmly by the client because the wife is assured that, if she can't take unfair advantage of her husband with the mediator, the husband won't be able to take advantage either. Most spouses believe the other controls the marriage, and each client is concerned that the other will develop a special relationship with the mediator. Indicating clearly that the mediator is not on either side is often a relief to the spouse who is trying, at that moment, to develop a special relationship.

Some callers try to elicit the mediator's aid in convincing a reluctant spouse to enter mediation. That is an unlikely outcome. The mediator might be able to convince a person to enter mediation with another mediator, but once the mediator joins one spouse in any way before establishing a working relationship with both parties, her usefulness as a mediator to that couple is compromised, and it is doubtful that the reluctant spouse will accept that mediator to handle the case.

Conveying the Message through Tone of Voice

When the mediator conducts her own telephone calls, the tone and manner of the mediator's voice is very important. The person on the other end of the line focuses on the voice. There are no body movements or facial expressions to support what the mediator says. The first contact requires a clear and concise statement from the mediator that avoids diffidence. I often meet couples who have talked to other mediators before coming to see me. When I ask why they choose to work with me, many reply that I sounded as if I knew what I was doing and did not sound clinical. With the permission of the caller, it is useful to record the intake conversation on audiotape and to analyze it afterwards to determine how you can make your presentation most effective.

THE FREE CONSULTATION

Many mediators offer a free one-half-hour consultation. This enables both spouses to meet with the mediator, get to know her, and ask any questions they have about the process of mediation and the issues of divorce. When a free consultation is offered, more initial telephone contacts result in an appointment, and my experience is that more than 90 percent of couples attending the half-hour consultation schedule mediation.

Maintaining Eye Contact

The mediator opens the session with a review of what was said on the telephone. If the mediator spoke with one spouse prior to the session, the review is directed at the spouse with whom she did not speak. This means that the mediator has more eye contact with that spouse to help to balance the relationship she has already established with the other. After the first few minutes, the mediator begins to even up the eye contact by frequently shifting eye contact between the members of the couple. In the intake session the mediator often breaks eye contact with the person speaking to sweep across the couch and check on the other spouse. This lets both of them know that she continually cares about both of them.

Constantly checking eye contact with each spouse has another benefit. If one spouse is doing a lot of talking and the mediator pays that person full attention, she will not notice the body language expressing displeasure at the lack of attention that is exhibited by the other spouse. If the husband if talking a great deal, when the mediator breaks eye contact with him and sweeps across to the wife, she will notice the wife shifting in her seat and making facial expressions indicating it is time to engage her in the process.

Four Goals of the Consultation

The half hour consultation has four basic purposes:

- Provide the couple with more detailed information about the process as well as the content areas of divorce by mediation
- Provide an opportunity for the couple to ask any questions they have about the process and content areas
- Provide them with an opportunity to assess the mediator
- Provide the mediator with the opportunity to assess whether the couple is suitable for mediation

Providing Information about the Process and Content.

The mediator opens the session by confirming the information the secretary has provided and confirming the purpose of the session. The typical session opens with the mediator welcoming the couple and then saying,

The purpose of our meeting this afternoon is for me to explain how mediation works and to give you an opportunity to ask any questions you may have about the process so that you can decide if it is appropriate for you.

She pauses while the couple confirm that they share her purpose statement.[4] When this is confirmed she continues,

I will work with you if it is clear you have decided to separate and I will help you identify everything that should go into your separation agreement.[5] I will begin by helping you do budgets to determine what it costs to live apart. Using that information together with your income information, I will help you negotiate the issues of support: if any, how much, in what form, for how long. I will then help you identify all of your marital assets: that is, everything of value you have

---

[4] If either indicate they had a different purpose in mind, e.g., the husband thought he was coming for marriage counseling, the mediator clarifies the real purpose and does not engage a client in the process of divorce if that client is not ready to divorce. This is a point of termination, if one spouse has been inveigled into mediation by the other spouse under some pretense such as going for counseling.

[5] This clarifies for the couple that your work with them is on their separation, not their reconciliation. It is important to make this statement, since one spouse is often reluctant to divorce and should not have any illusions about your role.

accumulated during the marriage. I will help you decide how to value those and help you to divide them fairly.[6]

Finally I will help you think through all of the future parenting issues for your children based on the idea that although you are separating as husband and wife, you will always be the mother and father of the children and they will always need each of you.[7] I will do all of that in the context that there should be no losers.[8] So, I will see that you cover everything. I will go into each area in great detail with you.[9]

I will manage the conflict between you, and obviously there is some conflict or we would not be here.[10] I will help you make that conflict productive rather than destructive. I will do that by keeping a focus on the tasks. I'll be looking to the future for each of you, not at the past.[11]

---

[6] This is the first use of the word *fair*. It is designed to establish a basis for making all decisions fairly and also precludes the mediator buying into either party's definition of the problem. For example, he might say, "divide them equally." But, the circumstances of their case may not call for an equal division but an equitable division of the assets. In any case, the actual division will take place based on data and the client's standard of fairness that is not yet available to the mediator.

[7] This is the first mutual statement, indicating a mutual parenting role in the future without any comment about either the quantity or quality of those roles.

[8] People often use the term *win/win* to describe mediation. However, most divorcing people do not believe it is possible to win in a divorce. They can accept that they should not lose and certainly believe that they should not suffer a loss at the hands of their spouse. Therefore, this comment is designed to speak to the fears about losing and establish the concept of fairness in the outcome of mediation.

[9] A reminder that you will take care of everything. At a time of divorce people need to know that the mediator will make sure everything is taken care of. It reinforces the idea of the mediator as manager of the process.

[10] The couple inevitably smile at this point with a sense of relief that you are not afraid to deal with conflict.

[11] A mention about the future focus of the mediation. This is helpful because a future focus is also nonjudgmental. No person coming to mediation is entirely faultless in the relationship, and each has been roundly criticized by the other for their actions in the relationship. Thus, a future focus is a relief

However, one thing I won't do is to tell you what to do. I will share ideas with you that other couples in similar situations have thought about to give you a wide range of options for each issue you must settle.[12] There may be times when you say to me, "Tell us what to do." But I won't tell you what to do because I don't have to live with your agreement, you do. So it must be an agreement that meets both of your needs.[13]

Predicting Behavior

The mediator attempts to predict some of the experiences that the couple will encounter during the process to help normalize the experiences when they actually happen. For example she says,

There will be times when you wonder why you ever chose mediation. You will want me to give you the answers, and you will say to yourselves that, if you had taken the litigation route, your attorney would have told you what to do and what not to do. When that happens, you will probably get angry with me and wish you had never come to see me. However, that too will pass and you will negotiate your own mutually acceptable agreement.

She further emphasizes the mutual problem-solving aspect of mediation and its voluntary character by saying, "Either of you may leave the process at any time it is not serving your needs." By giving them permission to leave, it is easier for them to remain in the process: Any compulsion or risk they might feel is minimized, and their control over the outcome is reinforced.

---

from the fights of the immediate past and an assurance that the mediator will not buy into the other's definition of the way the marriage ended.

[12] Obviously the couple cannot be expected to know very much about how divorce negotiations are conducted or how they normally turn out. Thus, the mediator's promise to share ideas with them relieves their concerns that they do not have the expertise to do it all themselves. It is also part of normalizing because the offer to share other's ideas with the clients also suggests to them that other people have been in a similar situation and have found solutions.

[13] This is designed to remind them that in mediation they are in control of the content at all times and that an agreement will not be imposed on either of them. It also reminds them that they must both agree or there is no agreement.

The Intake

As you proceed through the process and make agreements, I will keep track of them and I will draft a memorandum of understanding covering all of the agreements you reach in mediation. You then take this to your attorney. If you don't have a lawyer, we can give you a list of law firms that have handled mediated divorce agreements. The attorney will review the memorandum of understanding with you and incorporate the agreements you have reached into the formal separation agreement (or divorce agreement). The attorney files the separation agreement with the court, and after you have lived apart under the agreement for at least one year[14] either of you can convert it into a permanent decree under the *no fault* divorce law.

So, I will see that you cover everything, I'll manage the conflict, I'll provide you with a wide range of options, and I'll keep track of your agreements and draft the memorandum of understanding for you.[15] Now, why don't I stop talking and let you ask any questions you may have.

Obviously, there is a lot more the mediator could say in the opening monologue. However, the couple can handle a minimal amount of information in this session. Their minds are only half on what the mediator is saying. Many thoughts are passing through their minds at the same time. They are taking an inventory of the room, assessing the looks of the mediator, worrying about how the future will turn out, nursing an old grudge, feeling concern at what the spouse will say. Any one of these will distract the client. Therefore the mediator attempts to convey a *sense* of what will happen rather than detailed explanations. And she does it in the minimum time. The other issues that must be discussed are held in abeyance and develop from the questions the couple ask or are offered in the next session when the couple are more calm than in the first session.

Sometimes the mediator cannot cover all of the items on her agenda in the session. In that case she notes which items are uncovered so that she can deal with them at the next session.

---

[14] States vary as to the waiting requirements.

[15] A concise summary of the areas covered in the monologue.

The Fundamentals of Family Mediation

Clients' Questions

When the monologue is over the clients ask their questions. These are usually a mix of questions about the process and questions about their specific situation. Some process questions and answers include the following:

How long does it take?
About twelve hours, depending on the complexity of your estate and your dynamics. If you do more work outside the session, collecting the data, sharing it and discussing it, you will spend less time in the session. If you fight a great deal about the past, we will take longer than twelve hours. It's up to you. We move at whatever pace you set, always contingent, of course, on doing a thorough and careful job.

How much does it cost?
My fee is $100 an hour and I expect you to share in that fee in a ratio that is appropriate to you: (to wife) I want you to pay your share so you know that I am on your payroll, and (to husband) I want you to pay your share so you know I am on your payroll. How you share in my fee is up to the two of you. You know best what is appropriate.

Can we use one attorney or do we each have to have an attorney?
I recommend you each have your own attorney. That gives a second opinion on the agreement, which, after all, covers you for the rest of your lives. However, if it is relatively simple asset division, sometimes one attorney will handle it for both of you. But you don't have to decide on that until the end of the process.

What information do I need to bring into the sessions?
We will need a budget from each of you on what it will cost you to live apart. We will need a net worth statement from each of you showing everything you own and everything you owe, and we will need the last three year's tax returns. Of course, when we look at the net worth statement we will also need documentation of all of your assets. At the end of this

session I will give you the forms you will need to complete
before we get started.

Some Content Questions and Process Answers

In the initial consultation, the mediator carefully avoids getting
into any of the specifics. Obviously she does not have the facts, and
any specific discussions would be based on misinformation at this
stage. She responds to content questions with process answers that
assure the couple the issue will be covered without the mediator
becoming involved in the specific problems.

> *I want to stay in the house and he wants to sell it. Don't the
> mother and children always get the house?*
> Every couple has to decide what to do with the house and what
> the alternatives are. I will help you look at each proposal and
> weigh the consequences of each one so you can agree on the
> one that makes the most sense for your situation.

> *She inherited some money two years ago and keeps it secret
> from me. I don't care, but can she keep the money and still
> expect me to share all of my assets with her?*
> Well, we have two questions here. The first is, What is a
> marital asset? Marital assets, by and large, consist of every-
> thing you have accumulated during the marriage, with the
> exception of inheritances and gifts that have been kept
> separate. Obviously we need to know what each of you owns,
> and then we need to get agreement as to any of those items on
> each of your lists that are nonmarital. Then we focus on how
> to share the marital assets fairly. The second question relates
> to what is fair, and I will help you establish a standard of
> fairness for your family that meets both of your needs and the
> needs of the children.

As the half hour proceeds the mediator establishes that she is
in charge of the process by telling the clients that she will determine
the order of dealing with the issues and set the agenda for each session.
She also assures the couple that they are in charge of the content. She
does not accept either spouse's definition of the problem, preferring to
wait for a problem definition until its appropriate point in the process.

The Fundamentals of Family Mediation

Learning about the Source of the Referral

It is useful to find out how the clients learned about you and to share information about yourself, your professional background, special training in mediation, availability, and so forth. As the clients learn more about you and the process, they become more comfortable.

Assessing the Clients' Suitability for Mediation

While conducting the intake the mediator tests the suitability of the couple to the process offered by the mediator. There are several alternatives to accepting the assignment.

Refer to another mediator. If one member of the couple strongly reminds the mediator of a relative or a friend, she may suggest that they work with a different mediator. The same would be true if either one resonated with the mediator in a negative way, and the mediator doubted her ability to be balanced between the clients.

Refer to an attorney. Sometimes one person comes to mediation as a strategy rather than to mediate. For example, one client arrived with a fully drafted agreement that he wanted the mediator to look over and tell the wife that it was OK for her. Obviously this husband wanted to use the mediator to gain credibility for an agreement drafted by his attorney. He had no intention of mediating. After unsuccessfully attempting to engage the husband in the process, the mediator suggested to the wife that her interests would be best served if she was also represented by an attorney and terminated the mediation.

Refer to family therapy. On a few occasions, one spouse has brought the other to mediation under the guise of going to work on the marriage. In those cases the reluctant spouse indicates surprise when the mediator describes her role. The couple should decide whether they want to work on the marriage or the separation. If they choose the former, they are referred to a family therapist. If they choose the latter, they stay in mediation.

Maintaining Balance

Maintaining balance is an important aspect of mediation. However, every mediator has a personal history and a value system that clashes with the values or behavior of some clients. The mediator cannot like or empathize more with one party without having this bias work to the detriment of the other. Thus, when the mediator finds herself more attracted to or sympathetic with one party, she looks first at why she is so biased, trying to uncover what, in her own experience, causes this imbalance. Once this is understood, the professional examines the behaviors of the favored party that appeal to her. Finally, she looks at the behaviors of the unfavored party to identify what they are and how they impact on the mediator's biases. An understanding of this combination helps to prevent the mediator from becoming aligned with one person.

At times the mediator dislikes both parties. If the couple have a culture or value set that offends the mediator, she must decide whether she can overcome these biases to work efficiently with the couple. If she cannot, she must refer the couple to another mediator. There are times when the mediator dislikes a specific behavior of the couple and must develop an awareness of this dislike and focus on why she dislikes the specific behavior as the first step towards preventing this bias from lessening her efficiency as a mediator.

Assigning Tasks

Leave at least ten minutes at the close of the session to provide enough time to go over the data forms they need to complete. As the session draws to a close, the mediator provides the couple with a booklet describing mediation in detail, pointing out to them that they can read the booklet in the privacy of their homes (see page 221). The booklet provides a step-by-step description of the process so that they can know where they are at each stage of the process. It includes advice on how to prepare the data forms, some advice on parenting, and a section on how to negotiate.

The Information Forms

The other materials are

- The income data sheet showing income from all sources for the previous year (see page 68)
- A budget which the couple are asked to complete on what it will cost them for the next year (see page 73)

- the net worth statement showing all assets and liabilities (see page 94)

The mediator goes over the forms, answering questions about how to do the budget, assuaging fears that filling out the budget engenders in the clients, and suggesting they do their best to cooperate in completing the forms. But, if they get into a fight while doing the budgets, they can put it on hold and bring the dispute to the mediation session where "I will make it productive rather than destructive."

Setting the Order of Decision Making

In the very first mediation I conducted, I started with the budget and support issues, proceeded to the assets and liabilities, and finished with the parenting issues. That worked for me and I have used the same order since then. There is no magic or particular logic about this order. Some mediators begin with the parenting, believing that once those issues are worked out the economic questions are more easily dealt with. Others begin with the assets, believing that once the house and other assets are settled the rest of the package falls into line.

No one way is *the* right way. You, as a mediator, must experiment with the order that makes most sense for you because, if you are feeling comfortable about what you are doing, you will usually do a better job for the clients.

The Role of the Children

Some parents want to know how the children will be involved in the process. Individual mediators disagree about whether the children have any role at all or should become part of the process. We discuss this in chapter 5. I tell parents that we will make an opportunity available to them to bring the children into a session once the agreement has been reached. In that session the mediator reviews the parenting agreement with the children, giving them an opportunity to comment on the arrangements. The mediator suggests that the decision whether to bring the children in for a review session be made at the end of the process, after agreement is reached on the parenting.

Confidentiality and Privilege

Some clients ask about issues of confidentiality. Few states have provided for mediator confidentiality by way of legislation.

(Check your state legislation on this.) The mediator cannot guarantee confidentiality to the couple except in those states. But there is a more subtle issue involved here. While the mediator cannot guarantee confidentiality, she can note that the courts do not normally admit into evidence any offers made in a settlement conference. That is, when offers are exchanged in negotiations prior to the trial they are done so *without prejudice*. Counsel cannot reject an offer of settlement in the pretrial conference and then tell the judge at the trial, "Your honor they offered so much in negotiations. That is the least I should get." If judges admitted offers to settle into evidence in the trial, neither side would make any offer to settle for fear of having the offer used against them in the trial. If no serious attempts were made to settle the case before trial, the courts would become even more clogged. I share this information with the clients. But then I ask,

> What is it you are afraid of because, obviously, you will have to share all the information with each other during the mediation to make an intelligent decision. If you don't share that information in mediation, then you will share it when subpoenaed by the other's attorney, and if you don't share the information with the attorney, the judge will order you to share the information with him. So, the question is not *whether* you will share the information, but *when* you share it. Here voluntarily, at the attorney's in an adversarial arena, or in court under orders of the judge.

Making this very clear when the question is raised tells clients who were thinking of mediation as a possible arena in which to avoid full disclosure that they must share all of the data. It also tells the wife who might be concerned that her spouse is hiding information or not disclosing the data that in mediation she will receive full disclosure.

The Difference Between Therapy or Law, and Mediation

Almost every client is experiencing mediation for the first time. Most are experiencing divorce for the first time. Thus, they are neophytes about the process and content. Most people know how to behave in a therapist's office or a lawyer's office. If they have not experienced therapy, they have seen enough portrayals of therapy sessions in movies, TV, and the theater or read about them in books.

They have seen even more portrayals of legal clients in the media. But, so far, they have seen nothing about mediation. Thus they are not clear about how to behave. So the mediator helps the couple learn how to be mediation clients. She does it in three ways.

- Early in the interview she talks about the differences so the clients are clear what the mediator is not: she is not a therapist and not an attorney.
- She explains what the mediator is: the manager of their negotiations.
- The third way, which is more difficult, involves modeling appropriate mediation client behavior.

For example, when a husband advances some therapeutic tidbit or emotional need, the mediator carefully ignores the invitation to be therapist and focuses on the practical tasks confronting the couple. If the wife wants to know what her rights are, the mediator avoids being an attorney and points out that in mediation we are interested in meeting everyone's needs, which go beyond rights. If a client insists on knowing her rights, the mediator suggests that she consult with an attorney to provide her with such advice. I do point out that there are very few rights that either spouse has in a divorce. There are lots of responsibilities, particularly in the parenting area, but very few rights, except in community property states.[16] I point out that mediation helps meet the clients' *needs,* which are often greater and more important than their rights.

Spelling out Expectations

If the couple are to behave as mediation clients they must know what is expected of them as mediation clients. Thus, the mediator spells out her expectations very clearly. Different mediators have different expectations, but the following appear to be generic:

- Each spouse will do the work assigned outside of session. Thus, each will bring in completed budget forms for the support session.
- There will be full disclosure of all the information.

---

[16] See chapter 4.

- Clients will not cancel a session without appropriate notice, (twenty-four hours seems the most common minimum). If they do not show up for an appointment, they must pay for the time.
- The clients will treat each other with dignity. No cursing, no put-downs or denigrations of the other.
- Clients will pay for the mediation at the end of each session. No billing.

Consider Using an Agreement-to-Mediate Form

Spelling out these expectations at the first session helps the couple know how to behave and sets the stage for a productive mediation. Some mediators use an agreement-to-mediate form to spell out these issues. I do not use an agreement form because I believe it appears to be legalistic. In addition, if you have written rules you are required to enforce them whenever they are broken. I find that I can often ignore minor infringements of the normal rules of productive behavior if an infringement does not interfere with the process. Not writing rules down leaves me free to decide when to enforce them, which, for me, is when the infringement impedes the process.

Some groups give clients a set of rules. The Michigan Association of Court Mediators, for example, uses a simple set:

- Let each person speak without interruption.
- Be courteous in your manner towards the other person.
- Do not fight.
- Listen to what the other person has to say. You may find you can agree with some of the things they say.
- Do not accuse the other person. Just state the facts.
- Do not speak *for* the other person, or their intentions, motives or point of view. Speak only for yourself.
- Think about possible options for resolution of the issues. The more options you can think of, the more likely that you will find one that both of you can agree on.[17]

Obviously, not all of this can be accomplished in one half-hour consultation. The highlights are covered and each couple focuses on

---

[17] *Mediation Reference Guide* (Michigan Association of Court Mediators, 1991).

one or two areas for deeper explanation. When the consultation is over and the first session is scheduled, the mediator knows that the intake has only just begun.

THE FIRST SESSION

The first session is scheduled for the week following the consultation. It is useful to begin quickly, since the couple has decided to attend the consultation and made the decision to begin working with the mediator. Further delays at this point provide opportunities for second guessing and allow others to influence the couple. Bad things happen to most divorcing people. Their friends and families often urge war rather than reasonable solutions. Getting the process under way helps alleviate the fears of the unknown and keeps people moving forward. However, if the pace is too fast for the couple, the mediator can slow it down by suggesting sessions in alternate weeks rather than weekly. In this way the mediator engages the couple in the process as quickly as possible but always gives them space and time to move at a pace consonant with their needs.

When the mediator meets with the couple for the first full session, she has intake information to collect. We begin the session by collecting the basic data on the intake form (see fig. 2.1). Most of this is straightforward data collection, but how the data are shared with the mediator is also useful information.

1. Gathering the addresses independently determines whether the clients are living together or apart without asking the specific question. This is helpful when one spouse is very reluctant to separate. By not asking the question, are you living apart? the mediator avoids taking a stand on the issue, avoids stampeding the reluctant spouse, and stays out of the past.

2. The occupation, income, and education information rounds out the essential socioeconomic data.

3. When the clients provide information on the children (names, ages, and date of birth), the mediator notes who gives and how they give the information. In the typical family the mother responds to this question with the precise dates. If the father shares in giving the information, or is the sole provider of the information, it may indicate a more active parenting role on his part. The mediator notes who gave

The Intake

Figure 2.1 Intake Form

	Husband	Wife
1. Name	_____	_____
2. Address		_____

Phone: Home _____   Home _____
       Office _____   Office _____
4. Occupation _____   _____
Income _____   _____
Education _____   _____
3. Children   Name   Age/Birth date

4. Living arrangements _____ 4a. Separation date_____ __
Others in house _____
5. Marriage date _____   6. Referrer_____
7. Initiator _____   7a. Response_____
Gradual/Sudden _____   Feel Now _____
8. Therapist: Husband _____   Wife_____
Address _____

OK to send therapist brochure _____
OK to contact client for future research _____
9. Main issues:_____

the information and checks out its importance later. Sometimes the father begins to give the information but does not remember the dates. The way in which this is done and the mother's response to the father's providing the information often indicates the way the parenting issues will be dealt with in the session.

Obviously, all of the information the mediator gleans during this part of the session is tentative. It suggests areas to be explored more fully. Rarely does it both inform and confirm the hypothesis that the mediator develops in the same session. For example, if the mother provides all of the information regarding the children while the father sits passively watching the interaction, this suggests a typical family organization. However, the mediator does not make this assumption until the hypothesis that such behavior generates for the mediator has been confirmed by further information and/or behavior.

4. The answer to the living arrangements question also provides information about their readiness to divorce. If they are living in the same house but using separate bedrooms, this indicates they are further along the divorce process than people who are still living and sleeping together.

The separation date provides the mediator with an indicator as to their ability to conduct the negotiations. If they have been separated for some time, they have probably worked through a lot of their feelings. If they come to see a mediator shortly after separating, they may be still dealing with the emotional issues of separation and not be ready to get down to business in mediation. In that case, schedule the meetings less often than weekly to enable the couple to deal with the separation issues and, if necessary, refer them to a family therapist to work on these issues while going through mediation.

Check for others living in the house. When these are relatives and not tenants, it indicates an extra dimension to deal with in discussing future housing arrangements. It is also reminds the mediator to check the couple's income statements for any income contributed by the residents who are not members of the immediate family.

5. I ask the marriage date separate from questions about the children so that it does not concern parents whose children were born before or shortly after the marriage.

6. Asking about the referrer provides useful information. If the referrer is a therapist, it usually indicates that the couple has reached

the decision to divorce recently. If the referrer is an attorney, it usually indicates a high-conflict couple having trouble using the adversarial system. The profession of the referrer often informs the mediator of the couple's situation. The mediator notes the name to thank the referrer for the referral as part of the work in building a practice.

7. I ask four questions relating to the past. I usually preface these questions with the comment that, "I am going to ask you a few questions about the past. These will be the only questions I will ask you about the past because I am going to work with you in the here and now and the future. Now you may bring in the past, most people do. But I won't focus on it." The questions I ask about the past are

    a. Who initiated the decision to separate?
    b. When was that?
    c. How did the other partner respond when first told of the desire for the separation?
    d. How does s/he feel about the separation now?

The mediator needs to know this basic information to determine the extent of the difference between the couple towards the idea of separation. For example, the answers to each question may be:

The wife: a. "I suppose I did."
              b. "Last May" (three months prior to seeking the mediation).
The husband: c. "I was shocked. It came as a complete surprise. I was devastated and did not want it. I was utterly opposed to it."
              d. "I suppose if that is what she wants, I'll have to go along with it."

This tells the mediator the wife is the initiator and the husband is the reluctant spouse. However, there has been movement on the husband's part since first learning of the wife's decision, and he appears capable of not allowing his emotions to defeat his self-interest.

Preempting Some Dynamic Problems

At this point the mediator might say to the husband, "That makes it tough for you to negotiate an agreement because divorce is a goal you would prefer not to achieve." The husband nods in agreement. "Thus if you do anything to undermine your own self-interest in the negotiations, I will alert you of this." While such a comment may appear unbalanced, it is usually met with approval from the wife. She wants the separation and therefore will cooperate with any reasonable behavior of the mediator to achieve that end. She is aware of the husband's reluctance and welcomes the mediator's awareness of it and her commitment to the process of negotiating an agreement to separate. If the mediator's interventions are consonant with one spouse's goals, that spouse will overlook the mediator's identification with the needs of the other spouse.

The intake form includes an entry for Gradual/Sudden. This is space for the mediator to note from the information provided by the couple whether the decision to separate has been developing for some time or whether it has been recently sprung by one person. This helps the mediator understand the emotional impact of the divorce process on the mediation process.[18]

8.   The answers to the questions about therapy inform the mediator about the type of support each person is likely to be receiving outside of the mediation process. The question is also designed to gain permission to contact the therapist as a practice building strategy. Ask the clients for permission to contact them later as part of research efforts. You will rarely meet a person who denies this request.

9.   The Main Issues section, is space for me to note any issues that emerge during this part of the session that I cannot deal with then. This information helps me shape the agenda for future sessions.

Normalizing Ambivalence

Every couple exhibits a level of ambivalence about the divorce. In all probability, only robots could pass through divorce negotiations without some ambivalence. This is often apparent during the initial session. The mediator can recognize it and try to measure the level of ambivalence to determine whether to act on it or simply ignore the ambivalence as normal. In the latter case a simple comment to the couple, for example "I can see you are each a little ambivalent at times about divorce and that's true for every couple that sits in those chairs,"

---

[18] See J. M. Haynes, *Divorce Mediation: A Practical Guide for Therapists and Counselors* (New York: Springer, 1981).

lets the couple know you have heard them without having to act on it. It also tells the couple it is normal for them to have some ambivalence.

Ambivalence is not grounds for terminating the mediation. If the couple is truly ambivalent to the extent that neither really does not want the separation, this fact will surface most clearly in the session that deals with money. A mediator cannot divorce people who do not want to divorce. The worse that will happen is that those who really should not be mediating their separation will drop out of the process after the first or second session. There is no need to do any more than acknowledge ambivalence. If they really do not want to get divorced, nothing the mediator does will make them divorce against their will.

If you decide not to offer the free half-hour consultation, then the first session is usually an hour long. All that is done in the one half-hour consultation and the early part of the first session is replicated in the first hour-long session. Thus the first part of the session consists of the mediator's explanation of the process and the latter part handles the basic data gathering

Budget Forms

The session is brought to closure when the mediator gives the clients copies of the forms to be completed. The mediator explains each set of forms to the couple, going over each part step by step. I usually begin with the budget forms, since I start with the budgeting and support issues. I make sure each client understands

- exactly what information is needed,
- how to gather the necessary information,
- how to fill out the forms.

Obviously the budgets should be complete, but they will not always be 100 percent accurate. The role of the mediator is to enable the couple to develop information that is complete and accurate enough to be useful.

Figuring Out the Food Bill

Some people become upset when they see the budget forms because they have no experience in budgeting. However, budget information is required if the couple is to make rational decisions about their independent futures. In this case I explain to them not to worry if they don't have all the figures. "Do whatever you can and we will complete the rest together in the first session." The mediator may suggest ideas for developing figures such as asking each person how they pay for the supermarket bill. If it is by check, then they can look at their checkbooks and add to that figure the amount they spend each week at the milk store or deli or butcher to arrive at the total food bill. If they pay by cash, the mediator asks how much they usually take to the supermarket with them and how much they usually have left over. If each of these ideas draws a blank, the couple can be asked to make a reasonable guess for the budget session while keeping close records of actual amounts spent on food during the next few weeks. The spouse who is moving out (usually the husband) needs to establish an independent database from experience in deciding how much he needs for food in the future. In this session the mediator draws on her own life experience to assist the couple make the *best effort* to complete the budget forms.

Figuring Out the Clothing Bill

She may suggest that the couple decide where they purchase most of their clothes and whether, by and large, they charge them. The answer to these questions provides a source — the charge accounts — for determining the amount of money spent on clothes.

Telling the Children

It never ceases to amaze me that couples come to mediation, having decided to divorce without telling their children. Often they say, "Well, we thought we would tell them when we had it all settled." Here, the mediator puts on her educator's hat and points out that if they have decided to divorce, the children are probably aware of the fact or at least they are aware that the relationship is in serious trouble. Rhona Rosen's early work indicates that children are disturbed by being left out of the communication loop and having the decision sprung on them.[19]

One way of dealing with this is to suggest a family conference. The mediator suggests that the couple tell the children at least that they

---

[19] "The Importance of Parent-Child Communication in the Adjustment of Children to Parental Divorce," *Psychotherapeia: Journal of the South African Institute for Psychotherapy* 4, no. 1 (1978).

are meeting with a mediator to negotiate the separation. She helps the couple identify how best to do that.

My sense is that the disclosure about the divorce should take place at a family session with all relevant members present. I suggest to the parents that this session should take place in the room where such gatherings have taken place in the past, and both parents must be present. The clients then discuss what should be said, who will say it, and how each parent will be supportive of the other *as parents* and assure the children that the breakup is as adult spouses not as parents. Children need to be told the same story by both parents.

ISSUES AFFECTING THE MEDIATION

Other issues emerge that have an impact on the mediation process. These usually become clear in the first full session with the clients. However, the mediator should be aware of them at all stages of the process.

Have They Consulted Attorneys?

It is useful to know whether they have had a legal consultation and to learn, in general terms, what the attorney has told them. Any major misunderstandings can be clarified before the process gets under way. If one spouse has consulted an attorney and the other has not, the mediator suggests that the latter spouse also have a consultation so the spouses are on an equal footing at the start.

This recommendation helps establish the mediator's balance and prevents a later waste of time when one spouse insists the attorney stated some fact and the other must check it out.

Do They Need a Temporary Agreement?

If the wife says that the husband left three weeks ago and has not given her any money since then and she is destitute, or if the husband says that he left the house three weeks ago and has not been allowed to see his children since leaving, they have created a crisis. When one person forces the other into a difficult negotiating position, the other may make major concessions in the mediation to achieve a short-term goal. The wife may make concessions just to put bread on the table this week, or the husband may make concessions just to be able to see his children this week.

Neither of these situations is conducive to fair negotiations. Therefore, when the mediator sees that one partner has established a situation that could lead to an unfair bargain, she changes the agenda to negotiate an agreement on the immediate issue so as not to allow it to affect the long-term issues.

The mediator insists that the couple reach an agreement about the amount of temporary support to be paid or the schedule for the father's access before the other negotiations proceed. While doing this the mediator makes it clear that they are working on a temporary agreement and that the long-term agreement covering all of the issues will be achieved in the process.

Recognizing and Responding to Spouse Abuse

Every couple expresses some sense of ambivalence. This tends to make the neophyte mediator consider therapy referral as the *first* choice. However, there are dangers in this course of action. One couple came to see me and exhibited considerable ambivalence. I explored the ambivalence and suggested they might want to work on the marriage. They both agreed, the husband somewhat more enthusiastically than the wife. A few months later they were back in my office. The husband complained that "If only you had sent us to a competent therapist, we wouldn't be here now." Again I sensed a lot of ambivalence and made a second referral.

They returned three months later and, on the third attempt, the wife admitted that she had been abused and had moved out. I realized that in my anxiety to deal with their ambivalence, I had sent her back to an abusive household for more than five months.

Who Can Protect the Abused Spouse?

Spousal abuse is rampant. Some occupations seem to have higher incidence than others. However, abuse is present among all social classes and at all levels of education. It is, unfortunately, a fact of life in most countries. It is clear that although great strides have been made in the last decade, most women who are abused are also neglected by society. In Suffolk County on Long Island, where I live and work, three women were murdered by their husbands recently, and all three had orders of protection. The problem for the mediator is to know what the indicators of spouse abuse are, and what special provisions are required when spousal abuse is evident.

Indications that spousal abuse exists include:

- the abused spouse always waits for the other to speak first,
- the abused spouse glances at the abuser each time she talks, checking out his reaction,
- the abused spouse smoothes over any conflict,
- the abusing spouse speaks most of the time (often more than 75 percent of the time),
- the abusing spouse sends clear signals to the other, warning her by eye movement, facial expression, or words,
- the abusing spouse usually has a litany of complaints about the abused spouse, who offers no defense.

I do not believe it is appropriate to screen every couple for the possibility of domestic violence. Clients entering mediation do so in order to mediate not to be screened for violence, drug or alcohol abuse. I have developed a procedure that recognizes the women's rights and enhances her opportunities to negotiate a reasonable agreement when spouse abuse has been identified, and it is agreed upon. However, if the accused person denies the allegation and no agreement is reached on whether abuse is present, the mediator terminates the mediation, since she cannot establish the rules of conduct. But once I have their acknowledgment, I set the following rules for the couple as a condition for staying in mediation:

- The abused spouse must obtain an order of protection.
- The abusive spouse must leave the family home immediately and agree not to go to the family home while the mediation is in progress.
- Access for the children must take place *away* from the family home at some neutral spot. Usually this is the home of an agreed upon relative or a public place such as MacDonald's.
- Compliance with this arrangement is a condition of mediation. I check each week that it has been complied with.

Using Self-Interest

The abuser is often willing to agree to these conditions because, as I explain to him, "Negotiating an agreement can be tense at times, and you may lose control on occasion. If you do and your wife goes to divorce court with a black eye, you will surely get a tough deal from the judge. He is not likely to have much sympathy for you. You don't want to put yourself in the position of losing control and suffering for it; therefore, these conditions are in your best interests."

Some mediators object to this arrangement since it gives the abuser power to decide whether to use mediation and takes that decision away from the abused person. While I sympathize with this argument I also know that in every situation, one person has the right unilaterally to terminate the process — the husband, the wife, or the mediator. Therefore, I am comfortable with it. I reject the argument that abused women are not entitled to mediate because I believe that mediation gives all clients more control, and certainly an abused spouse needs all means to gain control over her own life.

There is no evidence that the legal route provides any better control for the abused spouse. She gives control of her case to her attorney and a county prosecutor who decide for her. She must still deal with all of her fears and aching desire to get the divorce over and done with as quickly as possible. Every person contemplating divorce must negotiate a separation agreement. That is a requirement the state places on every married couple. People should opt to negotiate the separation agreement as a free choice.

Remember Mediator Safety

The mediator must also assess her own safety. The mediator cannot guarantee safety for herself or the client. Yellott recommends "mediators should work out 'safety signals' with the party perceived at risk."[20] The safety signals need not unbalance the mediator, because there is no excuse for abuse. The mediator can say to both spouses, as Erickson and McKnight suggest, "There is never a valid excuse or reason for abuse and violence. Mediators do not mediate whether or not violence and battering was justified, nor do we try to determine

---

[20]   Ann W. Yellot, "Mediation and Domestic Violence: A Call for Collaboration," *Mediation Quarterly* 8, no. 1 (Fall 1990): 48.

what caused it or who started it. Rather, we try to help the two of you see what is needed to escape the violence of the past." [21]

Providing a supervised waiting room. Some agencies and mediators accept referrals knowing that abuse exists in the family. One well-administered program has developed a process where a male-female team meets with the spouses separately. The parents are given different times so they arrive separately and wait in a supervised waiting room. The abused spouse is seen first to minimize the ability of the abuser to signal her what to do because he knows what questions will be asked. [22]

In the initial session the female mediator asks the wife all of the questions, and the male mediator only asks clarifying questions. They reverse these roles with the husband. The following questions, which could be used in all individual interviews, are among those asked of each spouse:

- Has your partner ever hit, punched, slapped, pushed, or kicked you, pulled your hair, or used a weapon on you? [23]
- Has your spouse ever done the above things to your children?
- Has your partner ever forced you to be sexual with him or her against your will?
- Has your partner ever damaged or destroyed any of your belongings, or hurt any of your pets?
- Do you have any concerns about your partner's use of alcohol or drugs?
- Have you ever thought your partner had mental health problems?
- Do you have any fear about answering these questions?

By adding these questions to those of Yellott, the mediator can develop an instrument to use whenever abuse is suspected.

---

[21] Stephen Erickson, and Marilyn McKnight, "Mediating Spousal Abuse Divorces," *Mediation Quarterly* 7, no. 4 (Summer 1990): 377-388.

[22] Dennis Marthaler, "Successful Mediation with Abusive Couples," *Mediation Quarterly* no. 23 (Spring 1989): 53-66

[23] This specific list was developed in preference to a more general "Have you ever been abused by your spouse?" because the broad question left too many loopholes for the client to avoid the issue.

Recognizing and Responding to Substance Abuse

The right to choose the arena also applies to couples where drug and alcohol abuse is present. Where one or both spouses abuse drugs and/or alcohol, the mediator must establish specific rules to deal with that condition. I inform clients that they must come to each session substance free. I also declare that I will decide at each session if they are impaired and if either one is, the session will be canceled and the impaired person pays for the time scheduled.

Using self-interest to gain cooperation. The above procedure is explained to the clients in self-interest terms. I explain that if they are impaired they cannot adequately represent their legitimate self interest, and therefore the session must be canceled in their self-interest. My experience is that when these additional rules are applied in the context of protecting the self-interest of the people involved, most clients accept them. It is also useful to recommend that a substance abuser seek help from the numerous self help groups such as Alcoholic Anonymous. Again, the suggestion is made out of client self-interest in having additional help while going through the divorce.

Caucusing

Caucusing is particularly useful in cases where spouse or substance abuse appears to be present. A caucus is useful:

- to confirm or deny a mediator's suspicion that spousal and/or substance abuse is present which would interfere with one person's ability to negotiate a fair agreement,
- when one person is clearly not representing their own self interest, `
- when the level of hostility is so high that it prevents rational discussion,
- when continual ventilation by one person impedes the progress of the negotiations,[24]
- when response to events, external or internal to the negotiations, block or hinder productive bargaining in joint session,[25]

---

[24] Jack Heister, "Sequential Mediation: A Necessary Therapeutic Intervention Technique," *Mediation Quarterly* no. 9 (September 1985): 57-61.

- when one or both clients seem unable to make proposals and counter proposals.

The mediator uses caucus infrequently and engages in the following activities during the separate sessions.

- If the client maintains an obviously unreasonable position, the mediator can be a "Dutch uncle" and explain to him privately what he is doing that is not in his self-interest or is unrealistic.
- When the hostility is very high, the private session can be used to cool off the clients.
- If ventilation is clouding the issue, the mediator can allow a client to ventilate privately as a way of defusing the activity.
- When one or both clients cannot make a proposal or respond to a proposal, shuttle diplomacy can be used with the mediator taking a proposal from one client to another.

Other steps that the mediator can take include a separate caucus with each spouse whenever abuse is suspected. The mediator can assess the safety issues and help empower the victimized partner. Yellott suggests that in the separate session the mediator:

- explore what concerns the abused spouse has about her safety and that of her children, now and for the future
- assess the need for crisis intervention, referrals for shelter, and an emergency plan for safety during the mediation, if needed
- ask the abused spouse, "Is there anything you don't want to say in front of your partner? Are there hidden agendas I should know about?"[26]

Girdner suggests that each spouse be told in the caucus, "I will not share any of the information you tell me with your spouse unless I have your permission. Is there anything you would like to ask me or tell me before we continue?"[27] This gives permission to the abused person to talk about the abuse or about fears of abuse.

[25]   C. W. Moore, "The Caucus: Private Meetings That Promote Settlement," *Mediation Quarterly* no. 16 (Summer 1987): 87-101.

[26] Yellott, 39-50.

[27] Linda Girdner, "Mediation Triage: Screening for Spouse Abuse in Divorce

If abuse is suspected, meet with the abused person first and at the end of the caucus and ask if she wants to wait or leave separately from the spouse in the future. If the answer is yes, make separate arrangements.

Keep the caucus short. The caucus should be kept as short as possible with equal time given to each participant to maintain balance. Each session is task- and topically oriented. When the participants are brought back to the joint session, a brief review of the individual sessions is helpful in allaying fears that something special happened in the other's session.

Shuttle Mediation

In labor-management and international negotiations, the mediator frequently acts as the conduit for offers between the parties. The mediator meets with A, who suggests they may be willing to make an offer but they don't feel confident making it at this point. They may feel that making the offer would appear as a sign of weakness. So the mediator carries the proposal to B with the advice that "I think A would agree to this if you would accept it."

This activity, known as shuttle mediation, appears as a well-honored mediator role in other spheres. However, in family negotiations it is liable to undermine the mediator's credibility and give the mediator too much power, for nobody discovers if the mediator shades A's proposal to make it a little more palatable to B and then softens B's response to make it more acceptable to A. Shuttle mediation tends to put the mediator in control of the content.

Using the Caucus for Data Gathering

It is also possible to use the caucus as part of the basic data gathering. Some mediators meet with the parties individually at the beginning to collect each side's version of the data. This gives her an opportunity to press hard for information that the client is reluctant to provide. Also, the mediator can, through other questions, point out holes or weakness in a person's position. In the caucus the mediator can help the participants to move towards a more rational position more quickly, and she can do this without publicly undermining the people involved.

Mediation," *Mediation Quarterly* 7, no. 4 (Summer 1990): 365-376.

Thus, when the mediator pursues a hard line of questioning to gather all of the data and then points out the holes in a person's position that are created by this data, it is possible for one client to accept this without losing face in front of the other.

We can say that caucuses are useful

- any time spousal abuse is reported or suspected,
- at the intake stage if the mediator is having difficulty gaining information,
- during the negotiations if one person is holding on to an unreasonable position and the mediator wants to act as a Dutch uncle to the client,
- at the end of the negotiations if either party is afraid to make proposals or concessions in public; in this case the mediator engages in shuttle mediation, walking offers and counter offers between the parties who are in separate rooms.

Some Dangers

Using the caucus has inherent dangers and, except as noted, offers few benefits to the mediation process. The clients may reveal information to you that makes you share in their secrets. For example, at one time I regularly caucused with clients. One husband told me, "Look I have a friend but I don't want my wife to know about it." In the caucus with the wife she revealed, "I'm going to get married as soon as this is over, so I don't want any maintenance support, I want all the money in child support."

In each caucus I was told information that did not help me be a more effective mediator and, in fact, if I honored their requests to maintain silence, this made me a coconspirator with each spouse. The mediator can obviate this problem by stating at the beginning of each caucus that she will feel free to share anything said in the caucus in the full session, but that seems to undermine the purpose of the caucus.

It is more efficient to run the session so that everything is public between the participants and the mediator and no action appears to benefit one side more than the other.

The caucus may also tend to make the mediator lazy. If things are not going well in a session, it is easier to split into the caucus pattern than to stay in the consultation rook with the clients and figure out what the mediator can do in the consultation, with both clients, that will keep the mediation moving forward.

Organizing the Room

When the couple arrive at the office they are often surprised by the arrangement of the room: the way it resembles and differs from a therapist's or attorney's office. The room is furnished with a couch and a chair of equal height. There is no desk. The couple sit side by side rather than across from each other, and there is nothing between the mediator and the clients.

The seating arrangement has an impact on the negotiating behavior of the participants.[28] People who sit side by side tend to view the other less adversarily than people who sit opposite each other.[29] The couple has been cast into adversarial roles by their friends and family and their experience of other couples in the throes of divorce. The mediator helps to break that expectation and replace it with an expectation of mutual problem solving. She uses the physical arrangements of the room to help restructure the couple's expectations.

Now that they are sitting on the same side there is a danger that they will view the mediator as an adversary. The mediator's seat is arranged to minimize that possibility. There is no desk in the room and no furniture between her and the clients. The mediator's seat is at the same height as the couch and she looks at the couple at eye level, thereby increasing the mutuality of the process.

Finally, the mediator's chair is placed at the distance most likely to make the couple comfortable. The optimum distance seems to be from three to four feet.[30] The mediator sits between the clients at the apex of an isosceles triangle. All three people are equally spaced; each is from three to four feet from the others, sufficiently distant to be business like and sufficiently close to create a measure of intimacy.

You may not be able to arrange an office with a couch. In that case, two identical chairs can be used for the clients arranged in the same triangle.

---

[28] H. Proshansky, W. Ittleson, and L. Rivlen, *Environmental Psychology: Man and His Physical Setting* (New York: Holt, Reinhart & Winston, 1970).
[29] R. Sommer, "Further Studies of Small-Group Ecology," *Sociometry* 28, (1965):16-23.
[30] Edward Hall, *The Silent Language* (New York: Fawcett, 1959).

The Intake

In this chapter we have looked at the process of the intake for a divorce mediation. The next three chapters look at the other stages of the process: determining support, dividing the assets, and arranging the future parenting.

Chapter Three
Managing the Budget and Support Session

The income and budget forms are designed to provide the couple with a solid data base with which to make informed decisions. The couple are asked to bring in copies of the last three year's tax returns, in addition to the budget and income forms. The tax returns help verify the income information.[1]

The income sheet (fig. 3.1) is designed to show all forms of income for each client and to identify the mandatory deductions from the gross pay. In completing the income form, many people add nonmandatory deductions, which the mediator notes since they are expenses that the couple can eliminate. For example, if the husband makes a voluntary contribution to his pension plan, the amount of money contributed can be used to meet other expenses, if needed.

Notes on Completing the Income Form

Line 1. Each client is asked to produce a recent pay stub showing income and deductions. The mediator checks the items on the stub with the income form information to be sure that they match and that everything has been included. If the client is self-employed use the relevant tax return for the previous year to verify this information.

Line 2. Fees are often problematic since they are not always reported on a pay stub. For example, a self-employed person may receive consulting fees but not receive a pay check and stub. In this case refer to the tax return and the list of 1099 forms that the payer is required to file with the IRS.

---

[1] The tax returns are also used in the asset division session to verify data.

Figure 3.1 Income Form

Provide this information on an annual basis for the last twelve months. If you have weekly figures, multiply by 4.3 to convert to monthly. For further information consult your *Guide to Divorce by Mediation.*

Income

1. Salary (attach pay stub)   _____
2. Fees etc. from all sources   _____
3. Interest/dividends from all sources   _____
4. Other Income (include from items 11-16)   _____

Deductions

5. Number of deductions claimed ☐
6. Social Security Taxes (FICA)   _____
7. State/Provincial/Federal tax   _____
8. Other payroll deductions   _____
9. Total deductions   _____
10. Total gross income less deductions = net salary   _____

Complete any of the following and add the total to line 4 above

11. ☐Bonus, commissions, fringes   _____
     (such as use of auto etc.)
12. ☐Partnerships, royalties, sale of assets   _____
13. ☐Real estate income   _____
14. ☐Trust, profit sharing, and annuity income   _____
15. ☐Income from awards, grants,
     bequests, legacies, gifts, etc.   _____
16. ☐Other income   _____

Managing the Budget and Support Session

Line 3. Interest and dividends can usually be corroborated by the bank book, broker reports, and so forth.

Line 4. There are many kinds of other income, ranging from lottery winnings to any of the items listed on lines 11 through 15.

Line 5. There is a maximum amount each person pays towards social security. If the earnings of the client exceeds the statutory maximum contribution, then deductions are not made once the maximum contribution has been reached. That means that towards the end of the year many clients will not have social security deductions made giving them extra income for that period. Check the number on line 5 to see that it does not inadvertently exceed the maxim annual contribution.

Line 6. This line shows the taxes withheld. However, if the client files the long form tax return and takes the normal deductions there is a possibility that the actual annual tax is lower than this figure. On the other hand if the person under-deducts by claiming more dependents than he actually has (see line 7), the tax bill might be higher than this figure. Check with the previous year's tax return to determine whether there was a refund or tax owed which, if true for the current year, would revise the tax liability figure.

Line 7. This number should equal the actual number of dependents. Any difference is probably explained by the discussion for line six and is another indication of the need to check the tax returns.

Line 8. Other payroll deductions are usually voluntary. However, some companies unofficially require employees to contribute to the United Fund and/or buy U. S. Savings Bonds. Where it is unofficially required, consider these deductions as mandatory if the client indicates company pressure.

Line 9. The client adds all of the deductions and put the total here. The mediator checks for accuracy.

Line 10. This is the net figure also called "disposable income." That is the amount the client really has to spend each month.

Line 11. A bonus or commission usually appears on the pay stub or is supported by an IRS Form 1099. However, the value of fringe benefits is more difficult to determine. Discuss with the clients the level of the fringe benefits that have a monthly cash value. A company car, gasoline expenses, phone expenses, and so forth all put money into the employee's pocket. If they were not provided the client would have to pay for them out of current income. Therefore they are considered part of the disposable income and should be included here.

Line 12. Income from partnerships, royalties, and sale of assets is usually supported by reports to the IRS and filed with the income tax return. The mediator checks the tax return to verify the completeness and accuracy of this figure.

Line 13. Real estate income is more difficult to verify. However, use the tax return to check this.

Line 14. Trust, profit sharing, and annuity income are usually supported by appropriate reports to the IRS.

Line 15. This is a contentious area. Income from awards and grants is usually for a specific period and associated with a specific task. Do not argue with the clients as to whether the income should be included. Remind them that your job is to collect all of the data. Their task is to determine what to do with the data. Thus, there must be full disclosure of the information if they are to make informed decisions as to which monies to include and exclude.

Bequests, legacies, and gifts are considered in two parts. First is the claim to the asset, which will be dealt with in the next chapter, "Dividing the Assets." The income from these sources is subject to negotiation and is certainly included in all of the child support guidelines and, therefore, must be disclosed for the child support decisions discussed below.

Fixed and Flexible Expenditures

The budget sheets are designed to differentiate between *fixed expenses*, those expenses that cannot be changed, and *flexible expenses,* which can be changed.

The mortgage must be paid and cannot be reduced. On the other hand, entertainment can be modified. These budget forms have been designed to cover almost all of the items for a normal family. Some families will have additional items that they add to the budget under any of the *"other",* listings.

At the end of the intake session the mediator gives the couple budget forms to complete. He assigns the task carefully and clearly and anticipates any barriers that might be erected to prevent completion of the task.

Managing the Budget and Support Session

The first question for the budget and support session is, "Have you completed the budgets?" If the answer is no, find out which parts were not completed and why. Then assure the couple that you will help them fill in the gaps as the session proceeds.

Both Must Complete the Forms

At times one person refuses to complete the budget forms for strategic reasons. For example, the husband may say, "I didn't fill out the budget, it wasn't necessary," and turning to his wife he adds, "You just tell me what you need, and I'll tell you if I can afford it."

Such a stance, if allowed to be maintained, totally disempowers the wife and places her future income at the husband's discretion. The mediator, as controller of the process, insists that *both* spouses complete the forms since they can make intelligent choices only if they have all of the data. If the husband refuses to complete and submit his budget and income forms, the mediator terminates the mediation. To continue the mediation when one spouse defines the terms of the discussion is to allow that person to manipulate the mediation for his or her own interests. The mediator is clear that he will not allow the misuse of the process.

Encouraging the husband to participate in the process as an equal partner is best achieved by stressing his self-interest while insisting that the rules be followed. The mediator might say to the husband who resists completing the budget forms,

> I can't allow you not to complete the forms, John, because that would not be fair to Mary since she would not have important information. Also, it would not be fair to you. If you agree on a level of support without knowing your own needs, you could agree to give more than you can truly afford. I will not allow you to reach a decision without all the facts. That way each of you can assure that you have protected your individual self-interests.

Opening the Budget Discussions

A useful question is, "What issues emerged for you in doing the budgets?" The reluctant spouse will usually say that he is sure they cannot afford to divorce (and there may be a hint of triumph in

71

his voice). The mediator points out that most people feel that way; the numbers are always surprising and call for second thoughts. However, few people change their minds because of the money.

A wife may comment that she does not know how she will survive. She notes that she has gone through the budget several times, cutting here and there and still can't make ends meet. The mediator notes that this is true for most couples. However, the task at this point is not to try to make ends meet but to find out what each person needs for the *future*. As other issues emerge, the mediator deals with them by normalizing the concern and assuring the couple that he will help them deal with and overcome all of their problems.

When the mediator has the completed forms, he describes the purpose and agenda for the session. The purpose of the agenda is to collect the data to provide a solid data base from which informed decisions can be made. The mediator might say, "What we need to do first is to collect all of the data. Then we will verify it and share it with each other. The figures will give us a data base from which to make all of the decisions."

Figure. 3.2 on page 73 is a typical household budget form. Each spouse is asked to complete it according to anticipated needs for the next twelve months. Obviously, this requires both of them to make some assumptions about their futures.

The mediator explains that they need to complete the figures assuming what their needs will be for the next twelve months since that is a manageable time frame. She explains that adjustments can be made later for the longer span.

The couple will make assumptions about whether either of them is going to stay in the current residence and if so, which one.

They will have to make assumptions about such things as transportation. They may get by with one car now and be unable to do that in the future. The food costs for the resident parent will decline by the loss of the other parent but it is hard to know precisely how much it will decline.

If the wife is planning on working outside the home for the first time she will have a different clothing expenditure. The couple factor these thoughts into their respective budgets.

72

Figure 3.2 Expenditure Budget Sheets

Fixed Expenses

Household
Rent/mortgage _____
Property tax _____
Home insurance _____
Other _____
     TOTAL _____

Utilities
Gas/electricity _____
Telephone _____
Fuel oil _____
Water _____
Garbage pickup _____
Cable TV _____
TOTAL _____

Insurance _____
Life _____
Medical _____
Disability _____
Other _____
TOTAL _____

Installment Payments
 Auto _____
Furniture/
appliances _____
Charges accounts _____
Credit cards _____
Other _____
TOTAL _____

Personal loans
Christmas/
Hanukkah club _____
    Other _____
TOTAL _____

Education
Tuition _____
Room & board _____
Books etc. _____
Extracurricular _____
Other _____
TOTAL _____

Transportation
Auto license _____
Vehicle sticker _____
Parking/tolls _____
Commuting fares _____
Other _____
TOTAL _____

Memberships (omit if in
cluded on income sheet)
Union _____
Professional _____
Clubs _____
Religious _____
TOTAL _____

Expenditure Budget Sheets (cont.)
Flexible Expenses

Food
Supermarket _____
Meals out, lunches_____
Deli stops _____
TOTAL _____

Clothing
New clothes _____
Laundry/dry clean _____
Repairs _____
TOTAL _____

Transportation
Gas/oil _____
Repairs _____
Noncommuting fares_____
TOTAL _____

Household Assistance
Child care _____
Yard care _____
House cleaning_____
Other _____
TOTAL _____

Household Maintenance
Repairs _____
Replacements _____
Other _____
TOTAL _____

Noninsured health
Medical _____
Dental _____
Drugs _____
Therapy _____
Other _____
TOTAL _____

Personal
Allowances _____
Barber/beauty _____
Theater/movie _____
Sports _____
Hobbies _____
Vacations _____
Magazines _____
Newspapers _____
Alcohol _____
Tobacco _____
Aging parents _____
Lessons _____
Other _____
TOTAL _____

Miscellaneous
Gifts _____
Birthdays _____
Religious _____
Charity _____
Other _____
TOTAL _____

GRAND TOTAL _____

Notes on the Expenditure Sheets

Household expenses. Many people have the mortgage, taxes, and insurance paid by the bank, in which case, the cost for all three is included in the monthly mortgage payment.

Medical insurance. Cross check with the income sheet to see if the client has included the cost of the medical insurance in the payroll deductions. If so, eliminate one of the entries.

Installment payments. Check the asset forms to determine how many payments are due on each loan. For example, if an auto loan has only two more payments due, it would be reasonable to exclude it from the long-term budget. On the other hand, if the separation causes one of the clients to purchase an automobile, the projected payments for this expense should be included. The contributions to the Christmas/Hanukkah club can be stopped.

Education. Tuition covers college and/or private school expenses. Make a note of any expenses for tutors or special assistance. If a child is close to college age, the clients will have to discuss how to pay those costs. Most couples choose to share the college expenses in a ratio of incomes at the time the child attends college.

Transportation. There are two entries for transportation, one in *flexible* and the other in *fixed* expenses.

Food. Most people can identify how much they spend at the supermarket each week. However, many clients overlook stops at the deli, dairy, and other specialty stores such as the greengrocer or butcher, since these tend to be irregular and involve payments smaller than those made at the supermarket. Therefore, when reviewing this figure, the mediator prompts them to think about these expenses as well as the normal supermarket bill. Make sure the resident parent has included the cost of school lunches.

Household maintenance. Help the couple to identify major expenses they face in the next two years. They cannot always provide for a new washing machine, but awareness helps them in their planning.

Health. This is an area with a wide range of variation among different families, depending on the health status of the family. Note any special needs such as the health costs for handicapped children. Ask the clients whether they have included drugs in the food bill. Some people use a charge account at the drug store to buy nonmedical items. Move nonmedical items from the *drugs* entry to the *supermarket* entry.

In calculating the noninsured medical costs, you must know the amount of the deductible of the insurance plan. Most plans do not pay the first $50 to $250 of annual health care costs. In addition, find out whether the plan has a maximum benefit payable for each year. For example, most plans limit the amount paid for therapy to $1,000 or $2,000 a year. The clients need to include the deductible in this part of the budget. Plans pay a fixed percentage (usually 80 percent) of the actual cost. See that the clients include the amounts.

Personal. Most people don't think of what they spend as an allowance in the same way they think of the specific amount of money given to the children. They tend to overlook their own spending money. An adult allowance is often called "dribble money." Dribble is what happens to a twenty dollar bill after you break it. It is hard to determine the exact amount, but most people have some idea how much they spend each week without accounting for each part of it.

Contributions. This section is for contributions other than those deducted from the paycheck. Ask about office collections for showers, birthdays, accidents, and so on. These often add up and should not be overlooked.

Displaying the Budget

Before the couple arrives for the session, the mediator prepares a copy of the budget forms on the flip chart using the subheadings of each group of expenses. He has added two columns opposite each item and put the client's first names above the columns. He will use the space on the right of the sheet for notes or special children's expenses. The mediator's flip chart looks like the display in figure 3.3.

He has placed the subtotal names of each category of budget items on the display. This enables him to get all the items on one sheet so the total budget needs are observable at all times.

76

Figure 3.3 The Mediator's Budget Display[2]

ITEM	JOHN	MARY
Household	_____	_____
Utilities	_____	_____
Insurance	_____	_____
Installments	_____	_____
Education	_____	_____
Transportation	_____	_____
Memberships	_____	_____
Food	_____	_____
Clothing	_____	_____
Transportation	_____	_____
Household assistance	_____	_____
Household maintenance	_____	_____
Health	_____	_____
Personal	_____	_____
Miscellaneous	_____	_____
Contributions	_____	_____
Totals	_____	_____

Income:
John _____
Mary _____

The mediator begins by collecting his copy of the budget sheets and checking that each spouse also shares with the other a completed copy of the budget and income forms. He collects the data by asking each one for their figures on each item. The mediator takes turns, perhaps starting with the wife on housing and then the husband; then asking the husband first about the utilities and then the wife.

This method keeps both people involved in the process. If the mediator starts with the wife and goes through the entire budget collecting her numbers this gives the husband lots of time to sit and comment on each of his wife's numbers. However, if he is also

----

[2] The easiest way to display this information is to use a newsprint flip chart.

involved in giving information he must be preparing for the next item rather than thinking about remarks to make about his wife's numbers.

The mediator checks each number and the source of the data. In doing so, he verifies it. If the numbers look unusual the mediator explores more closely how the person arrived at the figure, helping them see if it is inflated or understated.

As he collects each number, the mediator enters it on the flip chart. We can now see a specific process unfolding, as he

- Collects the data from the couple
- Verifies the data with the couple
- Displays the data for the couple
- Shares the data with the couple

Very few couples share in the management of the family finances. They often divide the labor, with the most common division being the wife taking care of the weekly and regular expenses and the husband taking care of the larger, irregular expenses. Thus, typically the wife knows more about the food and housing costs, and the husband knows more about the vacation and insurance costs.

By checking each person's numbers and verifying them, the mediator establishes a common data base, which he displays on the flip chart. The display assures that the information is shared and that each person is empowered regarding the information they previously did not know or control in the marriage.

If there is a disagreement regarding any item, the mediator insists on documentation. Documentation can include the checkbook, bills, credit card invoices, bank statements, and so on. Sometimes this means that a number in dispute is entered on the flip chart and marked with an asterisk to indicate that it needs further documentation. The mediator returns to that item in the following session.

The goal of the session is to collect and display all the income and budget information providing the couple with the key information needed to make decisions about how much each needs to live separately. It tells them how much income they have and what the gap is between what they each need and what they currently have.

Once the mediator knows the size and nature of the gap, he focuses on the key mediation question, How can they close the gap between what they each need and what they each have? That is a remarkably different question from the one asked in legal negotiations. In the legal arena each spouse asks either, How little do I give? or How much can I get? Those two questions push the couple into positional bargaining. The mediation questions direct the couple towards problem solving.

Getting to the point in the session when the mediation question can be asked involves many diversions. As the items are discussed and displayed, numerous opportunities arise for the couple to engage in marital bickering about the past. The mediator's role is to keep the couple in the here and now, with a future focus to their discussions.

The mediator also observes the couple's marital dynamics, noticing those that interfere with their ability to negotiate a fair deal. The most useful way of dealing with any marital dynamics is to stay with the task, to discover what income each person needs in the future.

Closing the Gap

When the mediator completes the collection, verification, and display of the data he asks the question, "How will you close the gap between what you have and what you need?" The couple's answers move the discussion to a future focus and problem solving.

In general the couple have the following choices:

- Reduce expenses
- Increase income
- Liquefy assets

Reducing expenses. It is too easy for each person to solve the problem by requiring the other to reduce expenses. The mediator suggests that, in thinking about cutting expenses, each think only of their own numbers. In that way he limits the possibility of one spouse launching a fight about the other's expenses. It is useful to have each spouse reflect on the numbers for one week and to ask them to come back to the next session with some suggestions for cutting back.

The mediator also points out items in the budgets that have more flexibility, such as vacations, and items that are not mandatory, such as voluntary contributions to pensions. The mediator identifies them as areas for discussion. He does not propose that the couple make cuts in these areas. This is because the content is owned by the clients, not the mediator, and also because the mediator and the clients do not necessarily share agreement on what is flexible or voluntary.

The mediator avoids arguing with the clients by simply identifying options and pointing out areas for examination, not for specific action. One problem with looking at budgets is the difference between the mediator's money values and the client's values. It is hard not to make judgments about the way other people spend their money. Each couple has different priorities. Some couples never take vacations but have large entertainment expenses. Others spend a small amount on food at home but a large amount on food eaten out.

Each person has his own sense of what is important when it comes to expenditures, and the mediator is careful not to project his values on to the couple. I remember one case in which the wife spent sixty dollars per week on her nails. She had acrylic nails, which were reglued and manicured each week. I found this figure difficult to accept, but I also noted that it did not bother the husband at all. I accepted that such an expenditure, though frivolous by my standards, was acceptable by theirs.

Increasing income. This area has the greatest potential for cooperative action. When the size of the gap has been determined, the couple look to see whether they can increase their income. The mediator asks each of them to think only about what s/he can do, not what the other can do.

If the husband is the initiator, the wife has a difficult time thinking about what she can do. She is likely to articulate a position thus: "He wants the divorce, let him pay for it. Let him take a second job so that his kids do not suffer." If the roles are reversed, the husband will probably say, "She wants the divorce. She's Ms. Independent. Let her go out to work and earn it." Both of these responses are past focused and involve the couple in blaming rather than problem solving.

The mediator redirects the couple to the future by framing the question in a different way. Let us assume for a moment that the couple have two children, aged eight and six, and that the mother has not worked outside the home since the older child was born. The mediator might then ask her, "Mary, if you could write the script, what would you be doing two years from now?"

This is a powerful question. It moves the mother into a future focus. It is far enough away from the present to avoid the "I'm just living one day at a time" response and not too far away to be unimaginable.

The wife (particularly if she is the initiator) begins to think about her future and, after some thought, states a goal for herself. Once she has stated the goal, the mediator can explore with her the reality of the goal and the cost and the benefits of achieving it.

When both spouses accept this as a reasonable goal, the mediator has helped them develop a superordinate goal. A superordinate goal is a target shared by both parties that benefits both of them, that is, a goal they both wish to attain and one that will be used to measure all future discussions regarding support. All subsequent discussions and agreements must support the superordinate goal. The clients tend to cooperate on finding the solution to the problems raised by achieving the superordinate goal.

Let's look at an actual case. In responding to the mediator's question the wife says, "Well, I've thought about this and I would like to get a job teaching. I've always enjoyed working with children, and if I were a teacher I would be on the same work schedule as the children."

With that goal articulated the mediator explores the possibilities. He might ask, "What would you need to get a teaching job?" Once the answer to that question is clear he asks other exploratory questions such as,

- How many education credits would you need?
- Where could you earn those credits?
- How much would it cost?
- How long would it take to get the teaching certificate?

- How many teaching jobs are available?
- How much does a beginning teacher earn?

The answers to many of these questions will have to be obtained by the wife for a later session. The mediator explores the general numbers, trying to establish a ballpark figure of the cost of getting the teaching degree and the income benefits of having a teaching job.

At this point he turns to the husband and asks him the same question about his future. If he is established in his career he may talk of promotions or career changes, all of which are explored by the mediator in the same way as he did with the wife. In addition, he asks the husband, "Would you like to see Mary working as a teacher earning her own income?" When he replies affirmatively (as most husbands I have ever worked have answered) the mediator might ask, "What's in it for you if Mary becomes a teacher?"

There are significant benefits to the husband. First he will be less liable for support for his ex-wife if she is employed outside the home. Second, his children will enjoy a better standard of living if the total income of the wife's household is greater than the amount he could afford to provide in support. Last, he knows that she will be happier if she has her own career and sense of worth that comes from working outside the home.

As the husband ponders these issues the mediator asks, "John, if Mary needed some extra help while she was getting her teaching certificate, would you help her financially if you knew that the demands on you would be lighter once she was teaching?" He inevitably responds from his self-interest and agrees, usually cautiously, that he would help. This lays the ground work for a collaborative problem-solving session on how to achieve a situation where the wife is financially independent as an adult and leaving the amount of child support to be paid as the only remaining issue.

To assist the problem solving the mediator proceeds to examine the cost/benefit ratio of each of the choices. In this case, the couple should have a clear idea about the cost of the wife's education. The wife's cost/benefit ratio will consist of: the *cost* of tuition, books, extra child care, etc.; the *benefits* of having a teaching certificate; the likely starting income for a teacher.

Managing the Budget and Support Session

The husband's cost benefit/ratio will be: the *cost* of his share of her education; the *benefits* of his ex-wife having an independent income; shorter and possibly lower maintenance support, and a happier ex-wife, therefore a happier mother of his children.

As they weigh the costs and benefits they decide whether they are willing to incur the cost to attain a given benefit. In order for this to work each must have a clear idea of a cost and an understanding how they will share it and also the value of the benefit to each of them.

In this instance we looked at the wife becoming a teacher. Not everyone can become a teacher. Some wives settle for a teacher aide position. Others want to go to law school. The specific career choices are not important, provided they are practical. The mediator won't pay a lot of attention to the goal of becoming a surgeon if the person is in the mid-fifties and currently has a high school diploma.

The question for the mediator remains: Is the goal attainable and will it provide sufficient benefits to both spouses to justify their cooperating in achieving it?

No mediator in his right mind would suggest that a couple sell their assets to close the gap between income and outflow. Even the wealthiest clients would soon run out of assets. However, in the scenario above the couple may resort to selling some assets to help get the wife through her college program. In a sense they exchange assets. The assets sold would be replaced by a new equity - her teaching certificate.

Sometimes the couple has a budget or income problem that needs expert advice. The mediator is not an accountant or a lawyer and therefore does not take responsibility for providing the expert advice. He refers the couple to an expert for specific advice on the specific question. The mediator's role is to help the couple frame the question to be asked of the expert in a clear and concise way that both spouses find acceptable.

Assume that the husband is making a monthly contribution of one hundred dollars to his pension plan and another hundred dollars per month to the company-sponsored profit-sharing plan. He objects to thinking about these contributions as voluntary, arguing that dropping out of the plan will not save much because, if he ceases making the contributions, he will have to pay taxes on the amount not placed into the pension. To decide whether this is an important factor, the couple checks with an expert, in this case their accountant. The question for the accountant is, Assuming John did not make these contributions to the pension and profit sharing plans, how will his tax liability differ?

The husband may raise another objection: if he drops out of the profit-sharing plan, he will not be eligible to rejoin for three years. He says. "Since the company makes a dollar for dollar contribution to the plan, in the long run I'll lose a lot more than it's worth." This issue needs to be understood in two parts. The first is the veracity of the claim. To verify the waiting period before rejoining and an equal contribution by the employer, John is asked to bring in the booklet describing the plan and the last report from the profit-sharing plan. These two will verify the husband's claims.

The second part is to have the couple ask the accountant, Based on these facts, what is the total cost of dropping out of the profit sharing plan to John in (a) tax consequences and (b) missed contributions by the company?

Most couples can use the same accountant if that person has been completing their tax returns in the past. However, there are times when they should use a different accountant or each have his or her own accountant.

They should use a different professional if the tax accountant is also one of their business accountants. There is a danger that if the accountant earns income from representing one of the spouse's business interests, the accountant may not be entirely unbiased in the way he presents the data, and even if he is, the other spouse will have doubts about the balance of the data. Although this is more expensive, couples with a high level of mistrust do not seem to worry about the extra expense.

They should each use their own accountant where the level of mistrust is so high they are incapable of believing any data that the other could influence or control in any way. In these cases it is best for the mediator to suggest each take the same question to their respective accountants or lawyers.

The mediator assists the couple to frame the question so that it is mutual and provides answers that enable the couple to decide.

It is also helpful for the mediator to write the questions out so that each spouse has the same *written* information to take to the expert.

The couple bring the new information back to the next session. Agreement is reached as to the acceptability of the new information, and, once it is accepted by the couple, it is integrated into the other data and used to make informed decisions.

The Difference between Wants and Needs

There is an area that borders on value judgments in which the mediator must intervene. That is the difference between needs and wants. We all have needs. We also all have wants. However, we can live without all of our wants but cannot live reasonably without our needs. The mediator helps the couple distinguish between their needs, which, if at all possible, should always be met, and their wants, which need not necessarily be met.

The mediator helps the couple make this distinction by asking questions that reveal new ways of thinking to the couple. For example, the husband says, "But I need a new car." The mediator asks a series of questions about the reasons for needing the car. The answers usually include to get to work, to impress clients, to feel good, and so forth. The mediator asks, "To what extent can the existing car (or a good used car) meet your needs?"

The mediator's questions are designed to help the husband distinguish between *need,* which in this case is for a means of transportation, and *want*, which in this case is to impress others and feel good about oneself.[3] One can impress people with the top-of-the-line Mercedes or with a Honda or with a quality American car. The car does not have to be the current model: each of the husband's wants can be met by a recent model as well as by a new car.

The need can be met by any reliable automobile. So, when the mediator focuses on meeting the husband's needs, he helps him make decisions that are consistent with his needs on the one hand and his available resources on the other. We make these decisions every time we buy. For example, in purchasing an automobile we

---

[3] Helping people separate needs and wants is part of the problem-solving discussion in chapter 6.

may have the choice between a new car in the medium-price range or a used luxury car for the same price. We make the decision based on which car best meets a mix of our needs and our wants.

When we help clients make these decisions rationally, whatever decision they make will be acceptable to them and will help them be more satisfied with the total agreement, and that each will be more satisfied with the agreement over the long haul.

Child Support

Once the clients have all of the information they need in order to make their decisions, the mediator focuses on the issue of child support. Child support is mandated by law. Most states and provinces have a variation of the following formula:

Child support is determined by calculating each parent's gross income less actual social security payments and less any local (but not state) income taxes paid. The revised gross income is used to determine the amount of the child support: one child 17 percent, two children 25 percent, three children 27 percent, four children 31 percent, five or more children 35 percent.

Check the formula for your state. The child support guidelines were enacted because many women and children were falling into poverty as a result of receiving inadequate levels of support. The federal legislation requires the states to develop a formula for determining child support in the hope that the formula raises the level of support and makes support more uniform.

The mediator starts the problem-solving discussion by applying the child support formula to the couple's incomes. Once done, he addresses the remaining gap between needs and incomes.

Let us assume that the couple has two children and that the husband's gross income is $42,828 per year. If the couple live in a state where the support guidelines call for 25 percent of the net income, his child support payments will be calculated as follows:

Gross income	$42,828
FICA deductions	$ 2,052
Base income	$40,776
25 percent of base =	$10,200/ $850 per month.

Managing the Budget and Support Session

If we now assume that the wife has a budget of $21,600 then the difference between the child support guidelines amount and her needs is $21,600 - $10,200 = $11,400. If the wife earns more than this amount the couple usually agrees that there is no need for maintenance support. However, if her income is less than $11,400, the couple must negotiate how to close the gap between her needs of $21,600 and the available income (child support plus the income she earns.) The mediator helps the couple define a superordinate goal to guide the support negotiations. In negotiating the details of the support, the mediator keeps the superordinate goal in front of the discussions so the couple negotiates an agreement that helps each member to achieve a goal that is larger than the specific parts of the support agreement.

Inflated Budgets

When people complete budgets, they usually prepare them carefully and accurately. However, some people are advised to inflate their budgets to support a claim that they need more or can pay less. There is a simple way of determining whether the budgets are inflated.

When the budgets are displayed on the flip chart and the mediator believes that they are inflated, he deducts from the husband's (assuming he is the one moving out) budget those expenses that are a function of the separation. Once those numbers have been removed, the new combined totals are compared with the current income. If the revised expenditures match the actual income, the mediator assumes that no inflation has taken place. If the revised figures still exceed the current income, then he points out to the couple that they were not living beyond their income prior to the separation and, therefore, the numbers in the budgets must be inflated. He then suggests they each look at their *own* numbers and adjust any that have been overstated.

This is important because the wife may think that only the husband's figures are inflated. Experience suggests that when data inflation occurs, both sets tend to be overstated. The wife, although not moving into a new situation that incurs lots of new expenses may have some increases that are a function of the separation: for example increased child care costs, transportation expenses, or new insurance costs.

87

Let's look at an example. The mediator's board in table 3.1 shows that the combined budget needs of John and Mary are $1,233 + $1,631 = $2,864. Their current combined disposable income is $1,965 + $355 = $2,310.

Table 3.1 Mediator's Display of Monthly Budget Information

Item	John	Mary
Household	$ 460	$ 478
Utilities	100	149
Insurance	15	3
Installments	40	140
Education	0	0
Transportation	200	98
Memberships	10	0
Food	240	410
Clothing	60	60
Transportation	28	15
Household assistance	0	25
Household maintenance	0	10
Health	25	98
Personal	20	25
Contributions	10	40
Misc.	25	80
Totals	1,233	1,631

Income:
John   1,965
Mary   355

We now review John's list to determine which items in his budget are a function of the separation. We can identify them as follows (table 3.2).

Table 3.2 Increased Costs Due to the Separation

Item	Expenditure
Housing	$460
Utilities	100
50% of Food	120
Total	$680

When the $680 total increased costs are deducted from the combined budgets and compared to the disposable income, we find that the monthly expenditure becomes $2,184 (i.e., $2,864 - $680). This is less than the current disposable income of $2,310, suggesting that one or both spouses has already begun to trim the budget in anticipation of the separation.

If the figures show a substantial difference between past income and future needs (less those items that are a function of the separation), the mediator can be reasonably certain that the budget figures are inflated.

Child Support Enforcement

The Child Support Enforcement Amendments of 1984 require state child support enforcement agencies to initiate wage withholding when the parent obligated to pay support falls behind in an amount equal to thirty days of support payments.

All child support orders issued must include a provision for wage withholding. Therefore, each memorandum of understanding covering children should include a provision such as

In the event the child support is not paid and more than 60 days payments are due, the case shall be submitted to the (state) child support enforcement program for withholding as provided for in the (state) and federal laws.

When a case is referred to the Child Support Enforcement agency, the agency informs the paying parent and his/her employer. The employer must then begin wage withholding for the child support due and forward it to the agency, which then forwards it to the receiving parent.

Wage withholding of child support takes precedence over all other wage garnishments, and employers may not discipline or fire an employee because of the wage withholding order. The maximum withholding is 50 percent of disposable earnings if the paying parent has remarried and 60 percent if there is no second family. If the arrears exceed twelve weeks, then the withholdings can go as high as 55 percent and 65 percent.

This chapter has detailed the way the budget session is conducted. At times, money issues are also raised in the parenting session, and these are discussed in chapter 5. When the basic budget and support work has been done, the mediator turns to the question of how to divide the marital assets, the subject of the next chapter.

Chapter Four

Dividing the Property

Every divorcing couple has some kind of property that needs to be understood, discussed, and divided. Even couples who split up after a few months have wedding gifts to consider. Property in general can be considered as all of those things the couple has accumulated during the marriage. The only exceptions are inheritances of or gifts to one spouse.

States consider property division differently, but all use one of the following three methods:

- *Equitable Distribution.* The property is divided equitably based on criteria established by the legislature. Most laws require consideration of the length of the marriage, relative contribution of each spouse, and various other criteria, always adding "and any other factor considered by the court," giving judges wide leeway. It's worth remembering that people who want an equitable solution always want *more* than the other receives. If they wanted an equal division they would claim an equal, not an equitable, share.
- *Community Property.* The property is divided equally. The dominant idea is that marriage is an equal partnership and everything the partners accrue during the life of the marriage belongs to both partners equally.
- *Title.* Some states provide that whoever has title to the property is the owner. That was the prevalent system throughout the U. S.. in the first half of this century.

In addition, Louisiana and the Province of Quebec in Canada are guided by Napoleonic law, which places emphasis on what the couple agreed to before the marriage.

The Fundamentals of Family Mediation

The mediator needs to understand what the state law provides. However, people are not bound by the law. Neither is the mediator. One of the hallmarks of a free society is the right to enter into contract. We have that right and the state cannot take it away from us. Spouses have the right to enter into a contract, even though the contract may not provide the same terms that a local judge would incorporate into his award.[1]

So, we need to know the law but not to be bound by it. If we become bound by the law, mediation becomes a paralegal process that imposes the same outcome on the clients as a court would. Mediation is an empowering process that gives clients the right, the ability, and the process to determine what is right for their family.

The mediator's role is to manage the negotiations by organizing the discussion of the issues that emerge for each couple as the property is divided. The more coherent and organized the process, the easier it is for the clients to arrive at solutions that are appropriate to them.

A Four-step Process

Stephen Erickson[2] first developed a coherent four-step process for dealing with assets. This process, which is now widely used by mediators, provides for

- Asset identification
- Asset understanding
- Asset valuation
- Asset division

The mediator guides the couple through these four stages. Each step following in logical order, helps the couple to develop

- A database for decision making
- A complete understanding of each asset and the relationship of each asset to the total value

---

[1] The exception to this is a contract that, if implemented, would violate the law such as a contract to kill someone for payment, or a contract that is not in the public interest, e.g. an agreement that deliberately placed the wife on welfare.

[2] Co-Director of Erickson Mediation Institute, Bloomington , Minn.

- A knowledge of the value of each asset
- A criterion for dividing the assets in the most rational way

The mediator uses the same cycle of gathering, verifying, displaying, and sharing the data; defining the problem; developing and selecting options; and bargaining that is used at all content stages of the process.

To begin this cycle each spouse completes a net worth statement. A copy of the most commonly used form appears in figure 4.1, page 94.

The same rules apply to completion of these forms as with the others. However, in many ways, these are the most important forms the couple will complete since the information on these sheets is, in fact, their life savings. When reviewing these forms the mediator not only notes the information the couple have provided but also questions every blank item to be sure they have included everything. The mediator insists of full disclosure.

Notes on the Assets

Let's look at the form, line by line.

1. Bank accounts. This used to be a simple matter of looking at the savings bankbook and the checking account. Today there are many forms of bank accounts. Bank accounts now include checking accounts, regular passbook savings accounts, certificates of deposit, broker accounts linked with a money market fund, mutual fund accounts, and different types of savings accounts. The task for the couple is to identify each type of account together with the account number and the most recent balance statement.

2. Notes, accounts receivable. This is where people list monies owed to them. Normally these are monies owed to them personally. Business accounts receivable are listed under business interests.

3. Stocks and bonds. Most couples have these in a brokerage account and bring in the last account report to document the items. However, some people have the stock or bond certificates in a safe deposit box or at home and need to bring in certificate copies to document the items.

4. Real estate. The family home is the key item here. Check also for vacation homes and time shares as well as for investment real estate.

Figure 4.1 Net Worth Statement

List all of your assets:

1. Bank Accounts

Bank   Acct. #   Value/Cost

_____   _____

_____   _____

_____   _____

_____   _____

2. Notes, Accounts Receivable

_____   _____

_____   _____

_____   _____

3. Stocks and Bonds

_____   _____

_____   _____

_____   _____

_____   _____

4. Real Estate

_____   _____

_____   _____

_____   _____

_____   _____

5. Life Insurance (Cash Value)

Amount of Coverage.   Insurance Co.

_____   _____

6. Business Interests: include type, corporation
partnership, trust, capital contribution, net worth
of business, how the value was determined and
percent of interest (Bring in last balance sheet, Profit
& Loss statement, tax return, and buy-sell agreements)

_____   _____

_____   _____

7. Miscellaneous Property: patents, trademarks,
copyrights, and royalties (Bring in last income statement
and documentation)

_____   _____

_____   _____

_____   _____

94

Dividing The Property

8. Stock Options

_____   _____

_____   _____

_____   _____

9. Automobiles and Special Personal Property

_____   _____

_____   _____

_____   _____

_____   _____

_____   _____

10. Pension and Profit Sharing Plans (Bring in the
most recent statement and the booklet describing the plan)

_____   _____

_____   _____

_____   _____

11. Income Tax Refunds
State/City _____   _____
Federal _____   _____
12. All Other Assets

_____   _____

_____   _____

_____   _____

List all of your Liabilities
13. Mortgages on Real Estate
Lender _____   _____

_____   _____

_____   _____

14. Notes to Banks and Others

_____   _____

_____   _____

_____   _____

15. Loans on Insurance Policies: (Give policy #)

_____   _____

_____   _____

_____   _____

16. Other Debts (medical, charge accounts, etc.)

_____   _____

_____   _____

_____   _____

95

Fig. 4.1 (cont.)

17. Taxes Due:
State and City_____   _____
Federal _____   _____
                                      Total   _____

5. Life insurance. Term life insurance has no cash value; it is pure insurance and therefore cheaper. Whole-life or universal-life insurance builds a cash value (in effect both are forced savings plans). Although the policyholder can borrow against the cash value of the plan, the insurance company never lends the policy holder more than the cash value of the plan. Therefore, there is always some cash value to whole-life and universal-life insurance. The insurance company provides an annual report to the owner of the policy showing the account's status.

6. Business interests. Among the most difficult assets to deal with, and we discuss them at length later in this chapter. The instructions on the form are self-explanatory.

7. Miscellaneous property. Professionals often have one of these sources of income, and some can be valuable. Royalties, for example, might be small for a professional book and large for a best-selling novel. Some people think of these items only as income. However, after the couple separate, the owner of the item will receive the income. Therefore, a value is placed on the future income and considered an asset, unless the couple specifically decide to divide the future income when it is received. Owners of most of these sources of income also receive an annual report.

8. Stock options. More and more companies use stock options as a method of compensating employees. It is common at higher levels of management and is spreading to lower-level employees. A stock option is a right the company gives to employees to purchase stock at a fixed price. The employee does not have to exercise that right immediately and can be given a number of years to do so. Thus, if the price of the stock goes up the employee can exercise the right to buy it from the company at the earlier, lower price. For example, if the company grants an option to buy one hundred shares at two dollars per share and the price rises to three dollars, the employee can exercise the option to buy at two dollars and then own the one hundred shares worth three hundred dollars for which he paid two hundred dollars.

The clients bring in the employee handbook or contract describing the stock option plan and the most recent report from the company showing the status of the plan. The mediator makes particular note of the date the option can be exercised and the expiration date, if any.

9. Automobiles and other special personal property. The clients list their autos and any other items they think are particularly valuable, such as a grand piano or a Persian rug. This is the time not to list all of the personal property[3] but simply to identify unusual or special items.

10. Pension and profit sharing plans. Most people participate in a pension plan at the place of employment. Most plans are paid for in part by the employer and in part by the employee. Both contributions are deferred income and thus family property. Profit sharing plans are also growing in popularity and are usually jointly paid for by the employer and employee. Check the pay stub for any pension or profit sharing plan deductions. Profit sharing plans are usually restricted and cannot be cashed in at will. They are explained in the employee handbook along with the pension plan. Employers are required to provide plan participants with an annual report.

11. Income tax refunds. Depending on when the mediation is conducted this can be an important item. The closer the mediation is to either side of the tax filing time the more likely there is to be a tax refund or tax due. Check the previous tax returns[4] to see the history of the couple. Most people seem to get refunds and structure their tax payments to achieve this. If they received refunds in the past and do not report one on their forms, ask them about it.

12. All other assets. People seem to have other assets that do not fit into the listed categories This gives them a chance to list those items and to also question the whereabouts or nature of assets they believe — but are not certain the other has.

Notes on the Liabilities

13. Mortgages on real estate. Check here for the regular mortgage and for home equity loans. Cross-check with item 14 since many home equity loans are taken out with a different institution from the one that holds the mortgage. Since it will have to be dealt with along with the

---

[3] How to handle personal property is discussed later in this chapter.
[4] They should provide you with the tax returns for the previous three years.

house and its regular mortgage, move it to this item. The mortgage holder usually provides the borrower with an annual report on the status of the loan.

14. Notes to banks and others. Banks are clear. Other notes include money borrowed from friends and relatives, finance companies and so on. Most bank and finance company loans are repaid through a book system. The borrower is issued a booklet with coupons to mail each month with the payment. These coupons show the outstanding balance and the number of payments left to make. Ask for the documentation.

15. Loans on insurance policies. Since you can borrow from the cash value of the life insurance at very competitive rates, many people do so. The insurance company sends reports along with the premium bill showing the amount of the outstanding loan.

16. Other debts. These include debts to credit cards, charge accounts, education loans, professional bills, and so forth.

17. Taxes due. If you don't get a refund you usually owe money to the tax man. If the clients are not sure exactly how much they owe (or how large the refund will be), they can agree to divide this item by percentages rather than specific amounts and pay (or receive) their appropriate share when the exact information is known later.

Documentation

Among the documents to ask for in the identification stage are:

Wage stubs. Check all deductions noting any voluntary deductions for discussion in the budget session.

The last three years's tax returns. Check for any significant changes in unearned income or capital gains. Check the amount of the refund or taxes owed. Is there a pattern? Compare the amount paid last year with the amount deducted so far this year (from the pay stub) to see whether the current year is over- or under-deducted compared to previous years.

Insurance policies. Determine the type, and whether the policy is term, whole or universal life. Check for the cash value and the amount of any loans of whole- and universal-life policies.

Pension plan statements. Plans are required to issue annual reports. Check employer pensions, Keogh, IRA, and 401K plans.

Profit sharing plans. Ask for the last report on the status of the individual's plan and the booklet describing the plan.

Copies of net worth statements. These statements are submitted to lenders. While the value of items is often inflated to enhance the loan application, they are likely to list all the items the couple has.

Buy-sell agreements. These are often used when the business is owned by more than one partner. These agreements usually have a method for determining the value of the company each year and are useful information.

Business net worth statements. Such statements are often included in the annual accounting report of the business.

Bank and credit union. Check pass books and monthly reports.

Limited partnership agreements. These are often tax shelters, and the agreements explain the partnership.

Deeds. Check documents for all the real estate properties together with any mortgage agreements associated with the property.

Real estate appraisals. Check available appraisals of the properties.

The mediator prepares a copy of the forms on the flip chart, as in figure 4.2 on page 100.

Asset Identification

The completed forms contain the initial asset identification. The clients are asked to complete the forms independently. How they complete the forms provides the mediator with important information. If one spouse is precise, has the information on each item and knows the exact amounts, the mediator knows that spouse probably has controlled the finances of the family and will be familiar with the issues. If the other's form is incomplete and has estimates rather than precise numbers, the mediator knows that client will need help in gaining control of the information before moving to the next stage.

The way the couple completes the forms also tells the mediator about the power relationship between the clients. It informs the mediator how much time and effort she must expend to assure that the less-informed client becomes as well informed as his or her spouse. We will discuss how to do that later in this chapter. The mediator collects copies of the forms from each spouse and compares the two forms. Proceeding through the list, item by item, she[5] asks the clients to explain each item. As the couple explain each item, they help the mediator to understand the items and explain the assets to each other.

[5] In this chapter, the female gender is used for the mediator.

99

Figure 4.2 Mediator's Blank Net Worth Statement

Assets	Value/Cost	John	Mary
Bank Accounts	_____	_____	_____
Notes, Accts.			
Receivable	_____	_____	_____
Stocks and Bonds	_____	_____	_____
Real Estate	_____	_____	_____
Life Ins. (Cash Value)	_____	_____	_____
Business Interests	_____	_____	_____
Misc. Property	_____	_____	_____
Stock Options	_____	_____	_____
Autos, etc.	_____	_____	_____
Pension and Profit			
Sharing plans	_____	_____	_____
Income Tax Refunds	_____	_____	_____
All Other Assets	_____	_____	_____

Liabilities	Amount	John	Mary
Mortgages on Real Estate	_____	_____	_____
Notes to Banks and Others	_____	_____	_____
Loans on Insurance Policies	_____	_____	_____
Other Debts	_____	_____	_____
Taxes Due			
State and City	_____	_____	_____
Federal	_____	_____	_____
Total	_____	_____	_____

Asset Understanding

When it is clear that all of the assets have been identified the mediator moves to the asset understanding phase of the process. For this illustration, if we assume the husband has the more complete forms, as he explains the bank accounts entries he identifies the certificates of deposit. The mediator asks:

- Where are the certificates located?
- What is the interest rate?
- When do the certificates mature?

As the husband responds with the information, the mediator clarifies each response, checking to be sure that the wife understands the information. Thus, the wife learns about and understands the asset through the answers to the mediator's questions.

The wife may not know which questions to ask, and, even if she were to ask them, the husband might respond negatively, probably commenting on her lack of money management in the past. This could start a spousal argument. The mediator's request for information does not trigger a spousal response from the husband; he presents the information rationally. The wife hears it, the mediator checks that she understands it, and when the understanding is complete, the process has empowered the wife, since she now has the same information as the husband.

Understanding the assets also involves asking questions about the nature of the asset:

- Is it liquid or illiquid?
- Is it an income-producing or a growth-potential asset?
- What was the purpose of the asset when it was purchased?
- What are the tax ramifications of the sale of the asset?
- Who controls the asset?
- Where are the asset's records?
- What are the client's respective goals regarding the asset?

Liquidity

Some assets can be turned into cash very easily; others cannot. For example, the family home is generally regarded as an illiquid asset, since it cannot easily be sold and the proceeds (cash) used freely. Even if the house can be sold quickly, the proceeds are usually needed to purchase replacement housing. On the other hand, a stock share can be sold tomorrow and the cash used for any purpose. It is therefore considered a liquid asset.

As the couple think about their assets, they need to understand which are liquid and illiquid because each will need a mix of assets. For most people an illiquid asset is not the same psychological "cushion" against unforeseen events as money in the bank. Thus, most people need liquid assets to protect their cushion needs. The psychological cushion varies with each person. Some people are comfortable with only one week's pay on hand. Others are uncomfortable with less than one year's salary in the bank. The size of the cushion determines the amount of liquid assets they feel they need.

The actual mix of liquid and illiquid assets needed by each client can be a problem. Often, the mother wants to retain the family home with sole title. However, if the remaining assets are less than or equal to the value of the equity in the family home, it is unlikely she can negotiate the family home *and* additional liquid assets. In this case the client has to be helped to weigh the choices and understand the consequences of each choice so the choice she makes is informed and in her self-interest.

Income and Growth Assets

Some investments produce a good rate of return (rate of interest earned on the investment). A savings account earns a specific percentage of the balance each month or quarter. The account is an income-producing asset. Many real estate investments are growth assets: the investor does not expect a monthly return on the investment but expects the value of the investment to grow in the future. These types of investments are growth-potential assets. If the husband needs to increase his cash flow to pay the support, he will focus on the income-producing assets.

The savings account may earn seven percent interest, and, assuming the initial deposit is untouched and the interest is withdrawn regularly, the principal does not change over the years. If the interest is not withdrawn then, in approximately ten years, the total value of the investment doubles through the amount of interest. The real estate investment may only return a profit of two percent, but the value of the real estate grows so that at the end of the same ten years the total value of the investment grows by the profit plus the increase in the value (sale price) of the property.

Many investments — particularly stocks — are a mix of growth and income. The average stock earns approximately 4.5 percent dividends on its current price each year. Investors also expect the value of the stock to rise.

Clients need to understand their future needs and how best to meet those needs through the division of their assets. If the need is for immediate income, they opt for more of the income-producing assets.

If they have sufficient regular income, they are more likely to take the growth-potential assets.

Exploring and Understanding Each Asset

The goal of the asset when purchased. People buy things for different reasons. Sometimes they list jewelry as an asset. If the jewelry was a gift from one spouse to the other, it has one significance. If, however, it was purchased because it had good growth potential, the couple will probably look at the asset differently.

The clients might hold very different views about the asset. He may believe the purchase was an investment that should be treated in the same way as the stocks and bonds. She may believe the jewelry was a gift and therefore he has no right to claim it back. In either case, a discussion of the original reason for purchasing the item often clarifies the issue and helps them make a decision about how to treat it in the overall division of the assets.

Tax ramifications of the asset. Taking certain assets may have important tax ramifications. For example, if the asset was purchased many years ago and has enjoyed significant capital growth, there may be capital gains taxes to be paid when it is sold. Other investments made as tax shelters may carry future tax liabilities or benefits.

We will go into taxes later. The point at this stage of the process is for the mediator and the clients to understand the assets and all aspects of each asset, including possible tax liabilities or benefits.

Who controls the asset? You will notice the forms do not ask the couple to list assets by ownership. We don't ask for "title" of the asset. This is because we want the couple to think of all of their assets as belonging to the family and subject to division between them in a way that seems fair to them.

However, one spouse often thinks of an asset as his or hers. A person who does this usually has also handled the asset since its acquisition. Therefore he or she "controls" it. It is important to be sure that the person who controls the asset explains it carefully to the mediator and, therefore, also to the other spouse. The mediator ensures that the person who controls the assets is assigned the responsibility of bringing in all of the documentation regarding the asset.

Where are the asset's records? Discussing this question helps prompt memories and thus assist the clients gather information as to where further documentation might be obtained.

The clients' goals regarding the asset. Having each person discuss how he or she feels about the asset and any goals for it helps the mediator and the other spouse understand that position. The family home is often clear. Usually the resident parent wants to keep the home. The person with the pension plan usually wants to keep it. As this discussion takes place the mediator:

- notes the goals of each client,
- obtains a sense of priority for each person regarding the various assets, and
- develops a tentative hypothesis as to each person's goal regarding *all* of the assets (also known as a package goal).

In the asset-understanding phase the mediator learns a great deal about each asset and the overall net worth of the couple. She also identifies where more information is needed and assigns responsibility for obtaining the information to the appropriate spouse.

Deciding which spouse should be responsible for obtaining the information is usually based on which client has easiest access to the information. If the mediator needs a copy of the pension plan booklet, the spouse with the pension plan is in the better position to obtain the information. However, at times the mediator assigns responsibility with a plan in mind.

Let us assume the couple has a number of investments with a broker. The husband has handled the account in the past and knows most about it. The mediator might ask the wife to call the broker to obtain the needed information as a way of empowering her and helping her gain confidence in dealing with her future economic interests

When this happens the mediator is very explicit about what information is needed and how to gain the information. As this is discussed in the session, the husband is involved in helping the wife frame the right questions, so that she will know when she has the appropriate information.

This sharing has a power balancing function[6] as well as a data gathering one. It enhances the wife's ability to handle such matters after the mediation is completed and she is on her own.

Dividing The Property

Asset Valuation

When the clients have a clear understanding of the assets the mediator turns to the next stage of the process — asset valuation. Some values have been assigned to items during the understanding phase. The bank balances are known, the stock prices checked in the newspaper. The life insurance company provides the current cash value of the policies. However, many assets need special attention to determine the valuation.

Real estate. The family home has to be valued if the couple plans to trade it. For example, if the husband keeps the pension and the wife keeps the house, they must know the respective values of the house and the pension. If, however, they are going to keep the house as joint property for a period and divide the proceeds at some future sale date, they don't need to value the house now.

Other real estate properties need to be appraised. Clients have two choices.

- They can use the services of a licensed real estate appraiser; many are listed in the Yellow Pages.
- They can use the evaluations presented by one or more real estate brokers. Many real estate brokers provide a house evaluation at no cost.

The broker usually provides a computer-generated report showing the appraisal of the house and comparing it with six or more properties sold in the area during the previous six months. The comparisons show the asking price and the actual sale price of each property. The clients compare the sale prices of nearby properties to the evaluation of their property to see if it appears appropriate.

Most couples seem to prefer each contacting one real estate broker to do this work and then use an average of the two evaluations. If they choose a licensed appraiser who is not a real estate broker, they must pay a fee ranging from $250 to $500. In that case their task is to negotiate how to choose one appraiser, so neither feels the other controls the selection, while keeping costs to a minimum.

---

[6] J. M. Haynes, "Power Balancing," in *Divorce Mediation: Theory and Practice*, ed. J. Folberg, and Ann Milne, (New York: Guilford Press, 1988), 277-296.

Sometimes the clients state that they do not need the services of an appraiser, claiming that they know as much about the market as any appraiser. It is dangerous for them not to use an independent third party. Later, if one spouse does not like his choice of assets he can sue the other under the pretense of having entered into an agreement without all the facts.

I once had clients who owned a number of real estate properties that they jointly managed. I urged them to have the properties appraised before they divided them, but they both argued strongly that they knew the market better than anyone else. We finally divided the property based on the values they agreed upon. Two years later the wife discovered that an acre of land the husband took was sold for more than five times the price they had placed on it at the time of the mediation.

The wife sued the husband for fraud, claiming he knew of plans to develop adjacent property that caused the five-fold increase. The case was settled between them before the trial so I don't know the outcome of the second agreement. But it is a signal to mediators to insist on independent evaluations which are more difficult to fight when circumstances and minds change.

Business interests. When one spouse owns a business or an interest in a business, finding the correct evaluation is difficult. It is important to have some process rules to assure they obtain an appropriate valuation.

Let's assume the husband owns a business. He has an accountant who advises him, maintains his records, and handles all of his business tax matters. Let's assume that the wife is a teacher with no other income and that she has not been involved in the business. In this case the husband knows a great deal about the business and has access to professional accounting advice. The wife knows little about the business and has no access to independent professional advice.

This is the one situation in which the mediator *insists* that the spouse be independently represented by a professional. She must have her *own* professional, usually an accountant, to appraise the business. However, she probably does not have the money to pay for the professional, whose fees will be $5,000 or more, depending on the size of the business.

In this case the mediator invokes a process rule that the wife must retain her own appraiser, who must have complete access to all the relevant records (as determined by the wife's appraiser), and that the appraiser's fee must be paid by the husband's business. The wife then hires the appraiser, who meets with the husband to establish the fee and supply the data the appraiser may require. The appraiser is instructed by both husband and wife to report to and be responsible to the wife.

The wife's appraiser also assesses the value of the perks the husband receives from the business. This information is useful in determining the amount of money available for support. When the appraisal is completed the normal practice is for the appraiser to meet with the husband's accountant, and they try to settle any differences that may exist about the way the value has been reached. The agreed-upon evaluation is reported to the couple by both accountants at a meeting managed by the mediator.[7]

If the husband rejects an independent appraisal of the business, the mediator terminates the process. If the process is continued without full disclosure, the other spouse is at risk. I always say to the husband (or the wife if she owns the business), "This is a good way of getting it done. It is a question not of *whether* you will have the business appraised but of *when* you will have it appraised. You can have it appraised under a system acceptable to both of you. You can have it done when your spouse's lawyer files the papers, or you will have it appraised when the judge orders it."

Given this choice most rational people opt to have the appraisal done in civilized circumstances where they have some control over the process rather than give control to a lawyer or a judge.

Miscellaneous property. The difficulty of determining the value of patents, trademarks, copyrights, and royalties is that they are future benefits. That is, they will (or possibly will) provide an unknown income in the future. There are experts who, using common criteria, make reasonable assessments of the value of each of these items, and the couple should hire one to do that. The cost is shared equally by the clients, who often liquidate an asset to pay for it.

When the mediator assists the couple to develop the criteria of selecting and retaining an appraiser, the couple can be sure that they

---

[7] I have never had a problem in this regard. Accountants seem capable of gaining agreement based on their code of accounting practices.

will spend their money only for one appraisal not for two. It does not make sense to most people to spend hard-earned money on two separate appraisers who inevitably come in with two different appraisals and then spend more money having the lawyers negotiate how to split the difference between the two appraisals.

Stock options. Unlike miscellaneous property items, it is easier to determine the value of stock options because once the couple knows the price at which the option was taken and the price of the stock today then the difference represents its current value. The owner may not be able to exercise the option today. Often, options have limitation as to when they may be exercised. Thus, if the value is determined as of today, the holder of the options may argue that he cannot exercise the option for two years and, therefore, is unwilling to purchase them from the spouse at today's price because it will be two years before he knows whether or not they are worth the purchase price.

At this point the couple must understand and discuss the difference between current and future values, the value of a dollar today versus the value of a dollar in the future. Once they understand this, they can move towards deciding how to handle a stock option that cannot be exercised in the immediate future. The most common solution is to divide the option's profits when they becomes available.

A rule of thumb: When to appraise. Fortunately, there is someone, somewhere, who, for a price, will appraise the value of anything. The problem for the clients is how much they want to spend settling differences between them about the value of each item. I have a formula that says that clients ought to find noncost means of determining any item that is worth less than $20,000, or 10 percent of the total assets.

Automobiles and special personal property. The value of an automobile can be determined by going to the library and looking it up in an auto guidebook.[8] The one not owning the car should do this. If they both own cars, both should check the values of both autos so there is no doubt as to the accuracy of the numbers.

Vehicles such as boats and some special cars are not listed in the auto guidebooks. In that case the couple can agree to scan the newspaper "for sale" columns during the coming week and bring in

---

[8] The common ones are *The NADA Appraisal Guide* and *Galves Auto Prices*.

examples of advertisements for comparable vehicles that will give them a basis for agreeing on the value of the item.

Values of antiques, collector's items, and so forth, can all be found in books at the library[9] or through one of the magazines devoted to the particular item. The purpose is not to be able to settle definitively the precise value of an item but to provide sufficient data to enable the couple to make an informed decision.

Common sense should govern the mediator in helping the couple decide values. In one case the couple owned fifty vacuum tube radios. The husband wanted to keep them and claimed a low value for them. The wife, who in effect would be the seller, placed a high value on them. Neither produced any support for their respective figures. The task for the mediator was to help the couple determine a common-sense method for appraising the old radios.

The husband suggested that he get an appraisal from a friend of his who also dealt in old radios. The wife correctly rejected the proposal on the grounds that she could not trust the friend to be objective. The mediator explored all the options the clients had, and they finally agreed to select four radios, each choosing two sets, and take them to a dealer well known for handling antique radios but unknown personally to either of them. I assumed the husband choose two of the cheaper examples and the wife choose two of the expensive examples and, therefore, balanced each other out.[10]

The couple went together to the dealer with the four radios and accepted his appraisal, which was about double the amount the husband claimed and about one third less than the wife claimed.

Pension and profit sharing plans. Few companies provide an accurate number as to the value of an employee's pension. Most company reports project future benefits rather than current values. While it is good to know that you will receive a pension of $1,000 per month fifteen years from now, that figure does not tell you what the

---

[9] Check with the librarian as to the accuracy of the books. In a recent case, the couple checked the values of a collection of first class stamps from the 1940s. The stamp catalogue indicated a value of several thousand dollars but, when they took the stamps to dealers to sell them none would offer even the face value of the stamps. The couple used the stamps on their current mail.

[10] I base this on the concept that one is the seller of the radios and the other they buyer. For a discussion of this see chapter 6.

value of the plan is today; that is, how much money does there have to be in the plan today to guarantee the $1,000 fifteen years from now? Therefore, an appraisal must be done.[11]

You can usually understand profit sharing plans from the report from the employer to the employee when it shows the current value of the plan and details of when withdrawals can be made, and so forth. If there is any difficulty, a pension appraising company will also evaluate the profit sharing plan.

Liabilities

When the couple list their liabilities make sure they both understand each liability and associate it with the appropriate asset. When people talk about the value of any item they need to discuss its *net* value. That is, the proceeds they would receive from the sale of the item. Three factors must be considered when selling an asset:

- Discounting the sale price by the amount of any outstanding loan on that item
- Discounting the price by the cost of selling it, if that cost is significant[12]
- Discounting the tax consequences associated with the asset

Mortgages. If there is more than one property, make sure that they understand which mortgage or home equity loan goes with which property. Knowing this helps the clients understand the net value of each property.

Notes to banks and others. Have them bring in the current statement for each loan. Ask who took out the loan. Are they both signatories? Although both may be legally responsible for the loan, if one of them took it out, s/he may accept responsibility for it.

---

[11]One company that does good work at a reasonable fee (about one half of most other pension appraisers) is Legal Economic Evaluations, 1-800-2211-6826. They will advise the pension participant as to what information is needed to make the appraisal and provide the answer in less than one week.

[12] *Significant* is a vague term. However, this can be determined by the clients. Thus, they may ignore the broker's cost of selling one hundred shares worth $1,000 but agree that the real estate and legal fees (approximately 7 percent) in connection with the sale of a $150,000 house should be considered.

Loans on insurance policies   These are listed on their annual statement from the insurance company showing the cash value of the policy. Remember, since the insurance company won't loan you money you don't have in your policy there is always some cash value to a whole- or universal-life insurance policy. The sales office can also tell the clients.

Other debts. The way couples handle these debts matches the way they handled money in the marriage. If they considered all money as joint funds, they will probably consider the debts joint responsibilities. If each managed his or her own money and credit accounts, they will probably believe that the debt is the responsibility of the person incurring it.

The clients may have loans from members of the family. Parents sometimes loan money to help purchase the house. Although it is wise to make such loans in writing so there is no doubt about them, many parents simply loan the money to the children without using any documentation. I have yet to have a case in which one spouse denied that the other's parents loaned money for the house.[13] Once the loan has been identified and the amount agreed upon, the mediator leads the discussion of when and how the parents will be repaid.

Other family loans can be more difficult. A spouse may claim he owes money to his brother. The other spouse denies all knowledge of the transaction and rejects the claim. Absent some documentation the argument can go on forever. With documentation the argument is defined and simpler to manage.[14]

Dividing the Assets

Before the assets can be divided the couple must agree which items, if any, are nonmarital property. The law differs across jurisdictions but, in general, the following rules apply. Nonmarital property usually includes:

- *Property brought into the marriage by each spouse.* If the wife brought a house into the marriage, she is usually entitled to take it with her at the divorce. The husband has a

---

[13] This suggests that people who make claims to the other family's loan have probably been advised to do it as a negotiating strategy.

[14] Chapter 6 has a more detailed discussion of this issue.

claim to the added value of any work he did on the house that enhanced its value during the marriage or for part of the inflation in the price while he was helping to pay off the mortgage. But the asset would stay with the wife. On the other hand if she brought a car into the marriage she would take it with her in the divorce and there is no debate about the declined value.

- *Gifts and inheritances.* Inheritances are not considered marital property. However, as with the house, if one spouse helped the other increase the value of the inheritance, that spouse has a claim to a share of the increased value. Normally, gifts from the family of origin to one spouse are kept separate.

- *Business or investment interest obtained before marriage.* If the wife had a store before the marriage, she keeps the store at the divorce. However, the husband has a claim to the increased value of the store if he worked to help increase the value. For example, the wife had a shoe store before the marriage. She had inherited it from her parents. During the marriage both partners worked in the store. It prospered and during the marriage they took a lease on the store next door and expanded the business, which further increased its value. At the divorce the husband claimed a share of the growth that was related to his efforts which, he claimed, enabled them to expand the store.

- *Wedding rings, and other personal jewelry.* In some states gifts between spouses become marital (shared) properly. However, in all of my years of mediating I have never had a couple where one spouse sustained a demand for the return of a gift.

- *Personal injury settlements.* If one spouse has been injured and receives a lump-sum settlement of a claim, that money is considered nonmarital. However, you may have to separate the amount for pain and suffering from the amount for loss of services. The other spouse may have a claim to part or all the loss of services damage award.

Dividing The Property

Rely on Common Sense

Whenever there is a dispute about these items, use common sense and the family's individual values to find a mutually agreeable solution. Couples may, if they desire, include nonmarital property in the list to be divided for reasons unique to their situation. For example, one wife returned the husband's mother's wedding ring so it could stay in his family. The additional benefit of mediation is that it helps people consider what is right for them and their family regardless of what the legislation says.

Some people disclaim all interest in certain items of marital property that they consider the other's. For example some women who have not worked outside the home say, "I don't care about his pension, that's his. He worked for it. He can have it." The mediator must be sure that the wife understands what she is giving up.

The mediator says, "OK if that's what you want to do. However, you must know what it is you are waiving. Therefore the pension will have to be appraised. After all, if you discover that it is worth a couple of hundred thousand dollars you may want to change your mind. In any case you must know the value before you sign off on the agreement, otherwise you would have the right to come back later and claim the pension."

Stress the self-interest of both spouses in getting the plan evaluated: the wife's that she should know the value of what she is waiving and the husband's that the agreement should not be subject to a later challenge.

There are two other items that must be agreed before the couple can proceed to divide the property.

The first is the date they use to value all the items. The couple need to select a date that is autonomous of both of them upon which they will value the property. Steve Erickson coined the phrase "take a snapshot of the assets," to describe this.

The most frequently chosen time is the date of the physical separation. However, if the negotiations are conducted around the end of the year, it is easy to use December 31, since most reports are issued on that date. If the couple is negotiating at other times of the year, the end of each quarter is a useful time.

The mediator does not allow one person to set the date unilaterally since this may be done out of self-interest. For example, if the husband plans to negotiate for the stock portfolio while the wife keeps the house and if the stock market values increased in the past three months, he may suggest a date three months ago. If he is successful, he will get the stocks at a deflated price. The best course of action is to discuss these issues with the clients so they can choose a date that is fair to both of them.

The second point to reach agreement on is what to do about the personal property. You will notice that nowhere have we discussed personal property. Most legal forms have an entry for the household furnishings. Yet in real life it does not seem useful to value the bed and sofa and chairs. It does not make much sense to charge the mother for the children's furniture. In legal bargaining the spouse moving out often places a high value on the things he (it is usually the husband) is leaving behind. But this is often a negotiating strategy to enable him to gain more of the real assets of the family and does not reflect the needs of the two households.

Each spouse needs furniture after the divorce, and the best approach is to suggest to the spouse who plans to move out of the family home to make a list of the items he needs to start up his new home. The couple can then negotiate over that list. Many people have accumulated unused or duplicate items in their home and the list rarely causes disruptions to the resident parent's household. If there is a need to replace certain items, they can share in replacing those, each carrying part of the burden.

Fairness

So far we have discussed asset identification, understanding, and valuation. The mediator conducts one more discussion that is unique to the mediation process. She asks the couple about their standards of fairness. I usually ask the couple at this stage, "How will you know you have been fair to yourself and to each other when you divide your assets?" This is a startling question for most people who have not thought about fairness for many years. Probably the last time they discussed fairness was in Philosophy 101 the week after they discussed whether the tree made a sound as it fell into the woods.

Dividing The Property

Couples struggle with the idea of what is fair to them. The majority of people I work with opt for an even division of the property. They agree that the marriage was a partnership and that the divorce should be likewise. This is interesting, since most of my work with clients is done in an equitable distribution state where the norm is still for the wage earner to get a larger share of the assets.

I am often asked, Why are your clients different? I don't think they are. They are simply in an arena that does not suggest "smart" strategies. Rather, they are helped to focus on problem solving as the best means of negotiating a fair deal. Given the opportunity, people will generally rely on common sense and basic decency when making their decisions.

Taxes

Taxes vary and are frequently changed. Therefore mediators keep up with divorce tax changes. Below are the major tax issues in the asset distribution cycle.

Some assets and liabilities have tax ramifications. If an asset has appreciated in value, it will have a capital gain associated with it. If the asset has depreciated, it will have a capital loss associated with it. Factor in the tax consequences of the gain or loss when determining the true value of an item.

There are no tax consequences when an asset is transferred from one spouse to another in a divorce. Thus, if the husband transfers some appreciated stock to the wife as part of the settlement, she does not have a tax liability at the time of the transfer. She does, however, carry the tax liability forward and will have to pay the capital gain (or loss) when she sells it to a third party.

If the couple owes money to the IRS, one spouse cannot forgive the other for any responsibility to pay the debt. For example, if the husband agrees to pay any debts to the IRS and does not pay the IRS, the revenue service maintains the right to raid the wife's bank account or other assets to get its money.

There is a provision in the tax regulation called the innocent spouse rule which provides that if a spouse was honestly and truly ignorant of the other's dealings with the IRS in behalf of them, she will not be held responsible for the taxes. If a case appears to fulfill this standard, refer the wife to a tax lawyer for advice.

115

Dividing the assets is a process involving common sense and common decency. The mediator, in addition to managing the negotiations, creates a climate for self- and joint responsibility that appears to result in fairer agreements.

In the next chapter we discuss the final area of divorce negotiations, the parenting.

Chapter Five
The Future Parenting

The goal of this stage of the mediation is to determine the future *parenting* of the children. By parenting we mean all decisions that affect the raising of the children: their residence, access to each parent, schooling, health, extended family relationships, and so on.

The mediator focuses on the needs of both the parents and the children. One part of this is to educate the clients about their new parent roles. In this session, the mediator shares her[1] expertise with the clients, acting sometimes as a mediator and sometimes as an educator, but always in a way that helps the clients stay in charge of decisions.

A Short History[2]

Most people come to mediation with a set of ideas about what post-divorce parenting should be. Any deviation from the clients' "should be" is difficult for them to understand.

Up to the beginning of this century, when a couple divorced and litigated — a rare event — the children went to the father. That was probably because, in earlier times, children were seen as chattel or economic units. With the introduction of universal education, children ceased to be economic assets and became economic liabilities. Along with this change the courts introduced the concept of the "tender years doctrine" and began almost automatically awarding[3] custody of the children to the mother.

The economy changed in the early 1970s with the rapid growth of two-wage-earner families and no-fault divorce. If two-wage-earner families are to work smoothly, the father must provide

---

[1] The mediator is female in this chapter.
[2] A thorough and thoughtful history of divorce is Roderick Phillips, *Putting Asunder: A history of divorce in Western society* (New York: Cambridge University Press, 1988).
[3] The term *awarding* comes from the adversarial nature of the legal system. The children were thought of as prizes to be awarded to the "better" or winning parent.

117

more care and nurturing to the children than in a one-wage-earner, two-parent family. Since the children share two infrequently available parents, the father must play a more involved role and shoulder a larger share of the household obligations.

As the parent roles changed in the seventies and eighties, fathers' expectations in divorce changed to match their changed roles in a two-wage-earner family. One aspect of the change is more willingness to continue his increased parent role after the divorce. Another is the increased willingness of the mother to continue sharing the parenting role as she had done in the marriage. These changes led to an increased interest in shared parenting (joint custody).

Other changes in the economy have also influenced the way people think about parenting after divorce. The rapid increase of female participation in the work force is a result of more employment options for women. Twenty years ago many career options were not available. When young mothers divorce today, it is almost certain they will have to work outside the home to maintain a decent standard of living. As they look to a future of dual employment — outside the home and inside the home — many young mothers look to the fathers to take a greater share in the parenting.

The realities of this generation are played against those of an older generation. The experience of the older generation, particularly the parents of young couples currently divorcing, was very different. Up to the latter 1960s it was almost impossible for a father to obtain residency (custody) with his children. Fathers obtained custody only when the mother had significant problems such as mental illness, drug or alcohol abuse, and so forth.

People who grew up under those conditions entered marriage and watched others divorce knowing that only bad mothers lost custody of the children. Therefore, when young parents decide to share the parenting of their children or choose to have the children live with the father, they often must deal with the older generation's expectations that good mothers get the children.

It remains common for people to catch their breath upon learning that a mother has moved out, leaving the children with the father. Yet, those same people don't even notice when the father says that he left the children with the mother. Mediators hold many of these views and have their own prejudices about parenting. They must be aware of their own biases.

Changing the Language

The first step in dealing with prejudice is mechanical: change the language. Mediators avoid terms such as *failed marriage, broken home, custody* and *visitation*. They prefer non-judgmental terms such as *ending the relationship, mom's house and dad's house, parenting, access,* and *residence.*

The legal adversarial vocabulary refers to visitation. Most mediators prefer the term *access.*[4] In that way they reframe the question from *when does dad get to visit the kids,* to *when will the children have access to their dad?* The terms *custody* and *visitation* are legal terms. As such each has a winner-loser connotation and speaks about ownership of the children rather than supporting future parenting goals.

The choice of words is odd, for we use *custody* to describe prisoners in jail and patients in mental hospitals. Is there any wonder that the noncustody parent bridles at the language? Many fathers become antagonistic when asked how they might visit their children (we visit relatives in jail or hospital). Yet the same father is comfortable discussing how best to parent in the future.

The mediator has a choice. She can use the legal, adversarial language and provoke adversarial behavior or she can use normal language that speaks of their future parenting responsibilities, which invokes respectful behavior.

Educating the Parents

The mediator can be helpful as an educator to the parents about the future developmental needs of their children. She shares relevant information in general terms but not in therapeutic ways.

Children at each age group have different responses to divorce and different needs from their parents. Here are some useful ideas for each age group.

---

[4] Some people believe that *access* is a more impersonal word than *visit.* However, the mediator uses *access* in preference to *visit* because the latter has historical connotations the mediator seeks to avoid. Other terms could be used provided they do not have a negative history.

119

Preschool (ages 3-5).[5] This age group experiences increased fear, which is often expressed by crying when a parent leaves. The crying is repeated upon the parent's return. This is part of the child's normal striving for autonomy when separation anxiety is normally high. Therefore, both parents can assist the child to deal with the additional stress by being available to him/her on a regular basis. The child is likely to wake up at night. Parents need to be able to spend time dealing with the anxieties causing insomnia. Gentle talk and reassurance is helpful. If in nursery school, the child may try to avoid going. Parents need not only to reassure the child verbally but also to actually be there regularly, on time, to pick the child up. Regression such as returning to an old toy or a security blanket, is likely. If recently toilet trained, the child is likely to regress. Accepting this modified development is important and helps the child to get over it. Aggression increases towards peers, siblings, and parents. Providing care and firm guidelines without criticism helps the child control the aggressive behavior.

Young School (ages 6-8). Sadness is the hallmark of this age group for both boys and girls. Boys tend to increase crying. Children, especially sons, need permission to experience and express sadness. They will yearn for the other parent. Boys tend to be strongly loyal to an absent father, giving the resident mother a difficult time. The resident parent can acknowledge that the child misses the father (mother) and provide a time frame for the next visit with the other parent. The same calendar on the refrigerator door at each parent's home showing the schedule of times with the other parent also helps the child deal with time.

Aggression is usually inhibited with the absent parent but expressed at the residency parent. Loyalty conflicts abound as the child tries to decide with which parent to align. Regression is possible through age ten.

Middle School (ages 9-12). The child's peer group becomes increasingly important. Access arrangements for the parents must include a recognition of the importance of the peer relationships. The child continues to idolize the absent parent while expressing anger at

---

[5] Based on the work of Judith Wallerstein and Joan Kelly, *Surviving the Breakup: How Children and Parents Cope with Divorce* (New York: Basic Books, 1980).

the resident parent. Somatic responses include frequent headaches and stomach aches and/or increase in existing conditions such as allergies. These symptoms permit them to stay home to be with a parent. This age group tends to see everything in black-and-white terms. Thus these children tend to be extremely loyal and may align with one parent. Or, the loyalty may result in a demand for precise equality in the amount of time spent with each parent. Teachers often report day dreaming as children in this age group become lost in thought and concern about the absent parent.

Adolescents (ages 13-18). Teens have financial concerns, due to a keen awareness of the effects of the loss of money experienced by most divorcing families. Their anger is usually expressed in ongoing hassles with the resident parent. Sexual confusion is natural in this age group and can be exacerbated by a parent's new sexual activity. This is heightened if one spouse engages in a relationship with a younger person closer in age to the teen child. Loyalty conflicts abound as the teen tries to lay the blame and/or responsibility of the divorce on one or the other parent. The teen's emerging sense of identity needs to be protected by both parents. While access arrangements can be more flexible due to a teen's mobility, parents need to provide for clear accountability for a teen's whereabouts. Strategic withdrawal (where the teen lives and eats in his/her bedroom) is a normal development that can be helpful during the divorce by allowing them to escape from their parent's world.

Parent Reactions that Cause Problems for Children

Parents add to the problems children experience in divorce by:

- Sharing with the children their anger at the other spouse. This confuses them about the other parent and sharpens the loyalty conflicts they are already experiencing. Parents can be encouraged *not* to talk with the children about the divorce and the other spouse.
- Displacing anger at the other spouse on to the children. This is more likely if one child has a close physical resemblance to and/or behavioral characteristics of the other spouse. Making the parent aware of this is often enough to stop it.

- Failing to respond to the children's needs because they are caught up with their own needs. Most parents experiencing divorce become self-absorbed. The mediator can suggest the parents talk to friends to check out their relationship with the children.
- Using children as peers by confiding in them as adults rather than providing appropriate parent/child boundaries. This is most likely to happen with teenaged children, who are often happy to fill this role.
- Using older children as caretakers for the younger ones can force premature maturation in the older siblings and deny them their childhood.
- Viewing the children as "property" and claiming property rights in regards to them. This is the basis of many custody fights arising from legal ideas about parenting after divorce.
- Using the children as emotional pawns. Usually expressed by claiming that the children do not want to spend time with the other parent. These parents claim that their positions are really the positions of the children.

The Mediation Process Applied to Parenting Issues

The mediation process is the same for the parenting decisions as for support and assets. The mediator begins by collecting the data, asking, for example, "What are the important holidays in your family?" She then displays the data on the flip chart, verifies it with both parents and from this step emerges the problem definition; for example, "How will you share Christmas?" or "How will you share the Passover?" The clients, with the help of the mediator, develop options to solve the problem. They select which option is best for them, usually one that maintains important family traditions, and negotiate any differences. The mediator uses the same five-step procedure:

1. Collect, verify, understand and display the data,
2. Define the problem,
3. Develop options to solve the problem,
4. Negotiate the differences between the options chosen by each client,
5. State and clarify the agreement.

The Mediator As Manager of the Process

To help control mediator bias, the mediator should be clear about her function and repeat that she is the manager of the couple's negotiations about the future parenting of the children. Managers do not evaluate, judge, rate parenting competency, or decide who is the better parent. Neither are they advocates for one form of family structure over another. Managers organize the agenda, determine the order in which the items are to be taken up, help the parents define the problem, and develop options to solve the problem.

The mediator manages the negotiations, helping parents to devise a range of options and explore the risk/benefit (consequences) of each option. She does not decide for the parents which is the best option. Neither does she decide what is best for the clients' children. She manages the negotiations in a way that enables the parents to decide, just as she managed the asset division session in a way that enabled the clients to make the decisions around their house, pension, and other items.

Most parents who come to mediation do not have major issues involving the children. Single-issue disputes concerning the children are more likely to occur in court-ordered mediation where the couple have gone to court specifically on the issue of the parenting. Therefore, the remaining part of this chapter is divided into two sections: the first examines the mediation process for normal families, and the second examines it in difficult cases, emphasizing strategies for working with these families.

Managing the Negotiations for Normal Families

Parenting agreements should reflect each parent's interests in a continuing relationship with the children and define new roles while considering the needs of the children. The mediator's interventions with the family are minimal and designed to strengthen the two families that will emerge from the decision to divorce.

Most parents come to mediation with a vocabulary that is drawn from the courts because it is familiar to them. The mediator's task is to convert the language into nonadversarial terms. The terms most familiar to couples are:

1. *Joint legal custody.* In modern terms this does not necessarily mean shared residency. More and more couples opt for joint legal custody,

while providing for the children's primary residence to be with one parent, as a way of continuing to share the parenting. This allows the parents to share in the decision-making regarding the growth and raising of the children. While the residence is with one parent, the decisions continue to lie with both of them.

2. *Joint physical custody.* Under this arrangement the children share time at each parent's residence, often on a fifty-fifty basis.

3. *Sole parenting.* With this holdover from earlier times, one parent makes all the decisions and the other gets to visit.

4. *Split parenting.* The children reside with one parent primarily, and the parents divide the decision making on specific issues. For example, one parent may make the decisions regarding religion or education, and the other parent makes all the other decisions.

Developing New Language

The problem with all four designations just listed is that they pose the issues in ownership terms. Who gets custody? My experience suggests that most people want to pose the issue in parenting terms. How do we parent the children in the future? To help them focus on their parenting roles, the mediator uses language that eliminates talk of custody. In the next section we will look at how the new language is used in the process of deciding the parenting issues.

Residency and access. The mediator helps the couple designate the primary residence of the children and then discusses how the children will spend time with each parent. This is often done in the context of each parent having specific responsibilities for parts of the children's lives. The children may live with their mother and have access to their father in a way that allows him to be responsible for their sports activities. In that situation, the children are with their dad whenever they are in sports, and he is responsible for getting them to and from those activities.

In the marriage many parents shared responsibility for particular aspects of the children's lives. They can continue to share these responsibilities after the divorce. If there are practical reasons why one parent cannot do the same things s/he did in the marriage, alternative areas of responsibility can be determined. A way of explaining this is to suggest the following opening paragraph in the parenting agreement:

124

The Future Parenting

We have shared in the parenting of our children[6] in the past and will continue to do so. Therefore, we will maintain joint custody. The children will reside with their mother. We will each have access to all school, medical, and other professional records of the children.

The weekly calendar. Clients explore the access possibilities, and they work out a weekly or monthly schedule of the way in which the children will have access to and time with each parent.

The schedules vary from the standard alternate weekends and each Wednesday evening with the nonresident parent, to a variegated arrangement that does not repeat itself for weeks. In one case, a couple with three children developed a calendar providing times when each child could spend individual time with each parent as well as times when all three children could be with each parent. Alternate weekends and a weekday evening schedule would not work for this family.

The mediator prepares a blank calendar on the flip chart to show the days of the week for a four-week period. As the couple agrees to each point, she enters it onto the calendar. This visual aid is useful in keeping the couple focused on the agenda of deciding how to organize the parenting and demonstrates the impact of their decisions on their and the children's lives.

The calendar can also be used to identify visually an unfair position. Sometimes one parent takes a tough position that she wants the father to see the children only on the last weekend of each month and holds to that position, while the father remains quiet, unable to express his need. The mediator enters the father's name in the Saturday and Sunday boxes of week four. She then enters the mother's name in all of the other boxes. As the overwhelming preponderance of mother's name appears on the board, the visual impact often causes the father to argue more strongly for his position, and it can also cause the mother to soften her position. The visual effect can be enhanced by using different colored pens for each parent.

Access may not always be possible on schedule, and it is helpful for parents to recognize that their children's needs will, at

---

[6] The phrase "the children" is used in these examples. In the actual memorandum of understanding, the children's first names are used.

times, conflict with their needs. The following wording helps provide for such situations:

> All access to the children is based on their availability as affected by school and extracurricular activities. If they are unable to spend time with their father at the scheduled times, we agree to make equivalent alternative arrangements for them to spend time with him.

This wording helps to avoid a situation in which the resident parent determines when the children will and will not spend time with the other parent. If the resident parent and/or the children decide they cannot go to the other parent for the weekend because there is an important school event scheduled, an alternative weekend is arranged.

The holiday calendar. The parents develop a second calendar showing how they will share the major holidays. The mediator asks the couple to list all of the major holidays in their family. She lists them on the flip chart and asks one of her few past-focused questions, "How did you celebrate those holidays in the past?" This question is not as dangerous as it appears, since most families have a pattern of spending time with each of the parent's families of origin or friends on the same holiday each year. When the couple develops a list that seems shared and seems to have worked in the past, the mediator asks if the parents would like to maintain the schedule in the future.

The couple often keeps the same or a similar schedule. On the other hand many couples develop a new schedule to accommodate the changed needs of both parents.

Religious holidays seem to cause the most anguish. The Jewish holidays tend to be less difficult to share because many have two seders, and the children can spend one with each of the two families. Christian holidays are more difficult to divide evenly. The mediator begins by clarifying how the clients have celebrated a given holiday. Often they have spent Christmas Eve with one family of origin and Christmas Day with the other. If the arrangement worked in the past, she suggests they might want to consider it for the future.

If both parents want the same day, the most common solution is to rotate the holidays so the children spend the holiday with mother in the even years and with father in the odd years.

Vacations and holidays. The parents decide how to share vacation times: summer and winter. With two-wage earning parents, sharing the vacation time can be difficult. Most parents think about vacations in two parts: time with the children and time without the children. The mediation issue is to determine how each will designate vacation time.

Some parents do not have choices. The plant closes down for the last two weeks in July, and that is when they must take their vacation. If both have the same two weeks, they usually share the time, one week with mom and one week with dad. If one parent has a fixed vacation time and the other a flexible one, the flexible parent works around the schedule of the other.

Increasingly, people have more than two weeks' vacation. When they do, parents often opt to take part of the time in the summer and part of the time in the winter. The issue for the mediator is to help them determine *how* to decide what the children do during the vacation times. When the parents agree on vacation arrangements the agreement can be stated as follows:

> We will each be free to take the children on vacation for at least two weeks each year. We agree to give each other at least one month's notice of our intention to take the children on vacation.

Some parents need clear rules. These couples select a specific date, early in the year, by which they must inform each other of the desired vacation times. If they both select the same times and each has flexibility, a simple formula often solves the problem. Two examples are given below.

- If we both select the same times, the children will spend that time with the parent with whom they did not spend the same time in the previous year.

- If we both choose the same vacation period, the parent whose selection is chosen agrees that, in the following year, the other parent will make the first choice.

The impact of two wage-earners. When both parents are employed outside the home they also have to give special attention to the issue of school holidays. In most jurisdictions, education regulations mandate that children attend school for 180 days per year. The education department makes sure that the school year is no shorter than 180 days, and the teachers union makes sure it is no longer. Of those 180 days, approximately 10 are also national holidays on which one or both parents are also free and another 104 days fall on weekends. However, the children are not in school on approximately 66 days each year when both parents are at work. Add to that short days for teacher conferences, and so forth, and the parents have to assure parental coverage for the children for an average of 70 days each year when both parents are working.

If the parents have opted for the children to have prime residency with one parent, it is sometimes assumed that the resident parent is solely responsible for the nonschool days. That is fine if the resident parent does not also work outside the home or is employed in public education with a schedule similar to that of the children. However, the majority of parents work in other areas, and the two working parents need to reach an agreement on how to care for the children when the children are off school and both parents are at work.

Sharing responsibilities as well as rights. A similar situation emerges in caring for sick children. Is the resident parent always the one responsible for the children when they cannot attend school, or do the parents share in this responsibility? The answer to this question depends on the way the clients view their parenting roles. The way they view their roles will, in part, be shaped by the way the mediator manages the negotiations. If members of the couple look upon each other as adversaries, the custody (winner) parent will be left with all the responsibilities. If the mediator manages the talks in terms of problem solving, she is more likely to create a shared-responsibility atmosphere in the negotiations.

If a parent (usually the father) is marginalized in the negotiations, he will play a marginal role in the future. If his parenting role is honored, he will play a fuller father role. Because the adversarial system tends to marginalize his role, many mothers receive little help from the fathers after the divorce. In mediation both parents are assumed to want a role, and the task is to see how those roles might be organized in the future to ensure the children maintain the best and closest relationship with both parents.

The Future Parenting

The extended family. The needs of the extended family are considered along with the children's right to their grandparents, aunts, uncles, and cousins.

Most parents accept responsibility for ensuring the maintenance of their children's relationship with their family of origin. In addition, they often include a statement of intent so the children maintain their relationships with the other's family. Some grandparents have been denied access to their grandchildren and are struggling to gain legal recognition of their rights. Failure to provide for access to the grandparent after the death of a parent can lead to painful losses for the children. Increasingly, grandparents are seeking mediation of their disputes with the parent(s) over access to the grandchildren.[7]

Educational issues. With an increasing range of educational options, parents need to consider all aspects of their children's schooling.

The mediator helps the parents to think about how they will make future schooling decisions. How will they decide whether the children go to public or private school? If a private education, how will they select the specific school? How will they share the costs?

As children grow, they sometimes need additional education assistance. If the child has problems in the future, the parents must determine: How will they decide whether the child needs a tutor? How will they select the tutor? How will they pay for the tutor? On the issue of deciding how to pay for costs another useful formula is,

We will share in these expenses in a ratio of our gross incomes at the time the expenses are incurred.

This formula offers another way of making the agreement a living document. As their incomes and the ratio of their incomes change in the future, the amount each pays will be determined on the then current situation. The couple may need a method of determining these ratios. A simple method is to exchange the first page of their IRS returns showing the gross income for the previous year. This is normally done on May 1, just after the tax returns for the previous year have been filed. All shared costs for the following twelve months are based on this gross income figure.

---

[7]   J. M. Haynes, "The Use of Mediation in Grandparent Visitation Disputes," in *Grandparent Visitation Disputes: A Legal Resource Manual*, ed. R. Segal and B. Karp, (Washington, D.C.: American Bar Association, 1989).

The same formula can be used for determining how to pay for future college expenses. Parents must decide how they will choose a college and how they will pay for it. Some families have already saved money towards these expenses. The majority have not. Most parents rely on their borrowing ability at the time the children go to college to raise the money. The formula assures each parent will pay a fair share of the unknown future costs.

Religious education expenses. Families holding religion to be an important part of their lives have to decide about special religious education issues. The parents must decide who will take the children to their confirmation or Hebrew classes. Most parents agree that nothing is more onerous than taking an unwilling child to religious instruction.[8] By sharing the responsibilities, both parents send clear messages to the children that they both believe the religious education is important. When parents share this responsibility, they usually rotate the task or develop a similar workable formula. They must also agree as to how they will pay for the cost of the religious education.

Health care. Health is a major concern for many families in terms of determining how to pay for medical care, who is responsible for getting the children to the medical professional, and how to deal with any special medical needs.

With mounting health care costs, parents consider whether both of them should keep a family health insurance plan if their medical costs are above the norm. If they decide to keep only one family plan and the parent carrying the plan must pay towards its costs, the other can contribute towards the cost of the insurance coverage. The mediator helps the parents to look at the budget and estimate their total expenditures in the prior year for uncovered health care. If the actual cost of the health care exceeds the cost of the secondparent carrying a family insurance plan, she draws their attention to the pros and cons of both parents paying for the fuller family coverage.

---

[8] We do not discuss the issue of how to mediate when members of the couple disagree about the need or the appropriateness of the specific religious education, since that is usually presented to the mediator as a single issue, and she deals with it differently. Single-issue, high-conflict cases are discussed later in this chapter. A way of dealing with this specific issue appears in chapter 6, page 178.

Medical insurance. The child-support guidelines require the parent paying the child support to provide health insurance for the children if the insurance is available to that parent at a reasonable cost. Thus, all parents who are covered by health insurance by their employers and those parents currently carrying a family plan are required to maintain the family coverage.

Some families are beset with medical problems, and some children need special care. While much of this can be forecast and included in the budget when determining the support arrangements, many health care expenses cannot be accurately forecast. To cover this, parents can use the formula approach which provide the how to do it rather than specific numbers.

Other contingencies

When all of these issues have been settled the mediator engages in some "what ifs." Many parents find this part of the process difficult since, having reached agreement, they don't want to open new areas of disagreement. But, the long-term future requires examination.

What if one parent moves? In today's mobile society it is worth considering what would happen if one parent moves from the area. Of course, there is no problem if the parent wants to move; the problem arises if s/he wants to take the children along. It is not possible to provide for every conceivable contingency, so the couple relies on formulas for making decisions when the event occurs. One provision that has worked for many families is the following arc formula which can be adapted for your geographic location.

These arrangements are predicated on our living in close proximity. If either parent wishes to move from Long Island, we will change the parenting as follows: The parent making the move will notify the other at least three months prior to making the move. During that time we will renegotiate the parenting and access arrangements to provide for ample access by the children to both parents. We will assume the children will stay with the resident parent. At that time we will arrange for access on the following schedule. If the moving parent lives in an area bounded by an arc running through Washington D.C. then the access will be at least monthly for a

131

full weekend, from Friday after school through Sunday evening. If the moving parent resides in an area bounded by an arc running through Chicago then the access will be at least quarterly and for not less than one month each summer. If the moving parent lives beyond that arc, the access will be at least twice a year with at least six weeks in the summer. The moving parent will pay two-thirds of the cost of the children's travel.

The moving parent is assigned two-thirds of the cost on the grounds that the moving parent can negotiate with the employer or a new spouse to cover these extra expenses at the time of moving. It is difficult for the stationary parent to approach her/his employer requesting a raise because the ex-spouse has moved. Most parents find that this formula coincides with their sense of fairness.

The arc formula works if one parent (usually the father) makes no claim on the children being close by. Other families choose a limitation beyond which neither parent will move. Shared physical parenting agreements usually use a form of this since if either parent moves too far away then the shared parenting is disrupted.

We intend to live in close proximity, at least within the same school district while the children are growing up, in order to share equally in their parenting. If either of us decides to move so the current shared parenting becomes impractical, we agree that neither of us will move before negotiating a revised parenting arrangement. If one parent does move unilaterally, we agree the children will reside with the parent who stays in the current school district.

If the current mutual agreement cannot be continued or a new one negotiated, we will continue to share full and complete joint custody of the children and make arrangements for the parent with whom they do not reside to have liberal and reasonable access including, but not limited to, weekends and holidays. At a minimum the parent with whom the children reside during the school year will permit the other parent residence with the children during the summer and all other school breaks.

The Future Parenting

What happens if one parent remarries? Few people understand the difficulties of creating a family from two previously married families. There is always a chance that, if the resident parent remarries, one or more children will not be able to fit into the new family and may want to live with the other parent. While few parents have a specific agreement dealing with this, a discussion of these possibilities sows the seeds for the parents to think about these questions before embarking on a new marriage. This discussion makes it easier for the parents to understand the problem if it does occur in the future, since it has been predicted as normal.

The mediator shares with the couple the various problems that emerge for children upon the remarriage of one parent. She explains the different responses by age and sex and helps parents recognize that many problems that emerge upon remarriage are normal problems.

What happens if one parent dies? The death of one parent often places strains on the children's relationships with that parent's family of origin. Many parents include a provision accepting responsibility for helping the children to maintain the relationship with the dead parent's family. This discussion also reminds the parents of the need to provide insurance for the family in the case of the death of either parent.

At what age (if any) can the children elect to change those arrangements? Families have different styles of decision making. Some are democratic, involving the children in most decisions affecting them. Others are autocratic, never consulting the children about their wishes. The majority are somewhere in the middle of these two. The mediator recognizes it is unlikely the family decision-making style will change after the divorce.

However, as children mature, they demand a greater voice in decisions affecting them. The mediator leads a discussion of how the parents will respond to this over the years. The discussion rarely ends in a formal statement for the agreement. Rather, it promotes the parents' thinking about the future and reminds them that the agreement must be a living document that changes as lives, events, and people change.

Flexible and Structured Agreements

Different clients need different types of agreements. While most people prefer formulas that can be applied to future situations as they arise, other families need an agreement that spells out each point. In the latter case, the mediator dots every *i* and crosses every *t*. Some couples merely state that the children will spend alternate weekends with the father. Others spell out alternate weekends as meaning from Friday at 6:00 P.M. to Sunday evening at 6:00 P.M. A less rigid version of this is for the times to be Friday after school and Sunday one hour before the children's normal bedtime. The latter wording creates a living agreement that changes as the children's needs change. Returning the children at 6:00 P.M. is fine when the children are five years old but too restrictive when they are twelve years old. A flexible arrangement might be written:

We have decided upon open access by mutual agreement. If there is a disagreement between us, the children will spend at least one midweek evening and each alternate weekend from Friday evening through Monday morning with John (father). If they sleep over with John at any time, he agrees to be responsible for getting them to school in the morning.

We will share all the major holidays and the other three-day weekends by mutual agreement. If we have a difference, the children will spend the weekend with the parent with whom they did not spend the same weekend in the previous year.

We agree we can each take the children on vacation for up to four weeks each year but not more than one week at a time. When the youngest child reaches the age of five, we will each be free to take them for two weeks at a time up to eight weeks in any year. We will arrange the vacation time by mutual agreement. If we have a disagreement, the children will go on vacation with the parent with whom they did not spend the same period in the previous year.

As you can see, this wording provides for ongoing mutual decision making with formulas to use when differences occur.

The structured parent needs to know that, for example, the children will be with the father every Easter Sunday from 10:00 A.M. until 6:00 P.M. A structured agreement covers more details.

We will share the major holidays as follows. CHRISTMAS: In odd-numbered years the children will spend Christmas Eve with John, who will return them to Mary' house following Midnight Mass. In even-numbered years John will pick up the children at noon on Christmas Day and return them at 8:00 P.M. EASTER: In even years the children will spend Easter morning from 10:00 A.M. until 2:00 P.M. with John and the afternoon with Mary. THANKSGIVING: They will spend Thanksgiving with Mary in odd numbered years and even numbered years with John. Thanksgiving is defined as from Wednesday evening at 6:00 P.M. through Sunday at 6:00 P.M.

The children will spend Mother's Day and Mary's birthday with Mary, and Father's Day and John's birthday with John. We will share all three-day weekends as follows: beginning with this year we will rotate the three-day weekends so Mary will have the children on the Labor Day weekend and John will have them on the following three-day weekend and continue rotating in this manner. The weekend is defined as from Saturday at 10:00 A.M. to Monday at 4:00 P.M.

The mediator drafts the agreement the parents reach. She does not impose her standards of flexibility or structure on the couple. While directing their attention to the living document - one that can change as the children's needs change - she is perfectly happy to spell out each detail as a permanent factor if that is what the parents want.

Reviewing the Agreement with the Children

Many parents appreciate the opportunity to bring the children in for a session with the mediator so the agreements can be shared with them. In this session the mediator acts as family spokesperson and parent advocate while facilitating an open discussion in which the children's point of view can be heard and understood. It is important that this session be held *only* if the parents agree they are willing to modify the agreement to accommodate the children's legitimate concerns. It would be unfair to the children to invite them to comment on a fait accompli. When the children arrive and have settled into their chairs she engages in the following monologue.

> Well, it's good to see you here. I know this is the last place in the world you want to be and I appreciate your coming here, as do Mom and Dad.[9] As they have told you, I have been working with them for the last few weeks helping them negotiate their separation (divorce) agreement. In those talks you have been the center of most of the discussions as your parents have tried to reach an agreement that, as far as possible, meets your needs.

> We have spent most of the time talking about your best interests and how things could work best for you because both parents love you very much.

When the children appear to be comfortable, the mediator moves into the agenda and covers the following relevant points:

Your parents are getting a divorce. If appropriate, explain what this means. Many parents are not able to explain to younger children what they are doing and what divorce means. If the children do not fully understand what the divorce will do to their lives, they cannot decide how the proposed agreement will impact on them.

You did not cause it. Children are relieved to hear it was an adult decision and nothing they did led to the divorce. Most children secretly believe something they did caused or contributed to the divorce. Helping them understand it was a spousal decision helps relieve them of this responsibility.

Because of this, you could not prevent it in the past and *you won't be able to change it in the future.* If the children believe they helped cause the divorce, they will also feel able to help get the parents back together. It is helpful for the children to understand the irrevocable nature of their parent's decision, to relieve them of their omnipotence. If they believe their parents will get back together, they may do things to try to make it happen and be continually disappointed when it does not.

---

[9] This acknowledges their reluctance to be present – a useful first step to winning their attention.

The Future Parenting

Both parents want you to know that they love you now as they always have. This love will not change. Parents are encouraged to add, "I'll always be your mother," and "I'll always be your father." The children are very confused at this stage. The statement of mutual love from both parents helps lessen children's fears of being rejected by one parent.

Finally, explain that children *do not have to choose between parents.* Point out that the parents may still have arguments in the future — most adults, do but "you do not have to take sides in these arguments." Have the parents reinforce this point. The mediator explains the details of the future living arrangements and invites feedback. The mediator displays the access calendar on the flip chart for a three-month period so the children can see exactly how it will work. She also lists the major holidays and how they will be shared and says to the children, "Mom and Dad have asked me to explain those parts of the agreement that affect you so you can understand and comment on them. As you can see from the flip chart, we have worked out a calendar for the times you will spend with each parent." At this point she walks them through the calendar. "Now, before I go to the holidays, do you have any questions about the regular calendar?"

After discussing the calendar with the children, answering their questions and encouraging them to express their views, the mediator repeats the process with the holiday schedule. Some mediators prepare an eighteen-month calendar showing all of the holidays, how they will be shared and rotated.

Acknowledge each point any child makes, write it on the flip chart, and, when all the children have finished, invite the parents to comment. If the parents differ or if a substantial piece of the arrangement needs to be renegotiated, ask the children to wait outside and help the parents decide what to do.

Two Case Examples

The children often have useful contributions to make about the calendar. The case described earlier in this chapter of the couple who had a complicated schedule that did not replicate itself for over three months is an example of the value of checking with the children.

When I finished explaining the complicated schedule, the eldest teenager looked at his younger sister and said, "Hey, that's great. They'll never know where we are." When the children completed their comments I asked them to wait outside for a while; the parents agreed that they should know where the children were at all times and modified the calendar to a more simple schedule.

In another case, a couple had two children, a boy aged ten and a girl aged twelve. The arrangement was for the father to pick the children up on alternate Friday evenings and take them to his apartment for the weekend. When I finished the explanation of how the schedule would work, the boy turned to his father and said, "Dad, how will I get to soccer practice on Saturday mornings?"

The boy was very involved in the local soccer league near his mother's home. He was probably aware that once he was at his father's house it was unlikely his dad would bring him back to his mother's for the soccer practice and games. The parents looked at each other and admitted they had not thought about it. In front of the children they discussed how to get him to the soccer games and finally agreed that Dad would pick up the daughter on Friday evenings and the son on Saturday at noon after the soccer.

Most children have useful comments to make about the schedule, and most parents are willing to modify the schedule to meet the children's needs.

The mediator sets very clear goals and parameters for the children's session. The session is defined as a time when the children add their feelings and views about the parenting arrangements. Sometimes the children want to talk about money or other spousal issues. The children may raise an issue such as "Will my mother get enough money from my dad so I can live O.K.?" The mediator is quick to answer the question without permitting further discussion of the specific economic agreements.

She replies to the child, "Your parents have agreed on the financial issues and about support so that everyone's needs are taken care of. I know you are concerned about that because most kids your age are. However, it is a parent issue, and they have reached an agreement on it that meets everyone's needs."

Some children have questions about flexibility such as "Do I have to go with mom (or dad) if all my friends are having a party that Saturday?" The mediator replies, "When you have an event that conflicts with these arrangements and you are with mom that Saturday, you talk to her about it, and if you are with dad that Saturday you talk to him about it. You work it out as you have worked it out with your parents so far." This helps the children understand that they will negotiate with each parent independently in the future.

Integrating the Package

When making parenting decisions, clients often find it necessary to revise earlier agreements about support and asset distribution. When this happens, the mediator returns to the previous agreements and helps the couple modify them to conform to the parenting agreements.

For example, the clients may have omitted the cost of Hebrew school from their budgets. In the parenting discussion they realize the oversight and reach an agreement as to who will be responsible for taking the children to classes and who will pay for the classes. This item is added to the budgets, and the level of support is amended to reflect the costs or the cost is assigned to the nonresident parent.

This sometimes happens if the children are young and have not yet begun religious education. The parents agree on how they will divide the future cost and add that agreement to the support section.

Although the divorce mediation process is stated linearly - intake, support, asset distribution, and parenting - these areas are not discrete. The discussion frequently returns to an earlier agreement when that agreement needs modifying or amplifying in the light of information about another area. The mediator recognizes the final agreement is a total package that balances the couple's different interests on all the issues. I frequently remind them of Yogi Berra's famous statement, "It ain't over 'til it's over."

Mediation is a recursive, not a lineal, process. Each part of the agreement rests on the other parts. A change in one section often requires modification of an earlier agreement. The couple finally signs a complete package, and it is the complete package that must satisfy both sets of needs.

The Economic Considerations

Sometimes the parents find it easier to discuss some of the economic issues concerning the children at the point when they agree on the parenting arrangements. The mediator reviews any outstanding economic issues with them.

139

1. Child support
      a. How much? Use the appropriate guidelines.
      b. For how long? When will the support cease?
      c. Indexed to the cost of living?
      d. Indexed to children's developmental needs?

2. Health insurance
      a. The guidelines provide that parents must include health insurance as part of child support when private health insurance is available to the supporting parent at a reasonable cost. Thus if an employer provides insurance, the parent must include his/her children. Explore the value of both parents covering the children on their individual policies.
      b. How will uncovered medical expenses be paid?
      c. Is orthodontia provided for? What about other types of cosmetic procedures?

3. Religious expenses
      a. How will these be met?
      b. How will the social parts of major religious events such as Confirmation and Bar Mitzvah be paid for?

4. Extracurricular activities
      a. How will the parents determine which music lessons, sports activities, summer camps, and so forth, will the children participate in?
      b. How will these activities be paid for?

5. Private school and/or college
      a. How will the parents decide on how to determine where the children will go to school?
      b. How will the education costs will be allocated?

A Checklist of Issues Raised in the Parenting Negotiations

Custody. The mediator reframes the issue from "custody" with all of its negative connotations to "parenting" and how to share it in the future.

Residency. Which parent's home is to be the primary residence of the children?

Decision making. How will the parents share in the decisions regarding education, values, upbringing, and so on? Both parents can have access to all school, medical, and other professional records of the children. Each parent needs to be able to make emergency decisions regarding medical care for the children when they are with him/her.

Visitation. The mediator reframes the issue from "visitation" to "access," with an emphasis on the children's rights to access to both parents.

Schedules. These are developed showing when the children will be with each parent. Identify specific times, if needed, for weekends and weekdays. In general, younger children need shorter and more frequent access to the nonresident parent, and the time between access and duration of each access is enlarged as the children grow. Schedules also provide for which parent is responsible for getting the children to school following the nights they sleep over with the nonresident parent. Part of the discussion relates to which parent will be responsible when a child is sick and cannot go to school.

Access during illness of the children. It is particularly important to discuss this issue when illness is a feature of the family or a child.

Holidays. These days are important to families, and how they are shared is important. Many parents rotate the holidays annually.

Father's/Mother's Days. Consider these days as well as the children's and parent's birthdays.

Summer and school vacations. Pay attention to each parent's rights for vacation time and responsibilities for other school vacation times.

Open telephone access. This is an important item for the children, particularly when frequent access is not possible.

Extended family rights and obligation. These should be explored, with provisions made for the children to continue to enjoy access to important members of their extended families.

Geographic relocation. Moving beyond a reasonable distance can cause problems, and the rights of each parent to move must be tempered with each parent's rights and obligations to the children and the children's right of access to each parent.

Maintaining the family name. This often provides an important way to ease the father's fears about loss of his children.

Future changes. These need to be considered so that the parents can accommodate their arrangements to their children's changing needs. An arrangement that works for a five-year-old will not suit a teenager.

141

Managing Difficult Cases

So far we have dealt with the normal family negotiations regarding the future parenting of the children. We now turn our attention to difficult, high-conflict, and single-issue custody cases. These are typical of cases handled by court programs or referred to private practice mediators by the court

Separating parental from spousal roles. Adults fill many roles. The two major roles within the family are those of spouse and of parent. Ideally, we behave and react differently as parents than as spouses, and we are capable of keeping the two roles separate. However, a major cause of conflict over children is the inability of spouses to keep their spousal and parental roles separate. Too often a hurt spouse lashes back at the other parent. "He left us," is a frequent complaint of wives. But, he did not leave "us" he left her and wants to maintain a relationship with his children. However, as long as the wife joins the *mother* and *wife* roles together, or the husband joins the *husband* and *father* roles together, meaningful negotiations are stymied.

The role issues can be shown as lines as in figures 5.1 and 5.2. When communication and roles are appropriate (fig. 5.1), the discussion between the two parties is represented by a straight line.

Figure 5.1. Normal Family Roles

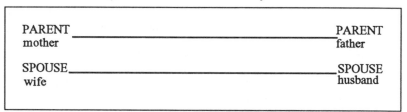

Figure 5.2 Confused Family Roles

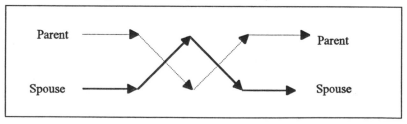

When discussing money they communicate as spouses; when talking about the children they relate to each other more as parents. When roles, and therefore communication, are distorted, the lines become confused (fig. 5.2).

The mediator's task is to unscramble them. A parent locked into a custody battle is often unable to distinguish between the former partner's role as parent and his or her role as spouse. Thus, all of the legitimate anger each has towards the other as a spouse is misdirected towards the other as a parent. When the mediator develops a sense that this role confusion exists, she checks it out by:

- Substituting the other spouse's name (mentally) when the parents are talking about the disputed children. If the name of the spouse fits equally with the name of the child, it indicates that the role confusion is present. For example, if the husband says "She neglects our son, she doesn't care for him," the statement might also make sense using " me" instead of "my son," if the husband also complains that she did not take care of him in the marriage.
- Seeking acknowledgment from each parent that the other is a good parent. When role confusion is present, parents resist giving this acknowledgment, even when all the evidence points to a positive parenting role by both of them.
- Educating the parents on the children's needs and rights.

Strategies for Mediators

Specific strategies for helping parents separate their spousal from parent roles emerge from the unique facts of each case. However, the mediator uses some universal strategies in most difficult cases.

Reducing defensiveness. Most people entering mediation arrive with a position they believe must be defended at all costs. This position may be a goal such as to *win* custody or it may be a fear of *losing* the children. The mediator reduces the fear early in the intake by asking the couple, "What is the worst possible outcome of working with me?"

When each parent articulates this fear, it is usually an unreasonable[10] concern. The mediator asks each parent if he or she can agree that the fear of the other parent will not materialize in the

---

[10] By unreasonable, I mean a fear that is based not in fact but in emotions.

mediation. For example, if both parents state that the worst possible outcome would be losing the children, the mediator asks each parent to affirm that the other will not lose the children in these negotiations.

As this is understood and accepted by each parent, the need to defend against that possibility is diminished, and each parent can spend the energy saved thinking about new solutions rather than defending against old fears.

Creating dissonance. In most high-tension disputes, neither party has seriously considered the other's point of view. Usually, each parent ascribes a view to the other that is totally unreal. The mediator tries to gain for each parent a clearer understanding of what the other parent seeks and needs by assigning tasks that help them think about what the other really thinks. Thus, an interim task might be for each parent to think about

1. What s/he would need from the other parent in order to agree to his/her position
2. What s/he could offer the other parent in order to get him/her to agree to that position

To prepare an intelligent response to these two questions, each parent must think about what the other really wants. In effect, they must "walk a mile in the other's moccasins."[11] In the process, two things happen:

- The legitimate aspects of the other's position cannot be ignored.
- Understanding the other's point of view creates dissonance in each parent. The dissonance can only be resolved by either terminating the thought process or by a change in an unrealistic view of the other's position.

A Case Example

John and Mary lived together during the late sixties and, when they became pregnant, formally married. Neither had a regular job, and both spent equal time caring for their son, Mark.

---

[11] Almost all of our folk sayings contain the accumulated wisdom of our culture. Thus, they are usually correct and useful and should not be dismissed as old wives' tales.

The Future Parenting

The marriage was not going well, partly because of the economic stress and partly for other relationship issues. John's parents called one day from Seattle with news of a job as an expediter on the docks. John and Mary talked it over and decided to make the move from Long Island to Seattle. John thought this was the opportunity he had been looking for. Mary saw it as a chance to restart the marriage in a new setting.

John's job on the docks required him to work an eighteen-hour shift when a ship was at dock followed by three days off. On his days off he maintained his close relationship as primary parent with Mark and continued to share equally in his nurturing. He was enjoying his new life.

Mary, however, was not. She was isolated from her support network, did not have any interests outside the home, and felt more and more oppressed in the relationship. After a year in the Northwest, she decided to return to the East coast. She told John she would like to visit her folks on Long Island and take Mark with her for the visit. At the end of the first week in New York, she called John and told him she was not returning to Seattle and would keep Mark with her.

John was devastated and, failing to persuade her to return, began divorce proceedings in Washington. Mary filed similar papers in New York and each waited for something to happen. John called regularly and spoke to Mark on the telephone.

The first legal action took place in New York, and Mark flew east to consult with a local lawyer. The case was, of course, postponed, and at the end of the week he had to return to Seattle. During the week in New York, he saw Mark each day, spending lots of time with him. On the final day of his visit he went to say good-bye to his son. Mary was working as a waitress, and there was a mix-up with the baby-sitter who thought John was staying in New York a few days longer.

When John arrived at Mary's house to say farewell to Mark he discovered his son asleep in bed with no baby-sitter. He wrapped Mark in a blanket, took him, in the car, to the airport, and flew back to Seattle. Once home, his parents cared for Mark while John worked and he settled back into a routine of nurturing father with total responsibility on his days off.

When Mary discovered what had happened she was devastated, but as helpless as John had been to do anything about it.

145

Two months later, the Seattle court heard the case, and Mary flew to Seattle to appear. The Seattle court held that the divorce would be heard in New York and the custody issue in Seattle. The New York court held likewise. Each parent felt stymied in the legal process, and each worried about losing in the other's court. People often feel at a disadvantage in a different court.

After the court hearing, Mary picked up Mark at John's parents's home to take him for a walk in the park. They went through the park to her car, into the car, to the airport, and back to New York.

Establishing mediation as the arena for settlement. When my phone rang, both parents, who were in New York for another court hearing, were on the other end of the line and gave me the basic information. I listened to their story and noted that each corroborated the other's information. They asked for an appointment, and I told them, "I will be able to see you twice for a total of three hours. The first meeting will be tomorrow, Friday, afternoon for an hour and one-half and then again on Monday afternoon. We will reach an agreement by then or an agreement will not be possible."

I gave this schedule since they told me they had engaged in this conflict for more than a year, and I wanted them to be clear that mediation was an arena to settle the case, not to continue the fighting. If clients are conflict habituated, they need a tight time frame to emphasize that mediation is a different arena from any they have used in the past. When clients inform the mediator they have been to see numerous lawyers and/or therapists, this information is an indicator the couple shops around for a professional to help them *continue* the fight rather than *settle* it. Setting well-defined and short time frames helps to sort out those who want to use mediation to settle and those who see it as another arena in which to maintain the conflict. John and Mary agreed to the schedule.

Eliminating worst fears. I then told them, "I want you each to think about something before you come to see me. What is the worst possible outcome in working with me? Don't answer that question now. Think about it until tomorrow; when we meet I will ask you the question again."

In asking the question about the worst possible outcome, I wanted to find out what it was they feared the most. My experience in cases such as this is that couples are driven to mediation by fear of the alternative arena, and their fear that their worst possible outcome will materialize in the other arenas.[12] We use enormous energy defending against our worst fears. If these fears are surfaced and negotiated early in the session, the parties can concentrate their energies on solving the problem rather than defending against their fears.

Confusion between parenting and spousal roles. I opened the first session by collecting the essential data and confirming the information they had provided on the telephone. As the session continued it became clear this couple had not separated their parenting and spousal roles. John complained that Mary did not take good care of Mark, did not mother him enough, and he repeated the story about finding him untended at the house while she was at work. John also complained about Mary's lack of care of him as a husband. As I listened, whenever John spoke about his marriage, I substituted the name John for the name Mark and realized he was really complaining about the lack of mothering he received from Mary during the marriage.

Mary complained about John's overpowering character. She said that during the marriage John felt any problem could be solved by talking about it, "as long as he does all the talking." Mary complained that Mark was beginning to grow up like his father, dominating women and believing that as long as he did the talking everything would be all right. As I listened, I realized Mary was complaining about John's *spousal* behavior not his *parenting* behavior.

I decided to see if each could acknowledge the other's parenting ability. No matter what I did I was unable to get Mary to acknowledge John's parenting just as I was unable to get John to acknowledge Mary's parenting. They were stuck in the spousal roles and marital fights. Any movement on the parenting issue would require their becoming unstuck.

Surfacing the WATNAs.[13] I turned to the question I had raised on the telephone and asked each of them their response to the question, "What would be the worst possible outcome in working with me?" John spoke first, saying, "I think the worst outcome would be if I would lose Mark. He is my only child, and I don't know what I would do if I lost him. The thought is unbearable."

---

[12] A fuller discussion of this phenomenon appears in the next chapter.
[13] WATNA is the client's **W**orst **A**lternative **T**o **A** **N**egotiated **A**greement. This concept is fully discussed in the next chapter.

I responded, "That would be an awful outcome and one you have every right to fear. Mary, how about you?" Mary replied, "I've thought about this a lot and I think the worst possible outcome would be if I lost Mark." Again, I responded, "That would indeed be an awful outcome and one you have every right to fear. Since you both fear the same outcome, could we agree that one outcome that is not acceptable is that either of you lose Mark? John, could you agree Mary must not lose Mark as a result of these negotiations? Mary, could you agree John must not lose Mark as result of these negotiations?"

They both replied positively and we had another agreement. This was their third; they had already agreed to mediate, they had agreed on using me as the mediator, and now they agreed that neither should lose Mark. I felt comfortable returning to the issue of the confused parenting/spousal roles. Even though the atmosphere was lighter in the room as a result of the agreement releasing each from their worst fears, neither parent was yet ready to acknowledge the other's parenting ability. Each seemed to sense that acknowledging the other's parenting meant they might possibly lose the argument about Mark's residency.

I pointed out we were no longer negotiating *whether* one or the other might lose him but *how* to share the time with him recognizing that, since he was almost five years old, he would have to live with one parent during the school year to be able to attend school on a regular basis. However, with time running out for the first session, I was unable to gain any significant movement from either of them towards acknowledging the other's parenting. I turned to the subject of the forthcoming weekend. They told me Mark was to spend Saturday with his father and Sunday with his mother.

Using dissonance theory. As I brought the session to closure I gave them a new task. I said, "I would like each of you to think about ways we could move towards an acceptable agreement. I would like you both to think about the following: John, what would you want from Mary to agree to her position that Mark lives primarily with her? Mary, what would you want from John to agree with his position that Mark lives primarily with him? And while you are thinking about this question I want you also to think about a second question, What could you offer the other to get them to agree to your position? Mary, what could you offer to John to get him to agree to your position? John, what could you offer to Mary to get her to agree to your position? Don't answer those questions now. Think about them and we will talk about them sometime during our meeting on Monday."

The purpose of asking these two questions was to get them to "walk a mile in other's moccasins." I knew that I had to break them out of the confusion between their spousal and parenting roles and that one way of doing it was through their own legitimate self-interest. Movement would come only when each understood what the other really wanted, rather than the motives they had each ascribed to each other. The motive each believed moved the other was a spousal motive, that is, "She didn't take care of me" and "He overpowered me." Each believed the other wanted to maintain that position.

A solution would emerge when each could see what the other really wanted: a meaningful, nurturing parent role with Mark. They needed to understand the other's position more clearly in order to reach an agreement on Mark's future parenting. To help them break out of the spousal role and understand what each wanted as a parent, I needed them to think about what the other wanted and needed *as a parent*.

Thus, with difficult couples, I get them thinking about what the other wants and needs as a parent. Hopefully what they see will not be as threatening as what they see in each other as a spouse. The purpose of the first question, "What would you want from the other to agree to their position?" is to have them think carefully about what each really wants and what the other is capable of giving. To answer this question, they must think about the issue from the other's point of view. If they are to accomplish this task they have to change their position since *(a)* they will have to admit to themselves the parenting needs of the other rather than the implied spousal motive and *(b)* they will have to understand the other's point of view.[14]

Understanding the other's point of view is the first step in moving towards an agreement. It uses dissonance theory to create change. Dissonance theory postulates that it is not possible to hold one

---

[14] An interesting use of this approach can be seen on a video tape available from the Academy of Family Mediators, 355 Tyrol West, 1500 S. Lilac Drive, Golden Valley, Minn. 55146. *The Case of Willie*, is a tape of a role play session conducted at an annual conference of the Academy.

position and argue another; the two are in dissonance and people modify one or the other position to lessen the dissonance.[15] When people modify their original positions, a negotiated agreement becomes possible.

However, not all people are willing to try to answer the first question; thus I ask the second question, which is a self-interest variation of the first. "Mary, what can you offer John to get him to agree to your position?" requires Mary to think about what John wants and accomplishes the same purpose as the first question. To know what John wants she must understand his position, and as each parent understands the other's position, the implied motive disappears and is replaced with an understanding of the other's needs. Many clients do not deal with the first question (possibly because it asks them to think about losing). However, most clients answer the second question (probably because it involves their winning). In either case, once each parent thinks about what the other parent wants, dissonance happens.

Acknowledging their parenting. When they returned on Monday each looked tired and drawn. I began the session by asking what each had done over the weekend. John began "Mark and I went to the beach. It was secluded, not many people there, and we flew a kite, built sand castles, and bought hot dogs. There was just the two of us, and we had a great time together." John talked about his day with Mark. I encouraged him to keep talking and provide every detail of the day. As he did, a picture emerged of one-on-one time with father and son. At the same time, the emotional climate of the room warmed up.

When John finished, I turned to Mary and asked her about the events of Sunday. "Oh, we had a great time with a bunch of my friends," she replied. "We went to the state park and had a picnic. There were a dozen of us and we spent the day playing volley ball and with frisbees. Then we had a great songfest; my friend Sally brought her guitar. We barbecued hamburgers and hot dogs, and Mark had a great time with all of my friends." As Mary talked about her day with Mark, I encouraged her to keep talking and provide every detail of the day. A picture emerged of a gregarious, social day with mother and son. The emotional climate of the room grew even warmer.

---

[15] Arthur Cohen. *Attitude Change and Social Influence* (New York: Basic Books, 1984).

Using a summary to mutualize. When both had finished I leaned forward and said, "Mark is a lucky guy. He gets the best of both worlds from each of you. From you, John, he gets the one-on-one attention, lots of special time and gets to do those things best done by just the two of you. And when he is with you, Mary, he gets the opportunity to socialize, to be gregarious and gets to do things best done in a crowd. Just as you are different as spouses, so Mark gets different things from each of you as parents. Each of the things he gets from you is important and he needs both of you if he is to grow up to be the young man you want him to be. In that way he is very lucky."

I had a choice of trying to weave this same/different idea in a way that would get them to acknowledge each other's parenting or of proceeding to my questions of the previous week. I felt that I had acknowledged each of them sufficiently for each to be nondefensive about their parenting roles. Further work was not needed at this point, even if they did not acknowledge each other's parenting. I turned to the assignment questions: "Tell me what your thinking has been about the two questions I asked you on Friday. I assume you have both thought about them." Mary replied first, "Yes, I thought about them a lot. It was very difficult to keep my mind focused on the questions. My mind kept wandering off them, but I did stick with them."

John replied, "You too? I had a terrible time. In fact I was awake most of last night thinking about them. But I finally came up with an answer, and I'd like to share it with you now." I replied, "OK, John, why don't you begin."

"Well," John began, sucking in his breath, "I thought about it a lot," he blurted out at great speed, afraid the words would get away from us all. "If you will let me take Mark back to Seattle until the first of January, I'll bring him back to New York and he can live with you during the school year and then spend the summer and Christmas holidays with me each year."

We were meeting at the end of May, and Mark was due to enter nursery school that fall. John's proposal meant Mark would miss the first semester of nursery school. I looked at Mary, who stared back at me blankly. I stood and wrote the proposal on the flip chart. "Is that correct?" I asked John. "Yes," he replied. I turned to Mary, and asked "What do you think about that?"

Mary studied the words and slowly nodded assent. "So you could agree with John's proposal?" I asked. "Yes," said Mary.[16]

With the basic agreement in place I pointed out that Mary could not let John take Mark back to Washington without a written agreement. I offered to draft the memorandum for them that afternoon so they could each take a copy to their respective lawyers for review and drafting into the legal agreement. They turned to each other and began talking about support and some other financial differences not previously disclosed, and quickly came to a fair support arrangement. We agreed to add a clause requiring mediation and arbitration of any violation of the agreement and brought the session to a close.

The parents have called me twice since the agreement to report that it was working well. I warned both of them that it may require rethinking as Mark reaches the age of nine or ten and his peer group becomes more important to him.

In this case study I have demonstrated the usefulness of identifying the couple's WATNA and then eliminating it from the talks, thus freeing up creative energy for solutions. I helped the couple separate their parenting and spousal roles in the belief that it is acceptable to dislike someone as an ex-spouse but not as mother or father of one's son. I helped them accomplish this through reducing defensiveness, using dissonance theory, and helping them understand what each really wanted. Finally, I validated their parenting and pointed out the unique attributes each gave to Mark. This combination of strategies helped the couple get over the kidnapping and begin to share parenting their only child.

Using these techniques also helped me to avoid dealing with the multitude of emotional and psychological issues behind their behavior. I was able to stay in the mediator role by using mediation strategies and avoid becoming seduced into a therapist role with a highly emotional couple.

---

[16] I am often asked why I did not ask for Mary's answer to the assigned question. Her original hesitance in answering and her agreement to John's proposal suggested that asking her to add a proposal would only complicate matters. I believe that, if she had a preferred proposal, she would have stated it then, rather than agreeing to John's.

Allegations of Child Abuse

When one parent alleges the other abuses the child, the mediator must take the allegation seriously. If the allegation is made and not withdrawn with an explanation, the mediator informs the couple that she must report the matter to the child protection services and explains to them what will happen. "An investigator will come to see you within forty-eight hours and interview you and the child, and, if the investigator determines the child has been abused, then child protective services will take the appropriate action." When the mediator is placed in this position, the parents terminate the session and the mediation.

If the mediator believes the allegation is strategic and is being used to gain a negotiating advantage but is not true, she devises a series of questions to help the alleging parent acknowledge that the charges are not true.[17] If the allegations are untrue, the adversarial system will only exacerbate the situation and make any future relationship between the parents even more difficult. However, the mediator always errs on the side of caution, and if there is a scintilla of question in her mind that the charges are true, she makes the report to child protective services.

Are the Problems Psychological or Negotiable?

If the conflict between the parents is the product of a serious psychological problem on the part of one, the mediator refers the couple to a family therapist to help them. The referral is to a family therapist even though the mediator believes the problem lies with one client. This destigmatizes the referral, and the mediator relies on the family therapist to deal with the therapeutic issue in the way the therapist determines is most useful to the clients.

When the mediator believes the conflict is negotiable, that is that practical solutions are available to solve the conflict, she can use strategies drawn from the next chapter, "Negotiating Behavior," to help the clients break the negotiating impasse and arrive at an

---

[17] An excellent source for information on these questions is Richard Gardner, *True and False Allegations of Child Sex Abuse* (Creskill, N. J.: Creative Therapeutics, 1990). Also see Richard Gardner, *The Parental Alienation Syndrome* (Creskill, N. J.: Creative Therapeutics, 1990).

agreement that is best for each of them and their children. The next chapter deals with the negotiating behavior of the clients and the role of the mediator as manager of the negotiations that take place at each stage of the mediation process.

Chapter Six
Negotiating Behavior

The best negotiator is not an advocate. The best negotiator is a man who could perform the role of mediator in the negotiations if he were called upon to perform that role. In other words, while he may have to engage in advocacy to reach a common ground, he should never be overly persuaded by his own advocacy. Advocacy should be a tactic and not an end in the negotiations.

— *Arthur Goldberg, former U. S. Supreme Court Justice*

For most people, bargaining is getting the best deal, and the way to get the best deal is to ask for more than they want or offer less than they are willing to pay and hope the others will adjust their figure. The problem with this approach is that it based on a series of lies, hardly a way to build trust in a negotiating arrangement.

A few years ago I was on vacation in Mexico and wanted to buy a rug for my office. I checked the various vendors in the market and choose one that had the rug I wanted. Realizing that haggling is the norm in this situation, I approached the stall with as much nonchalance as I could muster, casually looking at the pile of rugs. The seller came to me and, after an exchange of pleasantries, asked me what I was looking for. I told him and asked the price of the rug I wanted. "Ah, señor, you have chosen a very good one. That one, señor, is only one hundred and fifty dollars," he replied, smiling broadly.

"What!" I protested, as my part of the game, "That rug sells in the next market for just thirty-five dollars." "Yes señor, but this is good quality, not mass produced. If you really like the rug, perhaps I could sell it for one hundred dollars." "Oh no," I replied, "It is only worth sixty dollars." "But señor, I have a family to feed. However, since you are a Norte Americano, I will let you have it for seventy-five dollars." Having made movement which was reciprocated, I was stuck with the price and purchased a fifty-dollar rug for a bargain price of seventy-five dollars.

To arrive at that agreement we both lied to each other. I started by trying to suggest a low interest in the rugs, when I really was intent

155

on purchasing one, and quoted a fictional thirty-five-dollar comparison. His first lie was in asking for one hundred and fifty dollars.[1] We each acknowledged our lies by engaging in further concessions to each other until we arrived at a price that was acceptable to both of us.

My experience in the Mexican marketplace did no harm. I knew I was probably paying more than I should. The merchant was aware that his prices were inflated. We engaged in an amusing exercise, and, since we would probably never see each other again, no damage was done to our future relationship. In mediation, one of the mediator's prime responsibilities is to ensure that the disputing parties reach an agreement in a way that protects their future relationship. This is especially true in divorce, where the couple have an ongoing relationship as parents. It makes no sense to win a negotiating game if the cost is the loss of the parental relationship.

Most people set goals for themselves in the negotiations[2] that involve three positions:

1. Negotiators have an idea of what they want to achieve in the talks. This is called a "goal."
2. They exaggerate the goal either by adding demands they will give up if they achieve their goal or by increasing or decreasing[3] the value of the demand. We call this an "add-on." For example, if the goal is quantified as ten, the demand (add-on) might be thirteen. The other party may have a goal of eleven, so sets an opening offer (add-on) of eight.
3. Negotiators also have bottom lines. The bottom line is the point below (for the seller) or above (for the buyer) at which each will not settle.[4] It is also the point at which they will not stay in the negotiations.

---

[1] In a similar situation in the same market, I agreed to pay the first price a dealer quoted. He was so embarrassed that he gave me the wall hanging plus another, smaller one for the price I had agreed to pay.

[2] Most writers use the terms *negotiations* and *bargaining* synonymously; I use *negotiations* to describe the entire process and *bargaining* to describe that part of the negotiations process in which the parties engage in trading.

[3] The seller increases the price asked and the buyer reduces the price offered.

[4] We discuss the significance of the buyer-seller model to negotiations later.

Negotiating Behavior

The bottom line is determined by the individual's sense of fairness and general sense of what one could obtain in an alternative arena. Most mediation clients have a sense of what they can expect to gain in court and, if the expectation is realistic, are unlikely to settle for less in mediation. If the negotiator knows he can get at least eight in court, his bottom line in mediation would be close to that figure.

It is dangerous for the mediator[5] to explore the participants' bottom lines. If the bottom-line position of each party is known to the other, each will make offers just above the other's bottom line, sufficiently above to make it more attractive than the alternative but not attractive enough to enable the participants to reach a satisfying agreement. Since the participants are rarely evenly balanced in negotiating skills, revelation of the bottom line provides important knowledge to the one who knows what to do with the information and gives that person an unfair advantage. The mediator makes no attempt to discover or reveal the bottom lines for this reason. In addition, they are usually flexible and change during the course of the negotiations, and early revelation would fix them and make it difficult for the person to make changes.

The bottom line, the goal, and the add-on are all flexible points on a range, subject to change as new information is added to the body of knowledge of the participants. In one divorce case, the husband offered a substantial settlement for the wife's interest in his business. In part the offer was predicated on his fear of the alternative arena. He was concerned about the tax consequences if his business became the subject of a public trial, and he also thought the court would award his wife a 50 percent interest in the business.

The mediation fell apart when the husband's attorney convinced him that the court would not tell the IRS about the tax situation (how much he made off the books) and neither would the courts necessarily award a 50 percent interest to his wife. The husband withdrew his offer and established a new goal by offering less and also setting an even larger add-on. The wife, whose aspirations had been increased by the husband's earlier behavior, found it difficult to change her goal to incorporate the husband's new position.

---

[5] The mediator is female in this chapter.

As a result, they each developed new goals too far away from the goals of the other and set up a situation where each felt they would do better in court.

BATNA

Fisher and Ury[6] use the term **Better Alternative To A Negotiated Agreement (BATNA)** as a fuller explanation of the bottom line. Each person in dispute has an idea of whether a better alternative exists somewhere other than the arena in which the current negotiations are being conducted. Since this is a better description of the phenomenon than the term bottom line, from now on, we will refer to the participant's BATNA's rather than to bottom lines. Figure 6.1 demonstrates the way traditional negotiations take place.

Figure 6.1 Bargaining Areas Created by Participant Strategies

Husband		$	Wife
Defensive Zone	BATNA	125 120 110	Add-on
Creative Zone	Goal	100 90 80	Goal Creative Zone
	Add-on	70 60 50	Defensive Zone BATNA

In this example, the husband has a goal of paying $80 in maintenance support. His opening position, which includes his add-on, is to offer $70. On the other hand, if he is forced to pay more, he will go up to $125, his BATNA. Beyond that figure, he will take his chances in court where he has a better alternative to the negotiated agreement.

---

[6] Roger Fisher and William Ury, *Getting to Yes: Negotiating Agreement Without Giving In* (Boston: Houghton Mifflin, 1981).

Negotiating Behavior

The wife's goal is to get $100 in maintenance support. She has added $20 to that figure "to give herself room to negotiate." At the other end, if she is driven down, the minimum she will accept is $50. A mediation settlement of less than $50 would be unacceptable, and she would rather go to court where she believes she would fare better than in mediation.

The areas between the add-on of one and the BATNA of the other are where agreement is highly unlikely. The add-on of each party is too close to the BATNA of the other. In figure 6.1 this is $120 and $125, and $70 and $50. Since the numbers representing these positions are rarely precise, the person holding the BATNA is unsure when to exercise the option to move to an alternative arena. Thus, the husband may exercise the option to quit mediation before reaching $125, while the wife may leave prior to reaching her actual number of $50.

On the other hand, the husband could compromise in his defensive zone up to his BATNA. In this case, it is between $101 and $124. The wife could also compromise in her defensive zone between 79 and $51. Settlements in this zone do not provide satisfaction when the parties settle close to their BATNA, because their only achievement is having avoided going to court.

For this reason I have labeled the two areas bounded by the goals and the BATNAs as "defensive zones." The party closer to his or her BATNA will be in a defensive posture in the negotiations protecting against a poor deal. People defending against poor deals are unlikely to be creative. Creativity is most often seen when the negotiations are focused somewhere between the goals of the participants. This is the area in which a mutually acceptable agreement can be found.

If the participants open the negotiations with unreasonably high or low add-ons, new zone is created between the BATNA of one and the add-on of the other, making the negotiations very unfavorable to the person whose BATNA has been breached. We see this in figure 6.2 on page 160. A difficult situation also develops if a client has an unrealistic BATNA, although the latter can usually be remedied by suggesting the client consult with his or her lawyer as to their chances in court.

Figure 6.2 Bargaining Areas Created by Exaggerated Opening Positions

Husband		$		Wife
		145	Add-on	
Defensive	BATNA	130		
Zone		120		
		100	Goal	
Creative		90		Creative
Zone	Goal	80		Zone
		70		Defensive
		60		Zone
		50	BATNA	
	Add-on	40		

The extreme defensive zones in this figure are fraught with danger. Both parties have opened with unreasonable add-ons which places the opening position/add-on of each party beyond the BATNA of the other. When both have unreasonable add-ons and articulate them early in the process, each believes that movement to a zone of mutual agreement is impossible. When the parties open the negotiations in the pattern demonstrated in figure 6.1, the chances of movement are greater than in figure 6.2. This is because in figure 6.2 the BATNAs of the participants are above the add-ons of the other. When the add-ons are between the other's BATNA and goal (fig. 6.1), both participants see the possibility of reaching an agreement within a range that is better than their assumed alternatives (the court). Neither feels s/he will have to struggle to move the other away from their BATNA.

This is a major reason for not allowing bargaining to take place until all of the data have been obtained and understood by both parties. Clear data make it more difficult for either party to open with unreasonable positions, since the parameters of the bargaining are established in the data gathering and setting stage of the negotiations.

The bargaining areas between the goal and the BATNA of the other is designated as a defensive zone because, while the negotiations are taking place in these areas (between $100 and $130 and between $50 and $80 in fig. 6.2), one of the negotiators is busily defending against the breach of their BATNA. Little movement takes place here. The bargaining area with the greatest promise of an integrated agreement is between the two goals ($80 and $100 in figs. 6.1 and 6.2). This is the creative zone, where energies are devoted to creating a solution rather than defending against capitulation.

WATNA

So far we have looked at the content of the bargaining and how it influences the way people bargain. There is another important, dynamic factor that must be considered here: each client's Worst Alternative To A Negotiated Agreement (WATNA).[7] To discover that let's look at another aspect of bargaining: fear of the alternative.

While many clients opt for mediation because of its many positive attributes, others choose it because they fear the litigation route more. One person may fear that if the case goes to court, his business activities will be open to public scrutiny. Another may fear her earlier affair becoming public knowledge. Some people cannot bear the thought of being judged. Others relate horror stories of their friends' experiences. Most are concerned about the impact of a trial on their children. Whatever the reason, many clients are more negative about litigation than they are positive about mediation.

This fear of the alternative has important implications for mediation. If fear of litigation motivates people to mediate, they may be more willing to settle for less in mediation rather than risk going to court. On this end of the scale we could place the husband who thinks he would do badly in court: He concedes everything rather than end mediation. The wife who knows of this fear could refuse to make any concessions. Thus, when clients appear to be motivated by an unreasonable fear of the legal arena, it is useful to suggest they consult with counsel to gain a more normative view. Our interest in this matter is with the majority of people in the normative range. What effect does fear of litigation have on moving someone into the bargaining phase by making the other's proposal preferable to going to court? Let us

---

[7] J. M. Haynes, "Mediated Negotiations: The Function of the Intake," *Mediation Quarterly* no. 6, (Dec. 1984): 3-15.

use a situation in which the couple is bargaining over the amount of support and that the available resources are $800. The couple can settle anywhere on a curve between 0 and 800. Figure 6.3 displays the range of possibilities.

Figure 6.3 Range of Settlement Possibilities

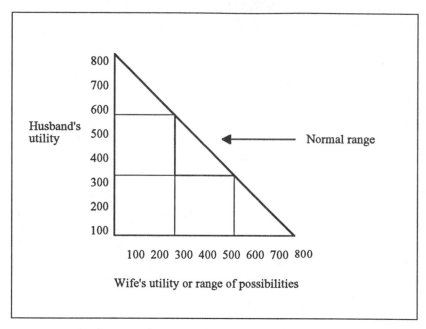

One factor that determines whether one party makes more concessions than the other is the fear of the alternative. Such fear is based on their respective WATNAs. We diagram this in figure 6.4.

To demonstrate this factor, we extend the couple's utility lines down and to the left and draw another line that pivots on their intersection. The utility lines below and to the left of the intersection become the pressure lines. Fear causes the pivoted line to move higher or lower on the settlement line. Thus, if the husband has a greater fear of the courts, his fear factor tends to push the settlement higher for the wife. If the wife has a greater fear, then this fear tends to push her to settle at a lower figure.

Figure 6.4 The Effect of Fear of the Alternative on the Settlement

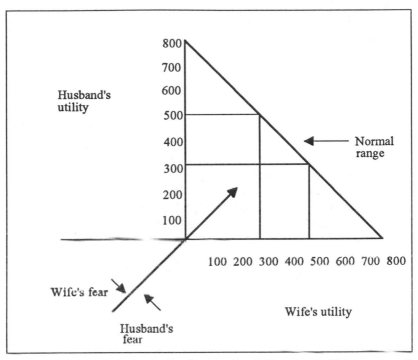

If a husband fears disclosing the full extent of his assets, the mediator makes it clear to him that mediation is not a way of avoiding the obligation for fairness, honesty, and the responsibility the judicial system places on him for full and complete disclosure. Indeed, the fear of giving the data is used by the mediator to clarify for the reluctant husband that he *must* make full disclosure and that mediation is the most private arena in which to do it.

On the other hand, if one of the clients seems to have an *unreasonable* fear of the court system and the fear prevents him/her from negotiating an agreement that meets the self-interest, the mediator devises strategies for relieving those fears through knowledge of the reality of the other arena.

The mediator engages in strategies to balance the power relationship between the parties by assuring them that each person has the same level of accurate negotiating information. The mediator maintains a balance between process control and content control. In maintaining process control he helps the clients understand how to negotiate, thereby removing constraints to a balanced process. He avoids telling the clients what do to in terms of the content of their negotiations.

Avoiding Premature Negotiations

I have seen a number of cases where the husband insisted on making proposals early in the negotiations only to have the wife reject them, adding, "If that's where you're coming from then mediation is useless. I'm going to my attorney."

In these cases I believe the wife made an assumption that she would spend most of her time trying to pull her husband up to her BATNA with little hope of achieving movement into her goal area. In that case she wisely exercised her BATNA and reminded me of the importance of holding all proposals until the data have been gathered and the problem has been defined.

Mediation structures the negotiations in a way that tends to avoid premature articulation of a goal. Rather than having the participants establish inflated positions, the mediator helps the disputants define their positions *based on the data*. In mediation we begin by gathering the data.

The mediator uses the process to avoid premature negotiating, which occurs when the participants look for solutions without first understanding the problem. The mediator avoids premature bargaining (such as, "you take the house and I'll take the pension," when neither party knows the true value of the house or the pension) by suggesting that the proposal be put on hold until all of the data are obtained. Using self-interest makes this acceptable to the participants. The mediator says, "It would be too early to negotiate right now, because, without all of the facts, you might give more than you can afford, or you might take less than is fair. So, in order to be fair to both of you, let's not make decisions until we have all of the data."

Proposals offered in the absence of complete data are ignored or "put on hold until later" so as not to commence the bargaining phase of the negotiations until the participants are in the creative zone.

The goal of the mediator, and the purpose of the process, is to help move both parties into the area bounded by their respective goals. This is done by basing the discussions on the data that are used to define the problem. Using data tends to limit the amount of each add-on, since unrealistic add-ons are exposed as such by the data.

In one sense we can therefore state that people move into the creative zone at the point they would rather settle on the other's terms than move to litigation, or, as Zartman and Berman suggest, "The moment is propitious for negotiation when both sides perceive that they may be better off with an agreement than without one."[8] In order to be in that position the aspirations of the each party must be public and within a reasonable distance of the goals of the other.

Negotiations Between the Buyer and Seller

Negotiations can be thought of as a transaction between a buyer and a seller. This is particularly true during the asset division negotiations. The person wanting an item is thought of as the buyer, who often understates the value of the item. The other spouse is the seller, who often overstates the value of the item.

A husband may overvalue his stamp collection because he is proud of his hobby. When completing the asset forms his pride may overtake his self-interest if he increases the value of the stamps. When the person who wants the item prices it above the value of the person who does not want the same item, it is usually because the buyer-seller roles are confused. The mediator insists on an independent valuation to assure that each party's self-interests are protected. Insisting on the documentation of the value of each item helps to prevent the game of buyer-seller from dominating the negotiations.

There may be intangible values each places on an item that cause different behavior on the part of each client. If one places a high intrinsic value on an antique rocking chair because it brings back pleasant memories of the day it was purchased at the Vermont auction, the other is entitled to accept that higher price, just as the payer is entitled to pay the higher price. In this sense the negotiations are modeled on the market economy: supply and demand fix value. As long as the parties have a reasonable idea of the market value of an item, the mediator does not interfere if they exchange that item for a value higher, or lower, than the understood value.

---

[8] William I. Zartman and Maureen R. Berman, *The Practical Negotiator* (New Haven: Yale University Press, 1982), 52.

Some people seem capable of trading economic and emotional items in the same deal. In one case the husband left his wife for a younger woman. The wife was reluctant about accepting the divorce and the negotiations proceeded slowly until they reached the sailboat on the assets list. Both wanted the boat, worth $30,000. Selling it and dividing the proceeds seemed the only option. The discussions became tense and emotional as each tried to negotiate to keep the boat. Finally, the wife broke emotionally and said, "You have your girlfriend, I want the boat." The husband thought about it and said "OK." While the wife got more of the assets, it was an equitable split for the couple; they traded the boat for the girlfriend and solved two problems at the same time — the emotional one of the wife being rejected and the practical one of distributing the boat. From then on, the negotiations proceeded smoothly and the remaining assets were divided equally.

I believe this was an acceptable trade. I checked it again the following week to be sure that the offer was not made on the spur of the moment, but the husband was clear he felt good about the boat agreement; it probably relieved his guilt. It seemed to settle the issue of the divorce for the wife, who became more cooperative. The bargain cost the husband one-half of the value of the boat. However, it is not possible to place a dollar value on the satisfaction he received in his wife's acceptance of the divorce and subsequent cooperative behavior.

Integrative Agreements

When people begin negotiations they tend to pay scant attention to the interests of the other. Most of their thinking has been about what they want and need. Therefore, the respective aspirations and BATNAs have not been developed with any thought of an integrated agreement. "An agreement is said to be integrated to the extent that it reconciles the parties' interests and thus provides high benefit to both of them."[9] An integrative agreement incorporates the needs and interests of both parties. The mediator's task is to structure the negotiations to enhance the possibility of an integrated solution.

---

[9]   Dean G. Pruitt and Peter J. D. Carnevale, "The Development of Integrative Agreements" in ed. Valerian Derlega and Janusz Grzelak, *Cooperation and Helping Behavior: Theories and Research* (New York: Academic Press, 1982).

The superordinate goal, discussed in an example in chapter 3, is often an integrative goal, since it gives both parties a higher joint benefit at a slightly higher cost than any other positions or solutions available to the couple. If, unlike the case in chapter 3, the wife does not go to college she will probably be forced into an unskilled job such as a cashier at the supermarket with low wages and few prospects for improvement. The husband then has an ex-wife and mother of his child in a low-paid occupation; therefore, he is always in danger of her pleading for more assistance. In this case the lower cost of not sending his wife to college is less desirable than a higher cost plan for college, because that plan has higher long-term benefits for both parties.

Information Exchange

The parties begin bargaining with add-ons that are based on an ill-conceived aspiration.[10] The mediator cannot dismiss these opening positions. Rather, she must help the couple revise them based on information made available in the discussions. She does this by generating information about

- Data such as an independent appraisal of the item
- Values, such as the importance of a given item to one party
- The strength of a given position

This part of the process is known as *information exchange*.[11] Information exchange begins when the mediator collects and shares the data. Since the positions of the parties are often faulty perceptions based on inadequate knowledge, sharing this information helps each understand what the other's view is. As they learn about the other's position, they assess the strength and weakness of their own position and the firmness of each other's stand. The mediator cannot expect either party to seek a solution at this stage (other than the one they came to mediation with) since they have not had an opportunity to hear the other's position. As they exchange information about facts, perceptions and firmness, they begin to modify their positions in order to defend their original goals. If one presents a solution at this early

---

[10] By ill-conceived, I mean one that does not consider the needs of the other disputant(s).

[11] P. H. Gulliver, *Disputes and Negotiations: A Cross Cultural Perspective* (New York: Academic Press, 1979).

stage it will probably be rejected by the other. The same solution suggested after the information is exchanged often meets with a more favorable reception.

While gathering the data and facilitating the information exchange, the mediator, through her choice of questions, creates doubt in the minds of the parties about the validity and the strength of their relative positions. This is the first step towards getting them to shift positions. The mediator might ask the wife who is demanding one-half of the husband's pension and all of the house, totaling 75 percent of the total assets, "When you both reach retirement age, what will you each have to live on?" The question raises an issue of equity. The tone and way it is asked determines whether the question is loaded (embedded with the suggestion she is asking for too much) or whether it is an information-gathering question (adding to the collective knowledge in the room).[12] If the husband maintains a similar position, the mediator might ask, "Do you think you should both have the same level of security in your old age?" This question places the issue entirely in equity terms and challenges the underlying assumption of the husband's position.

If they argue as to who should keep the house, the initial exchange takes place when they bring in their appraisals of the value of the house. The initial goal and add-on is based on the appraisals they received. Now they must incorporate the other's appraisals into the calculations.[13] This new information might cause them to stick firmly to a favorable price or be prepared to move from their original position, depending on the appraisal obtained by the other.

In addition, they have other interests in trying to obtain the house. Let us assume that the appraisals range from $85,000 to $100,000. The level of desire for the house tends to increase the amount each person is willing to pay for it. On the other hand, the ability of each person to handle the mortgage payments might decrease

---

[12] For a discussion of these question types see Haynes and Haynes, *Mediating Divorce,* chap. 2.

[13] Most real estate appraisals differ according to the criteria used by the appraiser. If there is no fight over who gets the house, the difference between the values is usually easily resolved. But when both parties want the house, the different appraisals are used to support the respective arguments.

the amount the bidder is willing or able to pay. The need to settle the housing question quickly could be another influencing factor. None of these factors are measurable; each person arrives at his/her own value to be placed on the house as a result of these competing interests. We can diagram this (fig. 6.5).

Figure 6.5 Factors Causing Movement in a Negotiator's Behavior

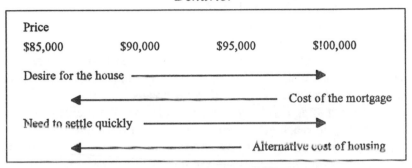

As the clients learn about each other's interests and needs, the process of information exchange continues. They become aware of their own needs, and the result of checking such items as the cost of alternative housing can cause a shift in each client's goal.

During the information exchange the clients also learn about the strength with which the other holds a position. In their planning they may not consider how strongly the other feels about the issue. Hearing the strength of the other's position articulated in the negotiations often causes a further adjustment in the client's positions. As a result they amend their goals and/or BATNAs, which, in turn, usually results in a change in the size of the add-on (fig. 6.1).

During this information exchange the parties may also begin to sound each other out. Sounding out is a form of information exchange. For example the husband might ask whether the wife would agree to let him take the washer and dryer if he had to move to a new location. This sends a message to the wife that he has thought of the possibility of *not* having the house. The wife may ask the husband if he would be willing to help her finance a new house if he kept the family home. If the husband hears this new information as an indicator of movement by his wife, he makes a suggestion of how he can help and how much cost he is willing to assume to help the wife move so that he can stay in the house.

The mediator listens intently to this information exchange since it also informs him of the respective strengths of the two positions and indicates directions she may pursue to reach an agreement. She checks to see that the other person has heard the information exchange. For example, the wife makes her query. If the husband dismisses it amid self-serving statements, the mediator interrupts and repeats the wife's question, asking him for a response. Coming from the mediator the question is more likely to be heard. The mediator frequently interrupts to be sure that each person has heard and understood what the other is saying particularly concerning *negotiating behavior and bargaining proposals.*

By listening carefully to these exchanges the mediator sees the path to follow to reach an agreement and points the couple towards the areas of possible agreement. By continually assessing the strength of each person regarding each issue, the mediator increases her efficiency in relation to the couple by focusing the discussion on where and how movement will take place. For example, if the wife has a strong position on an issue and the husband has a weak or no interest position on the same subject, it is not useful to spend time seeing whether the wife will change her strong position to a matching weak position. It does make sense to explore with the husband what compromise he would need to be able to accept the wife's strong position. The compromise may be on an aspect of the wife's position or it may be a compromise in another area where he has a strong position.

While movement between the parties resulting from information exchange is usually thought of as movement towards the other's position, under certain circumstances it can cause one person to strengthen a position. For example, if the husband suspects from her information that the wife cannot afford to keep the house, it may strengthen his resolve to propose a minimum price.

We can diagram the information exchange and sounding out stages (table 6.1).

Table 6.1 Information Exchange and Sounding Out Stages

Information Exchange During Negotiations Regarding the House	
Wife's Appraisal $85,000-$90,000	Husband's Appraisal $95,000-$100,000
Cost of other houses Ease of buying Location	Special features he had built in the house
Wife incorporates negative information she has gathered in the process	Husband incorporates negative information he has gathered in the process
Impact of husband's arguments	Impact of wife's arguments
Strength of his positive arguments	Strength of her positive arguments
Wife's desire to have the house	Husband's desire to have the house

When the wife is gathering her information she learns about the cost and availability of other houses in the area. How much are comparable ones selling for? How are they selling? Is it a buyer's or seller's market? Can she find a place closer to work? She decides, based on these data, how firm to be in her position which also helps her to clarify the range of options available to her. The possibility of increasing the range determines the extent to which she is willing and able to be flexible in the negotiations. When she hears her husband's information she learns further modifying data: How strong is his desire for the house? Is he willing to make concessions to get the house? She integrates into her thinking information (1) from her husband, including negative data such as the cost of maintaining the house, and

(2) from her own research about alternatives. She also assesses the impact of his arguments and compares them to her arguments.

By the end of this process she has varied her aspirations a number of times, at some times strengthening and at others weakening her resolve to get the house. The husband is engaged in the same process, making similar changes in his position. Changes in a person's goal often also causes change in their add-on and BATNA. The mediator maintains a focus on the aspiration rather than on the two negotiating positions.

The parties evaluate their respective desires to have the house. In this example it appears that the wife's desire lessens and the husband's increases. As her interest in the house decreases, her asking price increases. The husband's interest in the house remains firm, and, based on his wife's information communicated to him, he agrees to pay more. Thus, the wife's tactics change from getting the house at the lowest price to getting the maximum concessions from the husband in return for the house. The husband's tactics change to developing a package that allows the wife to concede the house to him.

Bargaining

As manager of the overall negotiations, the mediator interprets the changes to each of the parties and helps them focus on their self-interest and ways of achieving their self-interest. Let us now examine the steps in managing the negotiations and helping the parties reach the point where they can bargain.

Categorizing. Frequently, clients argue for or against ideas without providing any sense of the priority or importance of a proposal. The mediator helps the parties understand the relative importance of a given idea by categorizing it along a range from essential to nonessential. Within those two broad boundaries there are numerous subcategories that help the parties determine the *relative* importance of the idea. For example, the couple is arguing over whether the wife's figure for concerts in her recreation budget is appropriate. The wife says, "But I need to go the concerts. It helps me give better piano lessons, which means I get more pupils and earn more income." The mediator determines the importance of this item by categorizing it. She asks the wife, "Is it essential?" The wife replies "Not essential but. . ." If the concerts were essential to her piano lessons, she would have so

172

stated, and the mediator categorizes it appropriately. In this way the mediator tests the degree of importance. This form of question can be thought as a form of Twenty Questions. In this classic game the skill is asking questions that narrow the choices down to more and more specific groups. The question, Is it essential? is similar to, Is it bigger than a bread box? In the mediation game of Twenty Questions, the mediator is the questioner.

Determining the nature of the dispute. The mediator distinguishes between disputes about the *problem* and those about *how the problem is to be resolved.* Most couples do not discriminate between the two. Efran, Lukens, and Lukens note that "many disagreements between people are, at root, quarrels about the rules of precedence to be followed when data from disparate domains of experience conflict."[14] They underscore this: "From our point of view, when distinctions conflict, disagreements about which are to be sustained and which are to be discounted are inevitably political debates."[15] In mediating family disputes we see many cases in which the clients' conflict is the product, not of incompatible goals, but of incompatible methods for decision making.

Therefore, the more clearly the mediator distinguishes between the problem and the process, the easier it is for her to manage the negotiations. She controls the process, thereby neutralizing how the problem is defined and resolved. This leaves the parties freer to concentrate on the content of the resolution.

Case Example

One couple was fighting over whether the husband needed a two-room or two-and-one-half-room apartment. This argument is nonuseful, since it attacks the husband's interests without providing for the wife's interest. A real lose/lose debate. The mediator focused on what the husband said he *needed,* not on what he *did* with his money. By sticking to the agenda and the central goal, that is, answering the question, How do we close the gap? the mediator

---

[14] Jay S. Efran, Michael D. Lukens, and Robert J. Lukens, *Language Structure and Change: Frameworks of Meaning in Psychotherapy* (New York: Norton, 1990), 37-38.

[15] Ibid., 38.

avoided the wife's anger and made the two- versus two-and-one-half-room apartment a nonissue. Because if they close the gap, and the wife's needs are met, she will not care how the husband provides for his housing.

This type of conflict may also result from different styles of thinking. People generally use one of two styles of thinking: *Inductive* thinkers take each part of an issue and focus on the individual pieces. When working on a jigsaw puzzle, the inductive thinker sorts colors into groups and develops component parts of the puzzle, building the whole picture from each of the parts. *Deductive* thinkers seek the broad framework of an issue and then fill in the details within this framework. The deductive thinker starts the jig saw puzzle by collecting all of the straight edge pieces and building the outline in an effort to get a sense of the total picture before looking at the component parts.

Arguments are often the product of the differences in styles of thinking as much as the difference over needs. The mediator tries to understand the thinking methods of the client. If the mediator is a deductive thinker and one client thinks inductively, the communication between the two may be difficult. In addition, the mediator develops an unrecognized alliance with the deductive thinker to the discomfort of the inductive one.

For example, members of one couple were having a difficult time negotiating how to organize the physical exchange of the children. They agreed on the schedules but could not agree on how it should be done. The mother did not want the father entering the family home, and she framed the issue as one of independence and control over her own space. She was a deductive thinker. I also tend to think deductively and therefore understood the basis for her position.

However, the husband was focused on the details of the exchange. What if it was raining? Could he come to the front door or must he wait at the mail box? What if he was ten minutes early or late? He wanted the details settled before he could agree to the principle. The wife wanted the principle agreed to before she would discuss the details. My deductive thinking style led me to be more understanding of the wife's position. They were stuck.

Whenever the debate becomes stuck with neither client willing to move, the mediator must ask the question: What can I change to get the process unstuck? The mediator cannot expect the clients to leave their positions. But she can change her position and thereby change the dynamics of the situation. By changing my thinking style to an inductive approach I was able to say to the husband, "Well, John, if I understand it correctly, you feel that you may be able to agree not to enter the house to pick up the children if the details of exactly how you would do it under various circumstances are worked out?" John nodded affirmatively. "If that is the case, let us focus on those details so we can reach an agreement," I added.

John was able to accept this and, knowing he had been heard, deal with his needs on the details rather than oppose his wife's needs on the principle. As he began to move, Mary was able to handle the details on the understanding that if the details were worked out, the principle would be agreed to.

Real and Underlying Disputes

The parties may present an opening problem definition: they are in dispute about the times of the access of the children to their father. If the mediator accepts that definition and focuses attention on it without checking whether it is the core conflict, she might ignore the core conflict. Then no solution may be found. However, if she checks out the nature and scope of the conflict, she might find that the real dispute between the parties is an unresolved interpersonal dispute such as an affair. She can then identify and classify it while deciding either to work on resolving that issue or refer the interpersonal relationship to a therapist. When the therapist deals with the relationship issues, the business matters are more easily resolved in mediation.

Managed Reciprocal Concession Making

When couples come to mediation they are ending a relationship with all of the bitterness, frustration, disappointment, and anger the loss of the relationship entails. In addition, they have a low level of trust in each other. This makes it uniquely difficult for the mediator, who is asked to help them reach agreements on everything for the rest of their lives when they have been unable to agree on very much in the past year or so.

The mediator builds trust in the process and in him as a mediator which in turn helps them begin to trust each other while they are protected by the process. However, they may still be too untrusting to make concessions. Each is afraid that if they make an offer, the other will take advantage of this proposal. At the same time they reveal a great deal of information about where and how they might be willing to move on the issue, provided some reciprocal movement takes place on the part of the other.

Clients tend to articulate what they *don't* want easier than they state unequivocally what they *do* want. Thus the mediator listens carefully to the dialogue between the couple to determine

- What each party wants
- What each party wants to avoid
- What each party is willing to concede
- What alternative options each party is willing to consider
- The amount of movement each is willing to make on a given issue
- The relationship, if any, between the issue under discussion and other issues
- The strength of the positions
- What each can manage realistically

She takes all of this information and tries to develop a proposal that, *based on what the clients have clearly stated*, responds to their needs. The proposal must contain a benefit for each person and must clearly state the cost of the proposal to each person. In Michael and Debbie's[16] case, the wife said she would not allow the children to spend time with their father as long as his girlfriend was there. Her opposition was in two parts: she did not want the girlfriend sleeping over when the children were there, and she did not want her around at all when the children were with the father. The former position was firm, and the mediator assessed that the second position was more of an add-on.

The father's position was also in two parts: "I want the children half of the time." His position was firm on shared parenting with shared physical custody. The second part was that he did not want the wife controlling his life by telling when he could see his girlfriend.

---

[16] Haynes and Haynes, *Mediating Divorce,* chap. 4.

Based on these two positions and supporting information each shared with the other during the session, the mediator designed a reciprocal concession. "Let me ask you, Michael, could you agree that Jocelyn (the girlfriend) will not sleep over when the children are with you if you share in the parenting?"

This proposal by the mediator, presented in a question form to limit the imperative nature of the proposal, spelled out for Michael the benefit he would receive — sharing the children versus the cost he would have to pay — no girlfriend sleeping over when the children were with him. It stated the cost and benefit equally clearly to Debbie. The benefit was that the girlfriend would not sleep over when the children were with their father, and the cost was that she would agree to share the children with the father.

Each person knew, from this proposal, the exact cost and benefit. Each could weigh it and accept or reject the proposal based on this knowledge. Neither took any risk of making an offer that might be rejected. Neither of them risked making a unilateral concession in the hopes that the other would reciprocate. We can diagram this proposal (fig. 6.6).

Figure 6.6 Mediator Proposal Based on Client Input

cost	Girl friend not sleep over	benefit
Michael————————————————————————Debbie		
benefit	Share time with father	cost

The mediator opens the way for the parties to make further offers and counter offers by packaging proposals mutually. She takes information from the husband and information from the wife indicating how they are prepared to move or indicating what the terms of such movement would be. She notes what they want to avoid, loss of the children and involvement of the other woman; their respective needs, access to the children and sharing the children; and the firmness with which each held to their positions, Michael being more flexible than Debbie. The package balances wants, need to avoid, and firmness as evenly as possible. The mediator does *not* add to the package any item that has not been previously articulated by the clients. Thus the package comes from the fragmented statements each client makes, not from what the mediator would like them to say.

The couple's responses are risk-free. They know the cost and the benefit. They weigh the trade, and, if the mediator has accurately assessed the two positions, the reciprocal concession package should form the basis for meaningful bargaining.

Moving from Global to Specific

Many disputants talk in global terms and make global accusations that are not useful because they defy solution. Therefore, the mediator uses questions to move the global statement to a more specific one. For example, clients may say,

She wants everything.

He's cheap and won't give anything.

The more global the person's statement, the more specific questions you need to ask. In these examples the mediator begins by asking,

What is *everything?*

Won't give *anything?*

By asking for more and more specifics, these discriminating questions lead the parties to break it down.

Resource versus Value Disputes

Disputes over resources such as money, the house, or the amount of time spent with the children, are all quantifiable and resolvable. After all, a dollar can be divided one hundred ways, which provides considerable space for movement by both sides. However, value disputes are harder to resolve, since the values are not easily compromised. The mediator continually categorizes disputes into value or resource ones. Once clear that a dispute is over a value system, the mediator quantifies the value as a means of seeking agreement.

Case Example

When the couple married he was Roman Catholic and she was Unitarian. At the time of the marriage they agreed that the children would be raised Catholic. The agreement worked until they divorced, and their only son lived with the mother. She no longer wanted to take the son to Mass each week and instead, took him to Unitarian meeting. The husband was furious and demanded that the son spend each and every weekend with him so that he could attend Mass and be raised Roman Catholic, as the mother had agreed at the marriage.

Here was a clear value difference. The husband's values were shaped by his religion which meant maintaining the marriage agreement regarding raising the child Catholic. The wife's values were shaped by her religion and the belief that the son benefited from learning about his other religion. In addition she refused to take the son to Catholic church.

I divided the dispute into two parts. The first was the commitment they made to each other at the time of the marriage to raise the son Catholic. This was a written commitment, and I decided that it would not be appropriate to try to negotiate whether the wife could break that commitment. I focused instead on the second issue of whether the child should always attend Mass and who should take him. By disattending to the abrogation of the marriage agreement, I focused the couple's attention on the second set of questions.

The husband was adamant regarding raising the child Catholic, but was willing to look at the problem if that basic fact was not challenged. I asked the husband to quantify the issue by asking him, "In your church, are you allowed to attend ceremonies conducted by another religion?" The husband replied affirmatively. "Should your son receive a broad religious education about other faiths as well as his own if the basic tenets of his faith are not challenged?" Another affirmative answer. "How many times each month do you think it would be appropriate for your son to attend another religious ceremony as a learning experience, without undermining his essential Catholicism?" This was a more difficult question to answer since it needed both an affirmative response and a specific number. However, the father finally agreed that once a month would be acceptable. I turned to the mother and asked her, "If your son remained Catholic and attended Unitarian meeting monthly, would that meet your needs to share your religion with him?" After some thought the wife agreed that it would. The parents then negotiated how the son would share time with each of them around the church schedule.

The value question was unresolvable. But, once the value was quantified, both sets of needs could be met, and an agreement became possible. When the clients are directed away from the value or the principle of the matter towards the way they live their day-to-day lives, the argument often changes. When the discussion shifts, the meaning shifts, and the meaning of the parts cannot be changed without changing the meaning of the whole. [17]

Problem Solving

Mediating negotiations is really organized problem solving. A common method of problem solving is a means-end analysis. The analysis is conducted by first stating the goal to be achieved and then comparing the current situation with the desired goal. When the differences between the current situation and the goal have been defined, a search begins for methods to close the gap between the two. As the problem solving continues, it is useful frequently to measure the status of the process by restating the goal and the current situation and checking to see just how close the two situations have become or whether the two coincide, in which case the problem is solved.

Gardner describes an early computer program known as the General Problem Solver, designed to problem solve in this manner.

The art in the General Problem Solver lies in the methods of reducing this distance. A table is set up that associates the system's goals with operators that may be of use in achieving them. Once the difference has been computed between the present situation and the goal, the system then selects an operator associated with that difference and tests whether the operator is applicable to the current situation. If it can be applied, and if it produces a result that is closer to the desired end state, it is repeated again. If it proves inapplicable, then the system generates a sub-goal, whose aim is to reduce the difference between the current situation and the situation where the operator can be applied. This procedure is simply repeated until the goal is achieved or it has been demonstrated that it cannot be achieved with the information given, or with the operators available in the program.[18]

---

[17] George Lakoff, *Women, Fire, and Other Dangerous Things* (Chicago: University of Chicago Press, 1987), 230.

[18] Howard Gardner, *The Mind's New Science: A History of the Cognitive Revolution* (New York: Basic Books, 1985), 149.

One important task in problem solving is to be able to distinguish the difference between *means* and *ends* and between *wants* and *needs*. Doing this is an important aspect of helping the client clarify and understand his/her goals. For example the husband may say, "I need a new Mercedes." If the couple argue the pros and cons about the Mercedes, the argument will quickly drift back into the marriage. The mediator asks a series of questions designed to discover whether the Mercedes is a means or an end.

If we look at the statement, "I need a Mercedes," from the perspective of the husband's end we see that he needs transportation. If that is his *end,* he will be able to reach his goal by various means.

The husband's statements is analyzed in table 6.2

Table 6.2 Determining the Needs and Ends of the Statement

Statement: " I need a Mercedes."	
ENDS	MEANS
Transportation for work and pleasure	Feet Bicycle Scooter/motorcycle Car Bus/train
Status	Rolls Royce/Mercedes

We can define a *need* as the gap between current situation and desired situation (or end). A *want* is a desire not necessarily needed or required. The *problem definition* becomes a need or a gap to be closed. People can argue forever about means if they are unclear what it is they want to accomplish or if they don't define appropriate ends or outcomes they want from the negotiations.

The outcome should be measurable, so that moving from a need to an outcome can be seen and understood by both clients. For example, assume the divorcing wife wants economic independence. How will she know when she has reached that outcome? Helping her define how to measure the outcome clarifies the goal and also helps her to negotiate a realistic agreement. The wife may state that by earning $20,000 a year, she will reach economic independence. (Her *need* is met by $20,000 per year).

Using Ordinal Measurements

Not all problems lend themselves to nominal measurement. Some ends are best measured by ordinal (ranking) methods: if the wife is offered five different careers, each paying $20,000, she can't measure which one to take numerically. She must measure ordinally: various aspects of each job, such as the career path, could be scaled as greater potential than, equal potential to, and lesser potential than. Or she may use the same scale to measure how close the work is to home. When the clients are clear as to which method to use for measurement, the mediator lists the problem in two parts: 1. A statement defining the current situation, such as "a part-time job earning $7,000 per year" and 2. the desired situation, such as, "a full-time job earning $20,000 by January." The clients would then look at what it would take to achieve the desired situation.

When the starting and ending positions are agreed by the clients, moving from the current to the desired situation is easier to accomplish. Look at another example. The current position is that the wife does not have a pension plan. The desired situation is that she obtain a pension plan. The clients can then examine what steps are required to reach the desired situation and might come up with the plan of putting $150 per month into an IRA starting one year after the wife starts a full-time job.   Each step must meet the following criteria:

- Does it state the outcome to be achieved?
- Does it state when the outcome will be achieved and what criteria will be used to measure the achievement?
- Does it indicate what the achievement is and by whom will it be measured?
- Does each statement avoid ambiguity and confusion?

When the answer to each question is yes, the clients are ready to explore the methods and means available to get to the desired solution. They do this in a series of steps.

- Listing the gaps between the current situation and the desired situation

- Arranging the gaps (needs) in priority order
- Selecting the needs to be resolved
- Identifying as many possible ways and means to get there in the quickest time and the lowest cost

The mediator assures the clients maintain a reality base by continually checking with them the feasibility of each idea. She helps the couple avoid setting a goal of becoming a physician if the client is a high school dropout aged forty. Let's assume the wife's goal, to obtain a full-time job paying $20,000 per year by January 1, is realistic and well defined. The mediator

1. States the goal and gains agreement from the wife that it is her goal
2. Determines the husband's agreement with this goal and his needs in regard to this goal
3. Reconciles any differences regarding the goal
4. Lists the means of achieving the goal with as many alternatives as possible
5. Helps the clients determine which alternative is the most efficient/effective
6. Manages the negotiations on the selection of the best route when self-interests clash

It may be necessary to do this in parallel rather than con-jointly to determine what benefits are in this arrangement for the husband. In that case each completes (1) and (5) and the negotiations (6) are conducted around how both can meet their goals.

Splitting the Difference

Splitting the difference is a time honored strategy of mediators. When the clients are apart and no further compromises seem available, the tendency is to suggest the couple split the difference between them. If the husband offers $120 and the wife seeks $100, the mediator might suggest they settle for $110. However, this strategy has a serious limitation: it rewards the biggest liar. Let's go back to the case of the tube radios discussed in chapter 4.

The wife placed a value of $18,000 on the radios. The husband said they were worth only $8,000. If the couple reached a deadlock and split the difference, they would place a value of $13,000 on the radios, and the husband would buy them for that sum. But, if the appraisal showed the radios were worth $12,000, the husband would have paid $1,000 more in the split-the-difference deal. If the appraised value was $16,000, then he would have paid the wife $3,000 less than in the split-the-difference deal. Splitting the difference gives the advantage to the person who most over/under states the value of an item; it rewards the biggest liar.

Monitoring the Process

While managing the negotiations, the mediator continually asks herself a series of questions:

- What are the clients' positions?
- What are his/her interests, hidden agendas?
- What is the relationship between the parties?
- What are the parties BATNAs? WATNAs?
- What ideas do the clients have for settling the dispute?
- What objective criteria will they use to measure the agreement?
- What will it take to achieve a settlement covering all issues?
- What does each want the other to do?
- Why won't each do what the other wants?
- What ideas do I have for different ways of packaging an acceptable settlement?
- What is the highest (or best) joint payoff for the lowest joint cost?

Reviewing the Outcome

At times, while there are no negative feelings, neither party is quite sure how the other feels about the agreement. The time spent checking and dealing with feelings that have been generated in the negotiations helps ensure the agreements will be carried out. This step can make public new, positive feelings and helps build a new relationship. Thus the mediator asks herself:

- Does the solution reflect the clients' needs in both the short and long term?

- Does the solution reflect the ongoing relationship the clients will have to maintain in the future?
- Have the parties explored all the possible solutions that benefit one party with no adverse consequences to the other?
- Is the agreement more expensive to break than to maintain?
- Are the clients committed to the agreement so they will live with it without regret?

Using Questions

The mediator's primary mode of communication is the question. Therefore, we close this chapter with another way of organizing questions.

Ideally, the mediator's work is conducted in the question form. When asking questions the mediator cannot give advice or instructions on what to do. The clients provide the answers and therefore tend to own the answers. Using questions is one way of helping the clients maintain control of the content.

Different types of questions are useful at different stages of the process, and different question types are used for specific purposes. Here are question forms that help to keep the session moving:

Opening questions: Help to get things started
    What is the current situation?
    What are going to be the major issues in the mediation?
    What worries you the most about the mediation/negotiations?
    What experience do you have in dealing with this type of problem?

Information questions: Obtain facts and/or opinions
    Who is living in the house now?
    What is your mortgage payment?
    Where will the children go to school?

Clarifying questions: Make abstract and general ideas more specific
    What do you mean by "everything"?
    When do you want this to end?

Justifying questions: Clarify the reasons one party holds a position
    Why do you think . . .?
    How will this solve the problem?
    How will it work on a daily basis?

Hypothetical questions: Introduce ideas into the discussion

> Suppose you tried this option, what do you think would happen?
>
> If you could write the script, what would it be?

Leading questions: Suggest an idea within the questions

> Given the nature of the problem, is it possible to . . .?
>
> Is this the only option worth considering?
>
> I was wondering whether what another couple considered might be useful to you.

Stimulating questions: Encourage new ideas

> Are there other ways to solve this problem?
>
> What happens if you don't reach agreement on this problem?

Participation questions: Encourage expression of ideas/needs

> What do you think about that, Mary?
>
> How does that idea strike you, John?

Focusing questions: Bring the discussion back to the core issues

> Where do we go from here?
>
> How does this relate to the issue of the children?

Alternative questions: Compare two or more alternatives

> Which of these two options do you think is better?
>
> Do both work well for both of you?

Closure questions: Encourage making the decision

> Have we spent enough time on this issue?
>
> Do you want to think about it and decide next week?
>
> Have we agreed to the following . . .?

Evaluation questions: Help the couple assess their progress and future

> Why do you think we are blocked on this issue?
>
> What will happen if we do this?

In this chapter we have examined the negotiating behaviors of the clients and strategies for the mediator to maintain a balanced position while managing the negotiations. Each idea presented in this chapter is used at each stage of the process and within each cycle of the process. In the next chapter we will examine how to write up the agreements and draft the memorandum of understanding.

Chapter Seven
The Memorandum of Understanding

When agreement has been reached on the issues of support, asset division, and parenting, the mediator drafts a memorandum of understanding (MOU) explaining all the agreements. The memorandum is written in plain English so the contents are clearly understood. The memorandum explains what the clients agreed and, where appropriate, why they made the agreement. The spouses take the MOU to their respective attorneys for review, advice, and incorporation into the formal legal document that is ultimately filed with the court as part of the divorce decree.

The attorney needs to know the precise nature of the agreements, the supporting material on which the agreements were based, and the rationale for the decisions. This enables her to review the agreement and advise the client before she incorporates the contents of the memorandum into the formal legal document.

A legal divorce agreement includes pages of obscure information written in arcane language. For example, in some jurisdictions, three pages are taken up explaining how each will waive all claims to the dowries and courtesies of the other. This refers to the old custom of the bride providing a dowry and the groom providing a courtesy (the male equivalent of the dowry). It has nothing to do with being polite to each other.

The lawyer takes the memorandum that contains all of the agreements unique to the clients and integrates those agreements with the boilerplate material that is part of every divorce agreement. This process has two advantages:

1. The agreement is reviewed and the client has a second opinion on the work of the mediator; this makes sure that nothing is overlooked and keeps the mediator on his toes.

2. The legal document is the agreement referred to in the event of a legal dispute about the agreement. Since the attorney is responsible for the document, any questions and possible malpractice problems reside with her. Thus, the mediator's liability insurance costs are kept low.

This places an onus on the mediator to provide the counsel with all the background information and documentation, so counsel will be sure she has based her advice to the client on a solid database.

There is no particular logic to the order of the issues discussed in the MOU. It improves attorney-mediator relations if your MOUs are drafted in the same order as the attorneys in your area draft the legal document. When both documents are in the same order, it is easier for the attorney to incorporate your part of the work into her part.

The opening paragraph of the MOU explains the function of the mediator and that of the attorney. The wording supplied in this text was developed by the author and the Suffolk County Bar Association and has stood the test of use in almost every part of the U. S. and many countries overseas. Using this wording offers the best assurance that, as a mediator, you cannot be sued for the unlawful practice of law. If the mediator drafts the formal legal document as well as the MOU, the product could be defined as the unlawful practice of law. Drawing a clear demarcation between the role of the attorney and the mediator eliminates that risk.

Some sample clauses have been included in previous chapters to explain the process. This chapter provides the balance of different situations most mediators will face.[1]

Opening Paragraph

We have arrived at the following agreements in the process of mediation. These agreements represent a total package carefully balancing our mutual and self interests and the best interests of our children, Tom and Sue. They deal with the substance of our proposed Separation Agreement. We

---

[1] These examples do not come from the same case and should not be read as a coherent document. They are designed to show how different situations can be handled.

wish our respective attorneys to incorporate this substance into the formal Separation Agreement.

Background Information

The second paragraph provides the counsel with the essential information about the socioeconomic position of the clients.

We were married on December 16, 1978, and have two children by this marriage, Tom, born August 26, 1981, and Sue born July 15, 1984. John is a teacher earning approximately $35,000 per year, and Mary is a beautician earning approximately $18,000 per year. Mary will return to college to earn an undergraduate degree, and this agreement is designed to help her meet this goal.

The Children

Most of the standard provisions regarding the children are included in chapter 5. However, additional items crop up, and in the following situations these wordings have been useful.

Varying access. Agreements usually provide for some way to vary the access schedule based on the children's needs.

All access to the children is based on their availability as affected by school and extracurricular activities. If they are unable to spend time with their father on the scheduled times, we agree to make equivalent alternative arrangements for them to spend time with him.

Changing joint residency. When parents have joint residency and the children live with each parent approximately 50 percent of the time, the following explains the arrangement and provides for action if circumstances change:

We have shared in the parenting of Tom and Sue and will continue to do so. Therefore, we will maintain full and complete joint custody and residency. Tom and Sue will reside one-half of the time with John and one half of the time with Mary, the exact times to be determined by mutual agreement. If the current agreement cannot be continued or a new one negotiated, we will continue to share full and

189

complete joint custody of Tom and Mary and make arrangements for the parent with whom they do not reside to have liberal and reasonable access including, but not limited to, weekends and holidays. At a minimum the parent with whom the children reside during the school year will permit the other parent residence with Tom and Sue during the summer and all school breaks.

We agree that, if Tom and Sue accompany the moving parent, the moving parent may not effect the move until and unless the nonmoving parent has reasonable guarantees of all custody and access rights, a minimum of which includes not leaving the continental United States and access availability at an expense to each parent in proportion to our incomes for the previous year. If the children do not accompany the moving parent, the same guarantees will apply to the moving parent.

When the parents have plans regarding religious education and want them included in the memorandum, it can be stated as,

We agree, insofar as it is practical, to maintain Tom and Sue in a parochial school through high school, and John[2] agrees to pay for all of their tuition through high school.

Shared parenting/residency. A typical shared parenting/residency arrangement might look like this.

We have adopted the following access schedule based on agreement that the children should spend the maximum time with each of us jointly and individually.

Week	Mon	Tues	Wed	Thur	Fri	Sat	Sun
1 Mary	Sue	Tom	Tom	Tom			
1 John	Tom	Sue	Sue	Sue	S/T	S/T	S/T
2 Mary	Sue	Tom	Tom	Tom	S/T	S/T	S/T
2 John	Tom	Sue	Sue	Sue			

The purpose of this schedule is to provide for the children to spend some individual time with each of us and to spend

---

[2]   In this case, the father has significantly more income that the mother and is prepared to shoulder the entire cost. In most situations the parents share the education costs either equally or in a ratio of incomes.

some joint time with each of us. We will live in close proximity to allow for this schedule while allowing the children to maintain their peer group relationships.

Assigning shared costs. When parents have relatively equal incomes and plan to share in the costs of raising the children as well as in joint residency, they may choose to assign areas of responsibility.

> To facilitate the sharing of financial responsibility for Tom and Sue, we agree John will be responsible for purchasing their footwear, and school supplies. Mary will be responsible for purchasing the other clothes, and we will share equally in the cost of overcoats and similar outer garments. The cost of lessons and after school programs will be shared equally, as will the cost of any recreational equipment.

Assigning responsibility to a cost. Sometimes one parent agrees to pay a major cost such as the fees for summer camp. That parent usually wants to have the major say in determining how much the camp should cost. If the other parent is concerned that s/he may decide on a figure that is too low, a provision stating the minimum helps to break the log jam.

> John will be responsible for Tom's and Sue's summer camp costs and will have the primary say in what those costs should be but agrees that they should not be less than the cost of day camp (or a specific dollar amount) for Tom and Sue.

Teen flexibility. When the parents want a flexible arrangement for the children and the children are teens, the following wording seems to meet the needs of the parents and the teens.

> Given the children's ages we have made no schedule for the children to spend time with John. All access arrangements between him and the children will be made directly with the children and Mary will cooperate in implementing whatever agreement he makes with the children.

Support

Child support guidelines. The basic clauses in the support section refer to the child support guidelines and ways of implementing them.

John will pay to Mary child support equal to 25 percent of his gross which is $850 per month, calculated as follows:

Gross income	$42,828
FICA deductions	$ 2,052
Base income	$40,776
25 percent of base =	$10,200/ $850 per month.

Changes in the support. The agreement defines the circumstances under which the child support will change or cease.

The child support for each child will cease when that child reaches the age of majority[3] unless s/he attends undergraduate college, in which case support will continue until s/he completes undergraduate college or reaches the age of twenty-two whichever is sooner. The child support will cease if s/he graduates from high school and does not attend college, or if s/he joins the armed forces, marries, or is declared an emancipated minor or in the event of his/her death. When only one child is eligible for support, the support will be reduced to 17 percent of the adjusted gross income.

Support while in college. Even though the children are in college and away from home for about two-thirds of the year, the resident parent must still maintain a home for them. Most parents feel the following provision recognizes that the nonresident parent is paying a share of the room and board at college, but the resident parents continues to need extra money for the children.

When any child is in college and living on or near campus the child support for that child will be reduced by 50 percent.

Paying for college. When the parents have not made any provision for postsecondary education costs, they need to work out an arrangement to pay for them when the children go to college. The following indicates how the costs will be shared and defines the amount that is contractually guaranteed: the tuition level of the state university system. This is the guarantee. Parents can, of course, do more for their

---

[3] In most states the age of majority is eighteen. Parents who do not anticipate their children going to college normally expect the children to be self-sufficient at that age.

children if they wish when the children go to college. There is also a provision maintaining parental prerogatives. If the parents did not divorce, no court in the world would force parents to send their children to college. However, in divorce, courts frequently order one or both parents to pay for their children's college education. The provision maintaining parental prerogatives is a way of leaving the divorced parents with the same parental prerogatives they enjoyed when they were married and avoids giving the children rights they would not otherwise enjoy.

We will share in the children's college education in a ratio of our incomes for the years in question. We agree, for the purposes of this agreement, to define college expenses as room and board, tuition, fees, books, and transportation to and from a state college in the state the children are residing at the time of entering college. We agree that Tom and Sue should use their savings, scholarships, and reasonable tuition loans before our making expenditures for them. This agreement in no way waives our parental prerogatives regarding college selection and attendance.

Making future adjustments. When the amount of support is established the couple cannot forecast what will happen to the value of the support over the years. Inflation can reduce the true value of the support in the future. The child support guidelines make no provision for adjusting the level of support. One way of protecting the value of the support is to include a provision for automatic review based on changes in the Consumer Price Index.

We recognize that the financial circumstances of either of us may change in the future; therefore, we will adjust the child support annually. We agree to adjust the child support to reflect any changes in the cost of living as follows. Each year, usually in March, the Bureau of Labor Statistics (or the Canadian equivalent) publishes a Revised Consumer Price Index for the previous calendar year. On the first of the month following publication of this figure for the region in which Mary and the children are living, the child support will be adjusted by .5 percent for each 1 percent[4] change in the CPI.

Thus, if the consumer price index changes by 4 percent the support will change by 2 percent. Mary will be responsible for calling the Department of Labor, Bureau of Labor Statistics, to obtain the CPI figure and forwarding it to John with her understanding of the new level of support. If John agrees with the calculation, he will commence paying child support at the new rate on the first of the following month. If he disagrees, he will call the mediation service and obtain their figures. We agree to accept the figures determined by the mediation service using the above formula.

Some parents include an additional automatic review of the child support based on the recognition that the cost of raising a child increases as the child gets older.

We will increase the child support by 10 percent when Tom reaches the age of nine and another 10 percent when he reaches the age of thirteen in recognition of the children's increased needs as they grow older.

Medical insurance. To implement the child support guidelines requiring the parent paying support to also provide health insurance, parents add a clause to provide for it. In the following example, the resident parent is covered by health insurance from her employer and agrees to keep the children on her plan also.

John will maintain the children on his employer-provided health insurance plan for as long as permitted by the plan. He will maintain Mary on his employer-provided health insurance for as long as permitted by the plan.[5] Mary will maintain the children and John on any employer-provided health insurance plan for as long as permitted to do so by the employer.

---

[4]   The 50 percent adjustment is because the CPI is an index of a basket of prices. Not all families purchase everything in the index. The CPI is not an inflation index but a cost of living index. Most labor-management contracts provide for a similar 50 percent adjustment based on the same criteria.

[5]   If the other parent does not have health insurance, it does not cost the paying parent anything to maintain her on the policy also. The cost of family coverage is the same with or without the other spouse. Most insurance plans drop the spouse when the divorce is finalized.

194

The Memorandum of Understanding

A different approach for parents in a situation in which the wife/resident parent has coverage and the father does not is

Mary covers the children under her union-provided health insurance. She will continue to do so. If she is no longer eligible for this coverage, John will be responsible for providing the health insurance. Since Mary pays $50 per month in union dues, John will be responsible for the first $600 per year of uncovered medical expenses, including prescriptions, and we will divide the balance equally.

Methods of payment. Some couples spell out the way in which the support is paid, indicating the exact day(s) the payments are due.

The support will be paid semimonthly on the first and sixteenth of each month in equal installments.

Paying support can become a power game of slipped due dates and skipped payments. One way to avoid this is to have the payments made with a standing order to the bank.

We will each maintain an account at the same bank, and the payments will be made by electronic transfer.

When the parents have relatively equal incomes and share in the residence and cost of the children, one way of writing this up is:

Given the relative equality of our incomes and the fact that Tom and Sue will be living with each of us for an equal amount of time, we see no need for child support to be paid by either parent. If, for any reason the current living arrangements are changed and the children spend a majority of the time with one parent, we will provide for child support in accordance with the State Child Support Guidelines.

Joint checking accounts. When parents share the residency they can establish a joint checking account to handle the children's expenses.

Clothing, parochial, extracurricular and college education, recreation, child care associated with employment, and uncovered medical expenses: we will divide these costs equally. We will establish a joint account and pass all joint

195

expenditures for the children through this account each paying one-half of the costs. One parent will not incur an expense in excess of $50 without the prior agreement of the other parent.

Defining future incomes. When parents agree to share a future expense based on their future incomes, they need to agree how to define that future income. Here is one way:

> For the purposes of this agreement, gross income is defined as an amount consisting of gross income for federal tax purposes determined on an individual basis plus profit sharing or similar plans plus any tax exempt income. However, capital gains and losses shall be excluded from the calculation of gross income. Deductions shall not be made from the gross income for deferred compensation, pension or profit sharing plans of any corporation of which either of us is a member or for so-called tax shelters.

Maintenance Support

When one spouse agrees to pay maintenance support to the other, the terms of the agreement are spelled out. In this case the amount is defined, as are some additional, variable costs to be met by John. The clause goes on to define when the maintenance support will end and sets an income figure for Mary that, when reached, will also terminate the support.

> John will pay maintenance support to Mary of $12,000 per year. In addition, he will provide her with auto insurance and house insurance on her residence and pay for the accountant to prepare her annual tax returns. The maintenance support, accountant fees, and insurance payments will cease upon Mary's remarriage or death or if her gross adjusted income as reported on her tax return exceeds $50,000. Upon John's request, Mary will provide him with a copy of the page of her tax return (including W2, Form 1099, and other income reports) showing the adjusted gross income. She will provide this no later than April 30, following the request. The support will end as of the first of the month in which her adjusted gross income first exceeds the equivalent of $50,000 per year.

Assets

The most important asset for most people is the family home. When clients keep the family home as joint property, the events triggering its sale are spelled out. In the following case, the division of the assets is balanced by the division of the house sale proceeds.

We will retain joint title of the marital home, and Mary will reside there with our children until Sue[6] graduates from college or reaches the age of 22, whichever is sooner,[7] when we will place the house on the market at a price averaging at least two real estate broker valuations and sell the house to the first buyer plus or minus 10 percent of that price.[8] We will also sell the house upon Mary's remarriage if before that date. We will divide the proceeds of the sale 71 percent to Mary and 29 percent to John to reflect the fact that John will keep his pension and tax deferred annuity.

Buying out the other's share. The next part provides two formulas for how each might buy the house at the time of sale.

1. At the time of sale either of us may purchase the other's interest in the house, with Mary having first choice, as follows: we will have the house appraised by a licensed real estate appraiser who is not a broker and deduct from that figure the outstanding mortgage. The buyer will pay the seller the appropriate percentage of that amount.

2. At the time of sale either of us may purchase the other's interest in the house as follows: Mary will have the first right of refusal, and, if she does not exercise that right within sixty days of any of the above dates, John will have the right to purchase Mary's equity within sixty days from the day he can exercise the right. We will have the house appraised by a licensed real estate appraiser who is not a broker, and the buyer will pay the seller one-half of that amount less the outstanding mortgage.

---

[6] The youngest child.

[7] Some couples choose an earlier date such as graduation from high school.

[8] Setting a selling price eliminates the possibility of the resident rejecting all offers so that s/he may stay in the house.

197

Triggers to sell the house. Some couples add triggers to sell such as remarriage or changes regarding the children.

> We will also sell the house upon Mary's remarriage or cohabitation, as defined in the Domestic Relations Act, or the emancipation of all the children, if before that date.

Sharing future expenses. When the clients jointly own the house they, in effect, maintain a business partnership. The costs of the partnership in maintaining the house, which is an investment for both of them, needs to be considered.

> If, while we jointly own the marital home, it requires structural repairs, we will share in those repairs in a ratio to our share of ownership. If one of us is unable to meet their payment of such structural repairs and the other pays for the repairs, we agree that the person paying for the repairs will be reimbursed the amount of the expenditure for the other from the proceeds of the sale of the house.
>
> Mary will live in and have the exclusive use of the family home with our children until it is sold. In the interim, she will pay all expenses associated with the house including the balance of the mortgage, the real estate taxes, home insurance, and all normal maintenance expenses.[9] John will not be liable for any of these expenses associated with the marital home.

Protecting the interest of the nonresident. The nonresident is protected against loans being taken out against his/her equity.

> While Mary is residing in the house she will not borrow against the equity in the house or encumber the equity in any way without the prior agreement of John.

Unique situations. Some homes have a value that is difficult to assess. For example, one couple lived in an apartment that was built using state funds and rented to moderate income families. Legislation was pending providing that the apartment may, in the future, be sold to the tenants, in which case the resident would enjoy a windfall. In such a case the couple had to determine how to deal with the situation.

---

[9] These are the expenses that Mary will pay as her "rent" for living in the jointly owned house.

The Memorandum of Understanding

The apartment was built using Mitchell Lama funds. There is a possibility that it will be sold to the tenants of the building. If the apartment is privatized within five years from the signing of the agreement, Mary will compensate John. We will determine the potential capital gain to be the difference between the cost of the apartment as set by the state and the proceeds to Mary of an assumed sale of the apartment, at its then current market value as determined by a licensed real estate appraiser who is not a broker. Mary will pay to John one-third of the gain.

Tax considerations. The distribution of the assets can have future tax consequences. Usually, each takes the future tax liability with the asset. When the wife takes title to the family home, the tax liability is covered thus:

Mary agrees to carry forward the capital gains liability on the marital home and we will each pay our own capital gains liability from the sale of any of the other marital assets.

Listing the assets. The marital assets are listed in the agreement showing the name of the asset, its value, and, its disposition.

Our marital assets and liabilities consist of the following:
ASSETS

	Value	John	Mary
Savings account	$ 11,050	$ 6,324	$ 4,726
Auto (Chevrolet)	6,000		6,000
Auto (Honda)	10,000	10,000	
Marital home	170,000		170,000
Boat	3,000	3,000	
Pensions			
IRA/RRSP	12,700		12,700
Profit sharing plan	64,449	64,449	
Pension plan (John)	124,800	124,800	
Pension Plan (Mary)	33,897		33,897
Totals	$435,896	$208,573	$227,323

LIABILITIES

	Value	John	Mary
Mortgage	$ 21,500		21,500
Bank loan	1,800		1,800
Auto loan	4,200	4,200	
Visa	200	200	
J. C. Penney	150	150	
Totals	$ 27,850	$4,550	$23,300
Value of asset			
Distribution	$408,046	$204,023	$204,023

Describing the Distribution

The memorandum describes, in narrative form, the asset distribution, providing the reader with the rationale for each decision.

We have had the pensions appraised by Legal Economic Evaluation, Inc. John's pension has a value of $208,000, of which 60 percent was accrued in the marriage. Therefore we have used the figure of $124,800 for the marital value of the pension.[10] Mary's pension has a value of $40,840 of which 83 percent was accrued in the marriage. Therefore, we have used the figure of $33,897 for the marital value of the pension. We have used the same 60 percent to determine the marital value of the profit sharing plan, which has a current value of $108,500. Therefore we have used the figure of $64,449 as the marital value of the profit sharing plan. We have had the house appraised by two real estate appraisers and have used the average of the two appraisals, $170,000.

In the above example, the couple balanced the distribution through the liquid funds in the savings account. The husband took slightly more of this money to arrive at an even division of the marital assets. He also took responsibility for paying the two outstanding charge accounts.

---

[10] Both spouses had participated in their employment pension plans for a period before the marriage. Since marital assets are those accumulated during the marriage, the evaluations excluded that part of the pension accrued prior to the marriage. The value of the pension will vary depending on what assumptions the appraiser made about the value of the early contributions.

Auto loans. If the clients do not have individual titles to their autos, they may need to provide for how the loans will be paid off and the titles transferred.

> John will transfer title of the Chevrolet to Mary. She will also take over the loan for the car. The loan is currently in John's name. Mary agrees to either remove his name from the loan agreement or to take out a new loan or pay off the existing loan. John will keep the Honda and be responsible for the balance of the loan on the car.

Debts

> The clients need to confirm they have listed all the debts and describe what they will do with the joint accounts.

> There are no debts other than those listed above. We agree that any debts either of us currently has or incurs in the future will be the sole obligation of the person incurring the debt. We will close the joint savings account. We will close the joint Visa and J. C. Penney accounts. Mary will take over the Texaco and Macy accounts. We both agree not to make any charges on the joint Visa as of August 15, 1993. We will close this account as soon as the balance owed to Visa is paid off. If either uses the account after that date, the user will be liable for any payments.

Taxes

> The clients must agree on certain tax matters regarding the support. They need to decide how to take care of any future unknown tax liabilities. The most common method can be worded thus:

> If we owe any monies to the IRS or the State of New Jersey for any past jointly filed income tax returns, we will share in any liabilities equally.

They must also decide who will take the children as dependents for tax purposes:

> John will take the children as dependents for tax purposes for as long as he is contributing the child support. Mary will

201

claim head-of-household filing status, and we will cooperate with each other to accomplish these agreements.[11]

Resolving Future Differences

There is always the possibility the couple will have disagreements in the future. The division of assets cannot be reopened unless one person demonstrates fraud on the part of the other, such as when one has withheld information or misinformed the other about the value of an item. Most future disagreements will relate to support and/or to parenting. In either case it is better for the couple to find ways of settling the dispute quickly and as cheaply as possible while also maintaining the parenting relationship. The following clause provides a quick and inexpensive method:

> If we are unable to agree on the application of any part of the agreement or if there is a significant change in the status of either of us, we agree, before commencing litigation, to make a diligent effort to resolve our differences, including the use of mediation.

> If we are unable to resolve our differences, we agree to submit our differences to an arbitrator selected from the Family Disputes Panel of the American Arbitration Association[12] (or its equivalent) and to accept the arbitrator's findings as final and binding. If the arbitrator finds one of us has violated the agreement, the arbitrator may assign the costs of the arbitration against that person.

Legal Fees

The couple must decide how to pay the legal fees. In the past, when the husband was awarded a lion's share of the assets, it was also normal for him to pay his wife's legal fees. When couples divide their

---

[11] Current IRS regulations provide that if the nonresident parent takes the children as a deduction the resident parent must provide him/her with a letter agreeing to the transfer and the nonresident parent must file a copy of the letter with his/her tax return each year.

[12] For example, the American Arbitration Association charges a two-hundred-dollar filing fee, and the arbitrator works pro bono. Call the regional office of the Arbitration Association for details of the program.

assets equally and both have incomes, they usually agree to pay their own legal fees.

>We will pay our own legal fees in connection with the separation agreement and with any subsequent divorce.

If the husband is paying the wife's legal costs, most couples include a maximum amount. This keeps costs down and provides the wife with leverage in her negotiations with the attorney about the cost of converting the memorandum into a legal document.

>John will pay Mary's legal fees up to a maximum of $1,000 for the separation agreement and any subsequent divorce.

Future Financial Arrangements

Some parents are concerned to provide for the children if either of the parents inherit money. The children's interests can be protected by the following:

>If either of us inherits money in the future, we agree to draft our wills to make our surviving children the beneficiaries of at least 75 percent of any inheritances and to consult counsel and draft wills to assure this.

While couples feel this way when the children are young, their views about inheritance may change when the children become adults. Thus, they may also want to include a time when this part of the agreement would end. Some couples agree to leave their estates to each other.

>We agree that while we are unmarried, in the event of death of either of us, the unmarried parent will leave his/her estate to the other.

All states mandate a minimum amount of an estate that can be left to a spouse. The amount ranges from one-third to one-half of the estate. The following assures the children will receive the maximum permitted under this law.

>If either has remarried, we agree to leave the estate to the surviving children after any legal requirements to the next spouse have been met.

When the children are young and the parents have agreed to maintain the family home as joint property until they have grown up, some parents leave the house to each other as a way of assuring it will be there for the children.

> For as long as we jointly own the marital home, each will provide that the survivor inherits the other's interest in the home, in the event of the death of either of us. We agree to change our wills to this effect. If, at the time of death, our wills do not reflect this agreement, we agree that our respective estates will be responsible for this obligation.

Some couples agree to assist each other financially to achieve economic independence for both spouses. When one spouse needs some financial assistance from the other, they may agree the lending spouse will get the money back in the future.

> To assist Mary to achieve her goal of completing college and becoming a registered nurse, John agrees to pay an additional $225 per month to Mary for up to two years or until she completes her R. N. degree, whichever is sooner. One year after she has graduated with her R. N. degree, Mary will repay this money to John in equal monthly payments of $92 for five years.[13]

Life Insurance

Future support obligations must be protected. Therefore most couples agree on an amount of life insurance that the paying spouse will carry to protect the support payments in the event of his/her death.[14]

---

[13] Some lawyers argue that John has no guarantee Mary will finish her education and therefore he may not get his money back. In mediation we rely on self-interest to motivate the clients to implement and honor agreements. It is in Mary's self-interest to become a registered nurse and self-interest will drive her to complete the program. If she doesn't, John will have lost his investment and Mary will have lost her opportunity to earn more in the future.

[14] There are tax advantages to having the spouse who is receiving the support, own the policy. Many couples recognize this and agree on the amount of insurance, with the mother taking out the policy and the father adding the cost to the amount of support he pays.

John will maintain $75,000 in the equivalent of declining term life insurance, with Mary as the irrevocable beneficiary for as long as he has obligations to her under this agreement. Mary will maintain her employer-provided life insurance with John as irrevocable beneficiary for the same period. If the life insurance is not effective at the time of death and we have obligations under this agreement, our respective estates will be liable for the amount due.

If either of us is the recipient of funds from this life insurance, we agree to provide that Tom and Sue will be the sole beneficiaries of such monies.[15] We both agree to have our attorneys draft wills to provide for these arrangements.

Appendix

The appendix lists all the documents the couple used in the mediation. Copies of these are attached to the MOU and given to the lawyers. It is the clients' responsibility to make the copies and see that the lawyer has them.

The following documents used in the mediation are included with the Agreement:

The last three year's tax returns
The most recent wage stubs
The evaluations of the two pensions
The two house appraisals
All loan statements showing the current balance
List of items of personal property John is taking with him
Our wills
The mortgage
Health and life insurance policies

---

[15] This provides that if the resident parent remarries, the money for the children is separate from the marital estate. In that case, if the resident parent dies, that money goes entirely to the children, not to the new spouse.

Chapter Eight
Starting and Building Your Practice

Even the perfect product needs careful marketing, and mediation is no exception to this rule. A competent mediator needs to generate a client flow, and this chapter suggests ways of getting the clients to place that first call to you.

There are a number of steps you need to take to begin building your practice.

- Develop a brochure describing your practice
- Identify potential referral sources
- Determine how to reach these sources
- Contact groups and offer to present a program
- Send a press release to local media
- Use the Yellow Pages
- Maintain a network

The Brochure

Your brochure should describe you and your practice. Remember to include in your brochure descriptions of yourself and your background as well as the service. Here is a sample brochure:[1]

Divorce by mediation: a less painful path

Divorce mediation is an active process in which the mediator helps you identify all the issues that need to be covered in your separation agreement.

Your mediator will help you determine what it costs to live apart and, using that information together with the current income, help you determine the amount and duration of

---

[1] You may use this brochure in your own practice provided you maintain the copyright. The following copyright should appear on the brochure in not less than 8 point type: Copyright 1991, John M. Haynes, Ph.D.

support. We will show you how the State Child Support Guidelines apply to your situation.

We will help you identify all of your marital assets, figure out their value, and help you to divide them fairly.

We will also help you make all of the future parenting decisions.

Mediation is conducted so that there should be no losers - one spouse should not win at the expense of the other.

DIVORCE BY MEDIATION is a *nonadversarial* process helping people negotiate directly and dissolve marriages once the decision to divorce or separate is made. We provide you with the opportunity to negotiate mutually beneficial terms in total privacy.

DIVORCE BY MEDIATION helps identify key issues concerning the division of personal and real property, support, parenting, and plans for the future. It helps eliminate the painful win-lose atmosphere that is part of all adversarial divorces. The process is a mutual search for a reasonable solution; neither partner can win at the other's expense. Resolutions must emerge from the process with a settlement created and accepted by both. Mediation can also deal with specific limited issues such as times of access, what to do with the house, or other issues specified by you at the start.

The important aspects of DIVORCE BY MEDIATION are that:

It is nonadversarial. You are partners in decision-making.

It is mutual. You both must agree on solutions, or there is no agreement.

It helps clarify areas of conflict. Most couples have some conflict. The mediator helps you limit the conflict and discuss things productively.

It gives you power. You control your own decision over your own lives.

It is best for your children. All of the discussions are tempered by the fact that you are both parents of your children and you will have a continuing relationship as parents after you have ended the spouse relationship. Most other forms of divorce negotiations forget the best interests of the children. In mediation it is always paramount.

You owe it to yourself, your children, and your future to learn more about mediation.

Fees are moderate and on an hourly basis. We charge no retainers. You pay only for the actual time you use.

We ask that you share in the fees in a way that is appropriate to your situation, remembering that the mediator is working for both of you.

The average mediation takes twelve hours. Mediation of specific issues or for couples without children is shorter.

Jane Smith, ACSW, is a clinical social worker who has worked with thousands of clients in therapy and mediation. She is a member of the American Association of Marriage and Family Therapists, and the Academy of Family Mediators.

How to proceed. All you need to do is to call (your telephone number goes here) and arrange for a mutually convenient appointment for you and your spouse to come in for a no obligation, free consultation. At that time, a detailed explanation of how we proceed is described. Both of you receive the same information, and therefore each of you can rest assured that you will be on equal footing from the outset of the proceedings.

DIVORCE BY MEDIATION is not a legal service. The outcome of the mediation is a memorandum of understanding detailing all of your agreements that your attorney will review and incorporate into the formal legal documents. We can refer you to attorneys who have agreed to perform these services for modest fees.

Copyright 1978, 1983, 1991, John M. Haynes, Ph.D.

This text will fit on both sides of a standard 8½-by-11-inch sheet of paper. It looks good, set in three columns with the agency's logo and so forth on the front and the return address on the back fold. That way it becomes a self-mailing piece. Once your brochure is ready, identify all of the people in your community to whom people turn for advice when considering divorce. Your list should include

lawyers
clergy
therapists
medical professionals such as general practitioners,
chiropractors and homeopathic doctors
accountants
employee assistance programs

Lawyers. The majority of referrals may not come from matrimonial specialists. Such specialists may refer only to colleagues in their own profession. A good source of referrals are nonmatrimonial lawyers such as corporate, commercial, real estate, or wills/trusts lawyers. These lawyers are often asked to handle their client's divorces but prefer not to.

Clergy. Priests, rabbis, vicars and other religious leaders are always concerned about the welfare of their congregations and view mediation with favor, if they understand it. Many are afraid to deal with divorce lest they be accused of favoring it. However, when they know the benefits of mediation, many clergy refer their parishioners to mediators. If the religion does not favor divorce, clergy will refer parishioners for *separation mediation.* The mediator must be willing to accept the limitations of the referrer and the couple's religious beliefs.

Therapists. Therapist see many couples who decide to end their marriages. They are sad when this happens because the therapist senses a failure but also because they know the terrible toll the legal system takes on people. Most are anxious to find alternative methods of dealing with divorce.

Medical professionals. People in the throes of deciding to divorce frequently suffer from health problems. At that time they turn to medical professionals for help. Doctors are often frustrated in treating this type of patient because they do not respond quickly to traditional medical treatment. In recent years many practitioners have learned more about psycho-somatic conditions and have become increasingly interested in making referrals of these clients. Medical doctors, chiropractors, homeopathic doctors, and other health professionals are increasingly referring to mediators.

Accountants. Most people think of accountants as "number crunchers." Many are also family confidants and advise their clients on a wide range of issues. Many men turn to their accountants during divorce, and accountants are increasingly suggesting they use mediation as a way of preserving the family assets.

Employee assistance programs. Many companies have established programs to assist their employees deal with personal problems. Family problems become work problems if they are not resolved. Companies have found that it pays to help employees deal with their family problems. Mediation is particularly helpful to employers because it is faster and less expensive than the legal process. This means that the turbulence and turmoil people experience during the divorce negotiations is sharply limited when the couple mediate. The typical time for a divorce handled by two lawyers is nine months. That means that the couple are in anguish and distracted for a long period. The average time spent in mediation is six weeks. This sharply reduces the amount of time the divorce is central to the employee. Many companies recognize mediation means greater productivity.

The role of the employee assistance program is to identify appropriate community resources for the employees. A a sure way of receiving referrals is to become a referral source for an employee assistance program.

These are the main groups of referrers. There are many others such as hairdressers and bartenders for whom listening to customer problems is as much a part of their job as cutting hair and pouring drinks. Think of all the other types of people who other people turn to in times of crisis and you will identify potential referrers.

Reaching Out to Potential Referrers

Once you have identified the potential referrers, develop a plan how to reach them. Two main ways are by mailings and presentations. *Mailings.* The mail is used to generate initial referrals and to maintain a good relationship with a referring source. Here are some sample letters. The first is to a potential referral source. Similar letters can be drafted for the other groups identified above.

Sample letter to church groups:

The (name of religion) Church has long recognized the need to provide a Christian-centered family counseling service helping families through crises and overcoming problems. One of those crises is that of divorce. Approximately 40 percent of all marriages will end in divorce, and divorce seems to affect every group and every religion.

Traditionally, divorce has been settled in the legal arena through adversarial means. However, over the last ten years, divorce mediation has demonstrated that couples can be helped to implement a decision to divorce in a way that helps them end their spousal relationship while maintaining their parental relationship.

We provide divorce and family mediation services that are conducted in the context that minimal damage to family members should occur in a divorce and that the children should be assured of an outcome that protects their rights to both parents. We take as our key belief the word of Jesus, "This is my commandment that you love one another as I have loved you" (John 15:12). Loving does not mean necessarily agreeing, but it does mean being able to rise above disagreements and find solutions based on these words. We remind people, "When you have done it unto the least of these you have done it unto me" (Matthew 25:40).

We do not avoid conflict. Rather we work with the couple to make the conflict productive rather than destructive. We help them resolve all the issues: the amount and duration of financial support, a fair distribution of the marital assets, and the future parenting of the children. We accomplish this in the context that there should be no losers. That is, one person should not win at the expense of the other.

Mediation is more cost effective than the adversarial route. A typical mediation costs about one-third the same case would cost in the legal arena. The outcome is designed to maintain those relationships that must be maintained while allowing each spouse to move towards an independent future.

We are enclosing some brochures about the mediation service. If you would like to know more about any of these services, please call me.

Mailing is a key part to the process of maintaining good relationships with your referrers. You can keep your name and service in front of potential referrers by preparing and mailing pertinent materials on a regular basis. Here are samples of different letters you can send to professionals.

Sample letter to a new referrer —1:

Thank you for referring Mr. Robert Jones for mediation services. I have set an appointment for him and his wife to meet with the mediator for a free half-hour consultation.

I am enclosing a copy of the booklet we give to clients as they enter mediation; I think you will find it helpful. In addition, I am enclosing brochures for other potential clients.

Thank you for your confidence in our agency.

Sample letter to new referrer —2:

The following letter is sent if you did not send the above letter and you have started working with the couple.

Thank you for referring (client) to mediation. We have begun working with (clients) helping them to reach an amicable separation agreement. The process of mediation takes approximately twelve hours, and we will let you know when (clients) reach an agreement on the various issues.

For your use I am enclosing some divorce mediation brochures so if you have other clients contemplating divorce you can share this information with them.

We also offer mediation in a range of other family and business situations where the continuing relationship is more important than the problem. I am enclosing copies of our family and business mediation brochures and a recent press clipping about mediation.

No doubt (client) will talk to you about the process of mediation. If you would like information about the process or about our agency or our other services, please do not hesitate to call me.

Sometimes the clients come to you and you discover they are in therapy, but the therapist did not make the referral. After obtaining permission from the clients, you can send a letter to the therapist when the mediation is completed.

Letter to a nonreferring therapist upon completion of the mediation:

We have recently completed working with (client) in helping the (clients) reach an amicable separation agreement. The process of mediation has allowed them to reach an agreement that satisfactorily ends their spousal relationship while maintaining the parental relationship.

No doubt (client) has talked to you about the process of mediation. For your use I am enclosing some divorce mediation brochures that you can share with other clients contemplating divorce.

We also offer mediation in a range of other family and business situations where the continuing relationship is more important than the problem. I am enclosing copies of our family and business mediation brochures as well as a press clipping about mediation showing its wide use.

If you would like any further information about the services, please call me.

When the mediation is completed, send another letter to the referrer advising that you have completed the work. This lets them know the status and keeps your name in front of them.

Thank you letter to referring therapist upon completion of the mediation:

Thank you for referring (client) to mediation. We have recently completed working with (clients) helping them reach an amicable separation agreement.

No doubt (client) has talked to you about the process of mediation. I am enclosing some divorce mediation brochures so, if you have other clients contemplating divorce, you can share this information with them.

We also offer mediation in a range of other family and business situations where the continuing relationship is more important than the problem. I am enclosing copies of our family and business mediation brochures as well as a recent press clipping about mediation.

If you would like any further information about our services, please call me.

Letters are always useful; however, they will not be your main source of new referrals. You must get to know the people making the referrals. Everyone is more comfortable referring to someone they know in preference to someone they have heard about. Therefore, develop a plan to enable people to get to know you.

Presentations. Identify all of the groups that individual referrers belong to:

Clergy
> Diocesan Council
> Council of Churches
> Religious Leaders Conference

Almost every town or village has a Religious Leaders Conference, also known as the Religious Coordinating Council. This is how the clergy of all faiths in a specific area meet, usually monthly, to discuss common issues.

Mental health professionals in
> Private practice
> Family agencies
> Substance abuse programs
> Mental health departments of hospitals and prepaid health plans

Professional groups such as
> National Association of Social Workers
> Canadian Association of Social Workers
> American/Canadian Psychological Associations

American Association of Marriage and Family
Therapists

Employee Assistance Programs

Company offices
EAP Coordinating Committees

It is difficult to locate groups to which medical professionals and accountants belong and attend but ask your doctor and accountant where they learn about nonmedical or nonaccounting matters. Your medical professional may also be able to help you locate the right person to talk to at the mental health department of the local hospitals or group health plans.

While you are identifying these professional groups identify other service organizations such as Rotary and Kiwanis Clubs. They meet once a month for lunch and are always looking for speakers.

Once you have identified the groups that might include potential referrers, approach them with your availability to present to them. Agencies usually have regular staff-development programs and are always looking for good educational experiences for the staff. Your presentation should include the following:

- Why mediation? An explanation of the things wrong with the legal system in handling divorce
- What mediation is. A brief overview of the process
- The advantages of mediation. A list of advantages with special attention to those advantages that are important to the group you are addressing; for example, if you are talking to the religious leaders, stress the positive outcomes on the children and the maintenance of the ongoing relationship of the parents and the fact that people who mediate are more likely to both stay as members of the congregation
- Some good case examples. Stories always convey more meaning for the audience
- Use a video. You can obtain video tapes of the author for use in your own training and for selecting clips for general audiences that accurately portray the benefits of mediation.[2]

---

[2] Six tapes are currently available: *Not When She's Around, Who Makes the Decisions Here?, The Odd Child Out, Moving 100 Miles Apart,* and *A*

Each presentation usually yields at least one referral. But each referral that achieves a mediated divorce agreement has the potential of referring dozens of other people. The most useful referral system is a network of satisfied clients who tell their friends about the advantages of mediation as they experienced it.

Newsletter Articles

Every group that potential referrers belong to probably publishes a newsletter. Editors are always looking for relevant material. Prepare newsletter articles about mediation addressing the particular interests of the audience. Send the articles to the editor. You will be surprised how many wind up in print.

Using the Media

The media consists of newspapers, radio, and television. All three are available to you. It is unlikely you will get a spot on national television or radio, but careful research in your area will identify numerous possibilities.

Newspapers: Includes more than the dailies. Remember

> Weekly community newspapers
> Pennysavers[3]
> Advertising announcements

These publications make a living from printing news and, believe it or not, many people read everything that comes into the house and are likely to act on what they read.

Family Recovering from Alcohol, parts 1 and 2. Each tape comes with an annotated transcript, a trainer's guide and viewer's guide. For a description of the tapes and the training materials contact the Association of Family Conciliation Courts, 329 West Wilson Street, Madison, WI 53703 (608 251 4001). In addition, The Academy of Family Mediators has tapes made at its annual conferences. For information contact the Academy at 1500 South Highway 100, Suite 355, Golden Valley, MN 55416.

[3] The Pennysaver often includes "news stories" and articles of advice, and so forth, that help it to qualify for the newspaper delivery rate (much cheaper than the normal postage). Thus, any news item or article has double value to this medium, it helps fill space, and it helps meet postal regulations for lower postage rates.

217

Read your local newspaper and identify the byline of reporters who cover social issues and areas that include divorce and mediation. This will give you a name to send releases to and to call. Send an announcement to all print sources. Here is a sample announcement.

Divorce mediation, which is growing rapidly across the country, is now available in (identify your village, town, or country, whichever is most appropriate). Family mediation services are now offered by (your name) to meet the needs of couples who wish to separate/divorce without destroying each other and their children.

Mediation is a process in which couples work with a trained mediator to identify all the issues that need resolving for a legal separation in (your state). The mediator helps the couple resolve these issues in a win/win framework that enables people to end their relationship as husband and wife with dignity while maintaining their future roles as parents.

(Your name) was trained (add here the specific mediation training you have taken), (Your name) is a member of (list all of the relevant professional organizations you belong to as well as your relevant professional degrees).

Mediation is now mandated in a majority of states in the US. (Add a piece here about legislative developments in your state.)

(Add a paragraph here about your agency, its services, location, hours, fees and so forth.)

Send this release to all the papers you have identified. The news release has two purposes: It provides you with free publicity and also provides you with additional credibility.

Once you have a news article about yourself, clip it and copy it. Include the clipping with every letter, brochure, or information package about your service. It adds what is known as "third party validation" of your service and gives you additional credibility with the recipient of your letter.

You can follow this up whenever a national or cultural event about divorce happens. For example, when the movie *Kramer vs. Kramer* or *War of the Roses* is reviewed, send a release to the local press pointing out how mediation could have worked better in the situation. When a national celebrity such as Johnny Carson gets divorced, call your contact at the local newspaper and suggest a story about how mediation could have worked for him. Remember, every reporter has to write to make a living, and every newspaper must fill up the news pages to sell the advertising. When you call the paper with an idea for a story, you are doing them a favor.

Radio. With the increase in all-news and all-talk radio, many stations are looking for material. All-talk radio usually is also call-in radio. Listen to some of these programs. Get an idea of the kind of issues and stories they talk about. When you identify a host who is interested in family matters, listen to what others are talking about on the show. Call in whenever divorce is mentioned and talk about the advantages of mediation.

Many of these shows are on late at night. Conventional wisdom suggests that many of the listeners are single and lonely and many of them are in the throes of divorce. They are all anxious for suggestions on how to do it better.

Television. Local television is more than the three national networks. Also check your local cable network. Do they have a news show? Do they have talking head shows with a local personality? Identify all of the possible sources for your story. Call the editor or the show host and suggest an interview about mediation.

Building a practice is about being proud of who you are and what you do. It is about being willing to push yourself forward and to promote the idea of mediation.

Client Handbook

Prepare a handbook for the clients explaining the process of mediation. The handbook is helpful because it provides the clients with a written explanation of the process to support the verbal one you present at the intake session. Few people are able to hear everything the mediator says during the intake. So the client handbook can be read in the privacy of the client's home. It has an additional benefit. Clients often show it to their friends and to friends also going through divorce. Thus it is part of your marketing package.

The following sample looks good set on the 8½-by-11-inch page in landscape orientation folded once to make a booklet. The agency's name and logo appear on the front cover, and a list of services is printed on the back cover.

Client Handbook

Divorce mediation is a process of dissolving the marriage in a nonadversarial way. The framework provides you with the opportunity to negotiate your own settlement on the assumption that the decision to separate and/or divorce has been made.

You may decide to consult with a lawyer at the beginning of the mediation process to insure that you know your legal rights, even though you will negotiate directly with your spouse in the mediation process. You are free to consult with a lawyer at any time during the mediation process; and you will need to have a lawyer prepare the legal documents based on the mediation, as more fully described below.

This is not an avenue to resolve conflicts of the past. You may begin to understand some of those past problems in a different light, but we will not be working to resolve them. Rather, we shall, through the process of mutual negotiations, attempt to define a new life with new options for each of you. To do this, there must develop a sense of mutual respect among the three of us.

Too often divorce is placed in a win/lose framework. Given that situation, compromise is difficult, since it is seen as a loss. A smart, if less than honest, tactic is OK because it means a win. However, the result is a loss for both of you, since winning in this situation denies a part of the other's humanity. The divorce mediation process is designed to eliminate the win/lose atmosphere. Since the process is mutual, you can't win at the other's expense. Neither can you lose. You must come out of it with a settlement acceptable to both of you and controlled by both of you. We call that a "win/win" solution.

With control over the outcome you also experience a sense of power over the life decisions. The important aspects of divorce mediation are that:

- You emerge from these negotiations with a new sense of dignity and a clearer sense of self and what the future holds for you.
- You can place the past behind you and concentrate on the future.

My function is to assist you reach a settlement. I do not represent either of you individually. My commitment is to a settlement you can both live with. I will use my mediation skills to help you identify those areas of agreement and those substantive areas of disagreement. I will help you negotiate the substantive areas of disagreement to reach a settlement. I will also manage the conflict between you so it becomes productive rather than destructive.

The process

In the first phase I will help you to identify the parameters for negotiations. I will be working with you to define your short- and long-term goals. Obviously, you have given this whole matter considerable thought and you have many ideas on what the ultimate settlement should include. You can "sound out" ideas before proposing them. I can help by sharing my experience with you on what has worked in the past for other couples and what the norms are.

I cannot define the settlement, and I cannot impose an agreement. My role is to assist you reach your agreement. I will not take sides on the issues.

I am interested in the settlement as a principle, and I am interested in you as people. I feel for your pain and want to help you through this difficult process and help diminish this pain. Finally, I hope to help you use these negotiations to place the past behind you. The marriage is ending, but you have a life ahead of you. That new life can be marred by holding onto the anger of the separation, or the new life can be an exciting opportunity to redefine yourself.

I'm working for and with both of you to help you reach a settlement that permits you to concentrate on the future and the potential it holds.

There is a typical process we will use to reach a settlement; however, your individual needs may cause us to depart from a strict adherence to it. During the process we will:

- develop current and future income information
- develop budgets
- inventory marriage assets
- begin to define each of your short- and long-term goals
- define general areas of agreement
- define substantive areas of disagreement
- identify symbolic and emotional issues
- work through the parenting arrangements
- negotiate money differences
- develop a settlement.

Sessions normally last two hours. However, we do not limit ourselves. Rather, we attempt to complete the business scheduled for that session.

My role as mediator is to help you retain your power over the decision-making process that affects your lives. My focus is on the future and helping you define new options to you.

Budgeting guidelines

The purpose of this guide is to assist you in defining what it will cost for you to live separately. Obviously, your total expenses will increase. However, in developing a budget you may also identify areas of expenditure that can be reduced without significantly changing your essential standards of living. In addition, the process of budgeting helps you to develop a rational data base from which to begin negotiations.

Budgeting is difficult for most people. Some see it as penny-pinching, others as bookkeeping; Few of us like either of these activities. Yet, budgeting is financial planning, which enables us to make intelligent decisions and rational choices.

We will not try to account for every dime as we prepare your budget. Doing so will drive you to despair. Use your checkbook records as general guidelines to fill in the categories supplied here. Do not try to reconstruct every expenditure. Our purpose is to enable you to establish broad outlines, and by drawing on experience, to project future needs, recognizing that your future needs will be different from the past.

As part of this process, I will share some averages with you when a particular item is way out of line with general norms. This will enable both of you to develop budgets you can live with.

The assessment is in four parts

1. current income
2. future budgets
3. assets
4. liabilities.

There are forms at the end of this booklet that will help you to complete this assessment.

The budget

The budgets deal with anticipated expenses. They will differ for each of you depending on certain variables. For example, who will be primarily responsible for the children?

Will one of you continue to live in the family home? Often, the parent with prime responsibility for the child(ren) also remains in the home. The other, therefore, needs to calculate a budget based on an apartment rental or whatever other living arrangement is planned. These expenses are best calculated on a monthly basis. If your information is weekly, multiply one week's figures by 4.3 to get a monthly figure.

The prime purpose of completing this budget information is to provide you with a database with which to make decisions. I will work on these with you and we are looking for broad guidelines, not precise documentation. So, do not be overly concerned if you can't provide a specific figure - we'll work it out together.

In many marriages, one spouse has assumed responsibility for budgeting and handling the finances. This leaves the other "in the dark" when it comes to preparing this database. Doing the budgets provides both of you with the same data and enables you to make rational decisions about your futures.

There are times when the person who has most control over the money finds it difficult to share this information because knowledge is often equated with power. However, if you don't share this knowledge with your spouse now as the basis for reaching a mutual decision, you may have to share it later with a judge who will make a unilateral decision, thereby giving up all of your power. By sharing all of the information now, you assure that you will both keep and be able to exercise your power.

So, in a real sense, we are working together to provide you with the power to make your own decisions about your own lives. That means sharing data at this point so those decisions can be mutual.

Child Support

The Child Support Guidelines mandate that all child support be based on your actual income. It is assumed that you, as parents, will spend a specific percentage of your combined income on your children as follows:

one child	17%
two children	25%
three	29%
four	31%
five +	35%

The percentage is based on your gross income before deductions less money paid for FICA (social security) in the previous year.

It is assumed that each parent is contributing the same percentage to the children's expenses. In addition to the cash child support, parents are expected to share in the cost of child-care expenses incurred by the resident parent while working and uncovered medical expenses. (You are expected to cover your children under any employer-provided health insurance.) The ratio for sharing these expenses is the ratio of the two incomes less FICA.

We will start the process by reviewing the future needs as indicated by the budgets and then we will calculate and apply the child support guidelines. If you have a deficit following this part of the process, closing that deficit will be a subject of the negotiations.

As you collect all the data together, you begin to define the parameters of any agreement. You cannot divide what you don't have. You will begin to see that living separately costs more than living together. Therefore, there may have to be some reduction in the standard of living of *both* of you once the separation begins.

This leads to uncertainties and a sense of insecurity in you. That insecurity is as integral a part of these negotiations as are the emotional issues that led to the decision to divorce. Security will be sitting at the negotiating table with you, and you won't be able to leave until you settle its needs.

The data you have prepared enable you to consider some of the broad choices you need to make. Your final agreement will probably consist of maintenance and/or child support. There are pros and cons to each of these and to how payments should be divided. We will also consider the possibility of changing incomes and changes in the cost of living.

If you've been shopping lately for a new car or to replace furniture, you know just how expensive these items are. If you are just making ends meet and the washing machine breaks down for good, no amount of wishing will get you a new one. So, think about the cars, appliances, furniture and other high-cost items you have that might need replacement in the next two years and include them in the work sheet.

Your assets

Marital assets (everything you have accumulated during the marriage except gifts and inheritances) need to be identified, and an equitable distribution of these must be part of a mediated settlement. By and large, inheritances and gifts to an individual are considered nonmarital assets. This is an "equitable division" state, which means it may be equitable to divide property other than equally. However, the decision of how you divide the assets is up to you: you know your needs. We will work on identification of marital assets and how to divide them.

Considering your children

So far we have concentrated on the economic issues. But, what about the kids? In our society people generally think about children in three ways:

1. As chattels — "They *belong* to me." "I've invested all I have in them. I see in them my hopes for the future."
2. As weapons — "If he thinks he's going to see them whenever he wants, he's nuts." "If I'm paying for them, I'm going to decide who visits with her and when I see the kids."
3. As people afraid about the future, divided in loyalty, having feelings and needs independent from either of you and dependent on both of you.

Most of us have a combination of these feelings and sorting out which of the feelings are valid is difficult. The reality is that your children need both of you and you both need the children. You are the only parents they will ever have, and they need you to cooperate in the future as parents. I will help you keep this in mind as you negotiate an agreement that provides for a parenting role for both parents in the best interests of your children.

One family court judge has developed a Bill of Rights of Children in Divorce Actions. Among those rights are:

- The right to be treated as an interested and affected person and not as a pawn, possession or chattel of either or both parents
- The right to grow to maturity in that home environment which will best guarantee an opportunity for the child to mature to responsible citizenship
- The right to day-to-day love, care, discipline, and protection of the parent having custody of the child
- The right to know both parents and to have the benefit of such parents' love and guidance through adequate access
- The right to a positive and constructive relationship with both parents, with neither parent permitted to degrade or downgrade the other in the mind of the child
- The right to have moral and ethical values developed by precept and practices and to have limits set for behavior so early in life the child may develop self-discipline and self-control
- The right to the most adequate level of economic support that can be provided by the best efforts of both parents

• The right to the same opportunities for education that the child would have had if the household had not dissolved.

Neither of you wants to put the children at a disadvantage. You both want the best for them. However, if the children are viewed as bargaining tools or are ignored during the negotiations, then there is a danger of harming them.

For these reasons, it is important to determine how the children can be involved in the decision-making process. They are entitled to some input on the issues affecting their lives. The precise nature of that input should be decided in the ways you make family decisions. You would not admit a six year old to the bargaining table as an equal. On the other hand, a sixteen year old won't accept placidly a living arrangement that (s)he had no role in shaping. Part of the negotiations is about how to involve the children appropriately in those parts that have a direct bearing on them.

There are many options open to you regarding your children. They include:

Joint residency: In this arrangement you continue to live in close proximity (usually within the same school district) with the children spending part of each week or month in each household, coming and going according to some comfortable arrangement.

Joint parenting: Here you agree to share all parenting decision-making even though the children live primarily with one of you.

Single custody: The children live with one of you who makes all the decisions with either an "open" arrangement regarding access rights of the other parent, or you make specific arrangements detailing when and where the other parent has access to the children.

The joint residency arrangement might prove to be outside your realm of expectations. But if you plan to live close by and you can tolerate the essentially unstructured nature of this arrangement, then you should give it serious consideration.

The important thing to remember is that you will always be parents to your children even though you decide no longer to be husband and wife. There are some well-written, easy-to-read, and helpful books that address this issue. Ask me about them.

During the divorcing process, some people feel that whatever child contact they are granting the other parent is a concession. Such an attitude ties a stone around that parent's neck. In addition to normal access, each parent should consider the other parent's obligation to care for the children. For example, if your brother is sick in another city and you want to visit him, the children's need to stay at home for school may interfere. If you have a tight, carefully specified arrangement, you won't be able to ask the other parent to care for the children for a few days while you visit your brother.

You are both the parents, and while you may no longer be able to share the day-to-day responsibility of caring for the children, you can share the week-to-week responsibility.

Such an open arrangement also means that the children do not become a total burden on the freedom of one parent. This arrangement extends the parenting partnership theory of marriage into the post-marriage relationship.

The following points should be considered in determining parenting arrangements: the age and sex of the child, together with the interaction and interrelationship with both parents and siblings; the child's adjustment to home, school, and community; the mental and physical health of all involved.

So, in planning the future, think about these points. Your children have rights, and you have rights to frequent contact with them, or relief from the day-to-day burdens of child rearing. They have needs. You have aspirations for them.

How you work out the parenting issues will have a significant impact on the emotional life of your children and their future relationship with you as they mature.

THE NEGOTIATIONS
Preparation
Preparation is the key to successful negotiations. That is why we spend so much time preparing an adequate database

from which to start. As we get ready to negotiate here are some good ground rules to follow:

Know Your Case and Your Rights

You should be fully aware of your rights and, if necessary, consult with a lawyer to insure that you are. This does not mean that a lawyer should negotiate for you. You should define what it is you need in the settlement. Once you have a broad idea of what you need, begin to think through why you need it. Separate out each piece and develop in your own mind your reasons for it.

Review the Other's Position

Having prepared your case, try to review the other's case. What is his/her response likely to be to your proposals? What argument is (s)he likely to advance in opposition to your proposals? What things is (s)he likely to advance to support these claims?

Identify the Constraints

As you are thinking these points through you will also begin to identify those external constraints that must be recognized and factored in. For example you cannot divide more than is totally available. You can't ask for $15,000 and expect your partner to live on $10,000 if the total income is only $20,000. Or, if there is only one auto, and one income producer, and the only way to get to work is by auto, then this places a constraint on who gets the auto.

If you think these points through in preparation, you won't be surprised in the actual negotiations.

List Your Points

List the points you want to raise in each session; define your goals into an order of priority to help you decide what to emphasize in the session.

As you prepare for the negotiations, the task will often seem formidable. You will worry about not doing it correctly and many aspects of it will rekindle anger as it touches on some of the reasons for the divorce.

THE ROLE OF THE MEDIATOR

My role at this point is to help each of you develop your case. I do this by focusing on what is in your best interests without regard to the other party, since the give and take must come from each of you in negotiations.

Guidelines for Useful Behavior

There are some useful guidelines for behavior at the meetings. I will start the discussion from areas of common agreement, rather than from an obviously controversial area. Once you have secured a beginning base of agreement on which to build, you will find that subsequent favorable accommodations are more easily reached on disputed issues.

As you reach agreements, I make a note of them, and we remove those issues from the table. That does not mean we can't reopen those issues later, and obviously nothing is finalized until the actual settlement is signed.

During the talks my focus is on reaching a settlement you can both live with. Therefore, I will always be looking for the yes and trying to avoid reaching a premature no. However, each of you has the right to say no to demands that are totally unacceptable to you.

In mediation I help you to make a good effort to see the other's point of view without losing sight of your own position. At the same time, you should be well enough prepared to explain the reasonableness or acceptability of your proposals. To help you do this, I will ask you to state your proposals and then explain why they are beneficial to the other as well as yourself.

It is often difficult to decide, and the more important the decision, the more difficult it is to reach. One way of easing the burden of making a heavy decision is to offer a "forced choice" of two alternatives. Think about situations where you can suggest two alternatives of approximately equal value. Be careful not to offer a choice between a something and a nothing. Always remember the goal you have set can be reached in many ways. Be open to alternative plans or routes to your goal. Try also to determine which goals can be "traded" for a goal of your partner. Negotiating is the art of compromising — that means giving and taking.

When tensions are high, as they must inevitably be in this situation, it is important to work at minimizing them. Thus, if you win a point in the debate or if the other concedes an item, be gracious. Credit the other with sincerity. It will make it easier for both of you to make other compromises.

Try to maintain your own sense of dignity. Don't plead your case. You have invested as much in this marriage as your partner has. Explain your position, discuss the issues, try to persuade, but don't plead - you have rights too.

The real art of negotiating is listening. You know your spouse very well. Listen closely for clues as to when and how concessions are likely. *Don't talk more than necessary.* Many an agreement has been lost because one person kept on talking past the point when the other was willing to agree. Remember that you can't give anything away when you are listening.

If you are not ready to commit yourself at any point, don't get pressured. Say you need time to think it over. I will be watching this point and will help you to avoid reaching a premature decision.

Always try your best to keep the discussion problem oriented. Don't let it become personality centered. If it does, I will try to reorient the discussion to the issues. If that cannot be done, we will terminate the session, since a personality-centered discussion is detrimental to problem solving.

If a session becomes too difficult, feel free to ask that we end early. Your mediator will do that and you will be charged only for the time actually used.

Negotiating is a systematic search for solutions that will lead to a settlement you can both be comfortable with. It requires patience and some measure of good will. Even at its most successful, it cannot solve the problems that led to your decision to separate. However, it can help you implement this decision with less pain and with a sense of dignity and control over the process. Hopefully, it will also help you place the past behind you and help you focus on the future - a future you have helped determine, rather than one defined by a settlement imposed from the outside.

How to implement your settlement

When you have arrived at a settlement, I will prepare your memorandum of understanding. Each of you then take that memorandum of understanding to your respective lawyers, who incorporate your agreements into a legal separation agreement. Sometimes a lawyer will suggest minor modifications to your agreement that you feel change the intent rather than clarify an ambiguity. If this happens, you should check with each other and the mediator. This is important because the agreements reached in mediation represent a total package, carefully balancing your mutual and self interests.

If your lawyer suggests substantial changes, you should consider the changes in the context of a continued mediation. That is, you know what you gave and what you got in the negotiations. Weigh the overall outcome and, if you feel the changes are warranted, return to mediation to complete the negotiations. The more complicated your financial situation, the more likely your lawyers will contribute to the final structure of the memorandum of understanding. You should not attempt to convert the memorandum of understanding into a legal agreement without the advice of a lawyer, since it is not intended to be legal document.

Fees

The fee is paid at the end of each session for the amount of time used in that session. We ask that you share in the cost of mediation in a ratio appropriate to you. There is also a fee of three hours time charged for drafting the memorandum of understanding and work conducted outside of the session.

If you need to cancel a session, please call the office and reschedule your appointment at least twenty-four hours before the scheduled time. If you cancel with less than twenty-four hours notice, we will charge you for the time you have reserved.

Copyright 1978, 1989, 1991, John M. Haynes, Ph.D. [4]

---

[4] You may use this material provided you leave this copyright line on the front page of the brochure you develop and distribute.

Conducting a Survey

Every agency should conduct regular surveys of clients as a way of monitoring quality of services and levels of client satisfaction. In building a practice, the survey also helps to keep the service in the mind of the client thus enhancing the possibility of their making referrals of their friends.

The following survey is sent to the clients approximately six months after they have completed mediation. It provides good feedback to the agency and reminds the clients of your service when the memory of the mediation is fading.

Client Satisfaction Survey[5]

In an effort to improve our service and to meet as many needs of our clients as possible, we invite you to offer us feedback on your experience with mediation. Please complete as many of the questions as possible and make additional comments to any of the questions.

1. Name of your mediator _____

2. In thinking about the various stages of the mediation process, how were they handled for you? Please check the most appropriate answer. The stage was handled

	very well	well	adequately	poorly	very poorly
a) Initial phone contact	☐	☐	☐	☐	☐
b) Our brochures	☐	☐	☐	☐	☐
c) Intake session	☐	☐	☐	☐	☐
d) Asset data-collection	☐	☐	☐	☐	☐
e) Parenting discussions	☐	☐	☐	☐	☐
f) Budget/data	☐	☐	☐	☐	☐

[5] This survey was originally developed by Morna Barsky, ACSW.

Client Survey (cont.)

	very well	well	adequately	poorly	very poorly
g) Negotiations on child support	☐	☐	☐	☐	☐
h) Spousal support negotiations	☐	☐	☐	☐	☐
i) Asset division negotiations	☐	☐	☐	☐	☐
j) Written memorandum of understanding	☐	☐	☐	☐	☐
k) Consultations with lawyers	☐	☐	☐	☐	☐
l) Implementation	☐	☐	☐	☐	☐
m) Postlegal problems.	☐	☐	☐	☐	☐

3. Overall, how would you rate your mediator? Check one.
a) Was mediator fair? ☐to husband ☐ to both ☐ to wife
b) Was the mediator neutral? ☐Yes ☐ No
If no, why?_____

c) Did you think the mediation took :
☐ too long ☐about right ☐too quick

d) Did you make corrections to the memorandum of understanding
☐ too many ☐ a few ☐ none

4. If you were to change any of the agreements now, which would you change?
How?_____
_____
Why?_____
_____
_____

Client Survey (cont.)

5. Have you suggested mediation to any other divorcing person?
   ☐Yes   number of people _____
   ☐ No   Reason   _____

6. What was the date when the actual legal agreement was signed?

_____

7. Did you use a lawyer from the our list?
   ☐ Yes   ☐ No

8. What were the lawyer costs?
   For your separation agreement $_____
   For conversion to the divorce $_____
   Any other costs $_____

9. If you were to refer a friend to us, would you suggest we refer them to the lawyer you used?
   ☐ Yes   ☐ No
Why?_____

10. Your Lawyer's name:_____

11. Now that you have had a chance to live with the agreement are you
    ☐ highly satisfied   ☐ satisfied   ☐ dissatisfied

12. Overall, how do you feel about your mediation?
    ☐ highly satisfied   ☐ satisfied   ☐ dissatisfied.

13. Have any problems emerged for you since the mediation regarding implementation of the agreement?
    ☐ Yes   ☐ No

14. If yes how did you resolve them? (check all that apply)
    ☐ Talked directly to ex-spouse
    ☐ Went back to mediation
    ☐ Left it to my lawyer
    ☐ Went to court

15. Were you satisfied with the result of the choice(s) you checked above? ☐Yes   ☐No

Client Survey (cont.)

Thank you for helping us. Please feel free to add any additional comments about your experience.

Keeping Track of the Agreements

Some mediators find it useful to have a checklist to keep track of the areas covered and key points of agreement. Here is a useful suggestion.

Mediator Checklist

CHILD SUPPORT: Gross $ _____ Deductions $_____ Base $_____
Amount % $_____ Escalator Clause_____ College_____
Special needs_____ Health Insurance $_____ Moving Clause_____
MAINTENANCE SUPPORT:
Amount_____ Duration_____ Triggers_____
ASSETS:
House:
Ownership %_____ Resident_____ Sale Date_____
Other triggers _____ Loans_____ Repairs_____
Pension _____
Total $_____ Distribution (H) _____ (W)_____

DEBT:
Accounts to husband_____
Accounts to wife_____
Liabilities to husband_____
Liabilities to wife_____

TAXES:
Dependents to husband _____ to wife _____
House deductions _____

LIFE INSURANCE:
Amount for husband_____Coverage for wife _____
Amount for wife_____ Coverage for husband _____

ARBITRATION: _____LEGAL FEES: _____

PARENTING:
Residence_____Access_____
Holidays_____Vacations _____

Co-Mediation

When your service introduces mediation, it is useful if more than one person is trained to do the work. Many mediators find it helpful to begin mediating as a team. Teams normally consist of a man and a woman to balance mediators with the couple. Teams are often made up of professionals from different professions such as a lawyer-therapist team. However, many good teams are made up of same sex, same profession mediators.

The key to co-mediation is to create a team that works together and can model productive conflict resolution in front of the couple and does not engage in power games. That means having issues understood and agreed upon before meeting with the clients.
Teams should consider

- Who will lead and who will ask follow-up questions?
- How will you deal with differences of tactics and values?
- How will you alert each other to mediator caused problems?
- How will you signal when you don't want the other to interrupt a particular flow of questions?

When teams have asked these questions and worked out strategies to deal with them, they are unlikely to have open conflicts in the session. If a conflict between mediators occurs that appears to be unhelpful to the couple, take a caucus and get clarity on the direction each person is taking and how to conduct the remainder of the session. A legitimate disagreement between the mediators handled in a healthy way can be a useful modeling for the couple. Co-mediation offers several benefits

- Beginning mediators do not feel the entire responsibility rests on one set of shoulders.
- One mediator can identify the other's biases.
- The second mediator often thinks of a good follow-up question when the original one has not provided enough information.
- The team can share responsibility for leading: one might lead on the money and the other on the parenting.

237

Co-mediation should be considered a training tool, and mediators should work towards conducting the entire session alone. It is cheaper for the clients, and it forces the mediator to learn new ideas and fields of competence. For example, the lawyer-mediator must learn how to deal with difficult dynamics. The therapist-mediator must learn about taxes.

Supervision

Whether you start as part of a team or in solo practice, supervision is important. No professional should practice without engaging competent consultation from a professional mediator. Check with the Academy of Family Mediators for a list of approved consultants. I have written elsewhere describing a useful model of consultation that is used by many professionals.[6]

Supervisors of other mediators in an agency will find another piece useful in deciding how to assign cases and provide supervision for mediators at different levels of expertise. Mediator competence falls into three general areas: (1) context knowledge, the specific context of budgeting, support, asset division, and parenting; (2) knowledge of the role of the mediator as manager of the negotiations; (3) knowledge of the dynamics and relationships of the parties, and of the mediator to each of the parties individually and both of them collectively.[7]

Measurement of the first area is relatively simple. The mediator either knows or does not know whether child support is tax deductible. Measuring competence in the other two areas is much more subjective and requires expertise on the part of the supervisor/ consultant. The AFM provides training for consultants, and those who supervise other mediators should take it.

Starting a practice begins when you get the first client. Many professionals undertake rigorous mediation training and do not put it to use because they keep putting off the day they will really market their services and generate clients. The longer you put it off the more the

---

[6] John M. Haynes, "Consultation in Mediation," *Mediation Quarterly* no. 12, (June, 1986), 3-15.
[7] John M. Haynes, "Supervision Issues in Mediation," *Mediation Quarterly* no. 13 (Fall 1986), 31-42.

skills you learned in the training will atrophy and the less likely you will ever get started.

Mediation benefits the clients and society. It provides agreements that are integrated and preserve the ongoing relationship of the family members. It helps to assure children that they will keep both parents and it helps the parents move on with the independent lives. As such it is a worthy profession.

Annotated Bibliography

BOOKS

Instead of the standard listing of numerous books, I have included an annotated bibliography of the basic books every mediator should read. You will discover new ideas and different directions to take in future reading from these basic books. Depending on your current knowledge and areas of interest, these books will stimulate your thinking as to which areas to explore.

Ahrons, C. R., and Roy Rogers, *Divorced Families: A Multi-disciplinary Developmental View*. New York: Norton, 1987.
Almost all that is written about divorce is negative and blames every conceivable problem on people's decision to end the marriage. This book takes a healthier view. It examines divorce as a developmental stage and shows how most divorcing families manage the transition from married to divorced without great, long-term trauma.

Aspaklaria, Shelly, and Garson Geltner. *Everything You need to Know about Your Husband's Money and Need to Know Before the Divorce*. New York: Thomas Crowell, 1980.
Written for women, this book is very useful as a primer on how to look for and find the family assets. There are many good ideas for mediators in this book. However, it does seem to be based on the premise that all men are potential cheats and liars. Therefore, it is not a good book to suggest to clients.

Bolton, R. *People Skills*. Engelwood Cliffs, N. J.: Prentice Hall, 1979.
A perfect gem. Essential for all mediators who do not have specific therapy training. It explains in clear and jargon-free language how to handle people in difficult situations. The reader will learn how to handle difficult situations and pick up new ideas about mediation.

Filley, Allan. *Interpersonal Conflict Resolution.* Glenville, Ill.: Scott Foresman, 1975.

Wilmott, Joyce, and William. *Interpersonal Conflict.* Dubuque, Iowa: William C. Brown, 1978.

These two books complement each other perfectly and provide the reader with a good understanding of human conflict. You find out all you need to know about the why of conflict, how to manage conflict, and make it productive instead of destructive.

Fisher, Roger and William Ury. *Getting to Yes: Negotiating Agreements Without Giving In.* New York: Houghton Mifflin, 1981.

This paperback has sold more than two million copies around the world. It can be thought of as the bible of mediators. It develops a principled approach to negotiations and suggests how to negotiate agreements in which everyone wins. It forms the basis for much mediator behavior.

Folberg, Jay, and Ann Taylor. *Mediation: A Comprehensive Guide to Resolving Conflicts without Litigation.* San Francisco: Jossey Bass, 1984.

The title does not indicate that the contents are almost exclusively about family mediation. These authors have managed to synthesize a wide breadth of theory from different disciplines into one volume. It provides the mediator with a broad look at the literature and is the first serious attempt to develop a theoretical understanding of family mediation.

Haynes, John M., and Gretchen L. Haynes. *Mediating Divorce: Casebook of Strategies for Successful Family Negotiations.* San Francisco: Jossey Bass, 1989.

Based on annotated transcripts of video tapes, the authors analyze each step of the mediator's behavior from the first introduction to completion of the session. The book provides the reader with an opportunity to sit in on sessions and look over the shoulder of a master mediator.

Annotated Bibliography

Newman, George. *101 Ways to be a Long Distance Super-Dad.* Mountain View, Calif.: Blossom Valley Press, 1981.
An ideal book for parents who live far apart. It is full of simple things the absent parent can do to stay involved in the lives of his children. Very useful to suggest to clients.

Porter, Sylvia. *New Money Book for the Nineties.* New York: Avon, 1991.
Sloane, Leonard. *Book of Personal Finance.* New York: Times Books, 1985.
Either of these books will provide you with all you need to know about budgeting and family finances.

Pruitt, Dean G. *Negotiating Behavior.* New York: Academic Press, 1981.
This book examines the literature on negotiating. Most of it is devoted to structured situations created by psychology professors using students. Thus, some has little relevance to real life. However, the book is full of good ideas and postulations about negotiating behavior than can form the basis of a mediator's understanding of the theoretical aspect of the problem.

Saposnek, Donald. *Mediating Child Custody Disputes.* San Francisco: Jossey Bass, 1983.
Devoted entirely to custody disputes, this book is based on a systems approach to mediation. Some readers find some of the strategies callous. But every reader can obtain a bag full of ideas from this book in dealing with those difficult impasses creating high-conflict families in dispute over the children.

Tax Implications for Divorced and Separated Individuals. U. S. Internal Revenue Service Publication 504. Washington, D.C.: U. S. Government Printing Office.
This free publication covers all of the important tax considerations for divorce in the U. S. Replete with specific examples, it provides answers to almost every divorce tax question.

Wallerstein, Judith, and Joan Kelly. *Surviving the Breakup: How Children and Parents Cope With Divorce.* New York: Basic Books, 1980.
A longitudinal study of families who sought psychological help during divorce. The authors monitored the families and developed valuable material on the developmental needs of children in divorce. It provides the mediator with a basic understanding of the children's needs.

Wells, Theodora. *Keeping Your Cool under Fire: Communicating Non-Defensively.* New York: McGraw Hill, 1980.
Written for business executives it is a gold mine of help for the mediator. The author helps the reader understand his/her way of dealing with conflict. Then, through a set of tasks and further understanding, she helps the reader develop more effective responses to conflict and difficult clients. The mediator will find this useful in providing ideas on how to be nondefensive when dealing with emotionally charged clients.

JOURNALS

Mediation Quarterly, published by the Academy of Family Mediators and Jossey Bass. Every issue is filled with practical articles and information on family mediation. It is *the* way to keep up with the field.

Negotiations Journal, published by the Harvard Program on Negotiation and Plenum Press, is another invaluable source of ideas. The journal covers all aspects of negotiations and there is at least one article about family negotiations in each issue.

Family Advocate, published by the American Bar Association, Family Law Section, Chicago. Published four times a year, each issue is thematic, covering the latest trends in family law. Subscriptions are available to nonmembers.

Conciliation Courts Review, published by the Association of Family Conciliation Courts, an organization of people involved with family courts. The material tends to be focused on the family court with an emphasis on child custody issues and is very useful if your practice is in that area. It frequently carries research articles about mediation.

Annotated Bibliography

Missouri Journal of Alternative Dispute Resolution, published by the School of Law, University of Missouri-Columbia.

Ohio State Journal on Dispute Resolution, published by the Ohio State University College of Law.

These two legal journals are devoted to ADR with many articles useful to mediation. Of the two, the Missouri journal publishes more articles specifically about mediation. The Ohio Journal annually publishes a superb and thorough bibliography of all articles on ADR and is worth the subscription for this one issue.